NIGHTMARE IN DALLAS

Beverly Oliver

with
Coke Buchanan

NIGHTMARE IN DALLAS

Beverly Oliver

with
Coke Buchanan

Lovingly

Beverly Oliver

Credits:
Cover design by Bill Dussinger.
Cover photo by Marie Muchmore.
Text photo—credits appear with photos.
Text photos processed by Texas Photo Center, Duncanville, Texas.
Photo contributions by Robert Groden, Coke Buchanan and Beverly Oliver
Massegee.

NIGHTMARE IN DALLAS

First Printing, October 1994
Second Printing, August 2003
Third Printing, July 2014

ISBN: 1-931600-50-3
Library of Congress Catalog Number 94-66617
Printed in the United States of America.

Dedicated to the valiant soldiers
who fought for the ideals
of liberty and freedom
in
Vietnam

"The courage of life
is often a less dramatic spectacle
than the courage of a final moment;
but it is no less a magnificent mixture of
triumph and tragedy."

John Fitzgerald Kennedy

"... Perhaps the wisest thing that was said in the Bible were the words, 'Peace, be still.'

"I think it's appropriate that we should on occasion be still and consider where we are, where we've been, what we believe in, what we are trying to work for, what we want for our country, what we want our country to be, what our individual responsibilities are, and what our national responsibilities are.

"This country has carried great responsibilities, particularly in the years since the end of the Second World War, and I think that willingness to assume those responsibilities has come in part from the strong religious conviction which must carry with it a sense of responsibility to others if it is genuine, which has marked our country from its earliest beginnings, when the recognition of our obligation to God was stated in nearly every public document, down to the present day.

"This is not an occasion for feeling pleased with ourselves, but, rather, it is an occasion for asking for help to continue our work and to do more. This is a country which has this feeling strongly. I mentioned in the other room the letters which I receive, which the members of Congress receive, which the Governors receive, which carry with them by the hundreds the strong commitment to the good life also the strong feeling of communication which many of our citizens have with God and the feeling that we are under His protection. This is, I think, a source of strength to us all."

John Fitzgerald Kennedy

NIGHTMARE IN DALLAS

Contents

I V

V

V I

Preface

NOVEMBER 1963

Dallas Love Field–On a bright cool rain freshened morning, a young boy climbs above the throng of cheering people onto the shoulders of a friendly stranger, leaning forward to shake the hand of the President of the United States as he makes his way toward the chain-link fence.

Dealey Plaza–A young lady in a green and white polka-dot dress, tan overcoat and cream-colored headscarf, fidgets with her camera, trying to pick the best spot to stand for the perfect angle to film President Kennedy as he drives by.

Dallas Love Field–The young boy watches intently as the President and his wife take their seats in the back of a special car with flags on the front.

Dealey Plaza–The lady in the headscarf is pleased with the location she's chosen as she moves her camera in concert with the motion of the President's limousine as it glides towards her down Elm Street, the Presidential standard and the U.S. flag adorning the fenders, snapping in the wind.

Dallas Love Field–Traveling down Cedar Springs as it exits the airport at Mockingbird Lane, sitting on an imaginary cloud in the back-seat of his father's station wagon, the young boy feels the world is at his command. He'd just come face to face with the President of the United States of America. Who in school was going to believe him?

Dealey Plaza–In the slow-motion vision of infamy her camera films the final seconds of the great man the lady in the plaza came to see.

Dallas Love Field–As the light turns green, and the car slowly turns eastward, the radio interrupts the dreams of the young boy with the news flash that the President had been shot in downtown Dallas. The words were clear. His dream is shattered.

JULY 1966

Chateaubriand Restaurant, Dallas—After clearing the table, quietly placing each dish into the gray plastic tub so as not to upset the candle ambiance, a young man spreads a clean linen tablecloth, proceeds to arrange an array of polished dinnerware, spotless china and delicate stemmed glassware, when his attention is quickly diverted, his work stops, his face lights up as a lovely blonde singer, taking a microphone softly in her left hand, sweeping her right palm upwards, her eyes fanning the lonely recesses of the room, glowing her glow, lets flow from the fire in her heart, the magic that bewitched him every night, "The shadow of your smile when you are . . . ."

When the young man said good-bye to his summer job and the singer who never knew he was listening, he carried her song with him in his back pocket and replayed it from time to time in remembrance of a moment suspended in the time warp of his early teens. The singer also carried the song . . . in the shadow of her smile.

JULY 1992

Grabbing a large dinner fork in her right hand, raising it eye level, she looked him in the eye saying, "You're going to like this!" With a relentless passion she pounded the huge steak, opening a series of tenderizing holes bleeding juices onto the brown wooden platter.

The dinner guest felt privileged to have been invited over for a home-cooked meal. She did not grant interviews very often but agreed to the request with his friend, a journalist from out of town, wanting to color his article about the Kennedy assassination with the vivid memories of an eyewitness.

"I haven't seen a steak that big since I worked at the Chateaubriand Restaurant," the guest said, relishing the thought of it sizzling over a hot mesquite fire.

"Oh, when did you work there?" she asked, momentarily stopping her frenzied attack on the side of beef.

Visually picturing himself moving from table to table, pouring water, running back to the kitchen for more breadsticks, he calculated backwards from graduation day. "Summer of '66."

"Really?" she remarked, "I was the singer there at that time."

"The Shadow of Your Smile?[1]" he threw in the air.

Looking him fixedly in the eyes, glowing her glow, she let flow the sweet charismatic melody that he carried in his back pocket, "The shadow of your smile when you are gone . . . . "

The young boy at Love Field, the young man at Chateaubriand, the dinner guest, were all the same person. The young lady in the scarf at Dealey Plaza, the singer of songs, the eyewitness, were all the same person.

Three months later, in the late hours of the early morning, he opens a file on his computer and writes a short abstract of her experience in Dealey Plaza, written as if he was standing there looking through the viewfinder of her camera. Weeks later, while visting with a friend one evening, he was asked to read it to her over the phone. After the reading, they both were quiet. He didn't quite know how she liked it. She didn't quite know what to say. He handed the phone back to his friend.

Two weeks later, amid the commotion and reverence of the JFK Symposium, she asked him to help write her book. He is Coke Buchanan. She is Beverly Oliver.

1 *The Shadow Of Your Smile*, love theme from the "Sandpiper,"
   Copyright 1965 Metro-Godwyn Meyer, Inc., New York

Foreword

"... we are not afraid to entrust the
American people with unpleasant facts ..."
— John F. Kennedy

"... truth is fallen in the street, and equity cannot enter."
— Isaiah

The name Abraham Zapruder has become almost synonymous with the assassination of President John F. Kennedy. Mr. Zapruder, as an amateur photographer, stood on a low concrete pedestal in Dallas' Dealey Plaza and focused his newly-purchased camera on the presidential motorcade. He recorded the horrifying event that many now refer to as "The Crime of the Century." The Zapruder film, described by some as "The Greatest Home Movie Ever Made," is approximimately thirty seconds in length. But contained within those thirty seconds of film is a vivid portrayal, depicting in brutal reality, the tragic and final moments of our young, vibrant, and charismatic President's life. This historic film was purchased by Life magazine. Life placed in a locked vault, refusing to allow it to be shown to the American people. In what has to be regarded as an attempt to sell the public on the official "lone assassin" conclusion, news commentators and writers lied about what was actually portrayed in the film. Vital and revealing visual evidence of the Presidents's murder was withheld from public scrutiny.

However, Mr. Zapruder's film was not the only important photographic record of the assassination taken that day. There was another motion picture recording of this tragic event; one which could be even more revealing. Across the street from Mr. Zapruder's position, and observable in the background of his film, is another amateur photograper—a woman wearing a long coat and head scarf (babushka). She is filming from a position which would undoubtedly record some of the most significant aspects of the assassination. For, not only would her camera record the last cruel moments of the President's life; it would also capture, in its background, the Texas School Book Depository building and the infamous Grassy Knoll during the strategic period of the ambush. The FBI took full note of this photographer, and in a November 25, 1963 memo reported:

". . . one of the 35mm slides (taken by a bystander and in possession of the FBI) depicted a female wearing a brown coat taking pictures from an angle, which, undoubtedly, would have included the Texas School Book Depository building in the background of her pictures. Her pictures evidently were taken just as the President was shot."

It is possible, even probable, that these "pictures," taken by a "female wearing a brown coat," could answer—once and for all—some of the more troublesome thirty-year-old questions about the President's murder:

- Were shots actually fired from the sixth-floor window of the Depository Buiding?
- Was Lee Harvey Oswald the shooter?
- Were shots fired from *other* windows of the Depository Building?
- Were there assassins firing from other buildings which overlook Dealey Plaza?
- Was there an assassin—as many eyewitnesses have so forcefully asserted—firing from the Grassy Knoll?

For these reasons alone, this film is extremely important. The significance of the other films and photographs, including Mr. Zapruder's, all pale in comparison. It is a vital piece of evidence.

Beverly Oliver was the "female wearing a brown coat" taking that vital film. It was not until late 1970, seven years after the President's death, that Miss Oliver first told me the story of her film. Prior to that time she had not confided this to anyone outside of her immediate family and a few close friends. The reasons for her silence are understandable. Miss Oliver was 17 years old at the time. She had just seen her President murdered. She watched in horror as her friend, Jack Ruby, shot and killed a man she believed to be his cohort—suspected assassin Lee Harvey Oswald. On the day following Oswald's execution, the same day above FBI memo was prepared, two men identifying themselves as FBI agents confiscated Beverly's film. She had not yet had it developed and was never able to view her historic and valuable footage. It has never been seen by the American people.

And why have the American people never seen it? The answer to this question is simple. It is also disturbing. The answer is simple because the film could have settled the question of whether or not there were multiple shooters, thus establishing that a conspiracy was involved in the President's murder. Therefore, the film *had* to be confiscated, and its existence kept secret. It is possible that it was so revealing that it had to be destroyed. The answer is disturbing because it has been the actions of people within our own government, with assistance from the major news media, who have steadfastly refused to inform the American public of the film's existence and importance. The reasons for this dereliction can only be surmised. That these actions were criminal—perhaps even treasonous—is without question.

Shortly after the assassination, Abraham Zapruder, as noted, was able to sell the rights to his film for more that two-hundred thousand (1963) dollars. Those rights were later returned to the Zapruder family. Today, the Zapruder family demands and receives large sums of money for its use. In contrast, Beverly Oliver, with the criminal confiscation of her film, *lost* her opportunity for any monetary gain.

But, as Miss Oliver is quick to point out, the real *loss* is not in the thuggish-like theft of her film, thereby depriving her of potential profit; it is the sad fact that a vital piece of evidence remains unseen, hidden from view—evidence which from its treatment may, and probably does, hold the key to unlocking the secrets of Dealey Plaza.

Therefore, the American people suffered the **real** loss.

J. Gary Shaw

J. Gary Shaw is a long-time researcher/critic of the Warren Report. He is co-author of two books on the JFK assassination; *Cover-Up,* with Larry Ray Harris, and the bestseller *JFK: Conspiracy of Silence,* with Dr. Charles A. Crenshaw.

I

John Fitzgerald Kennedy

Dallas

The Search For Tomorrow

Luwanna Jean

Interlude

Along the Watchtower

CHAPTER ONE

John Fitzgerald Kennedy

Washington D.C. was chilled to the bone. Twenty-two degrees and falling. The eight inches of snow, which silently blanketed Pennsylvania Avenue and the rest of the inauguration parade route the night before, had been miraculously shoveled into large frozen mounds by thousands of hurried servicemen, and served as natural barricades for the tens of thousands of well-wishers lining the streets to catch a glimpse of the historical moment. The Capitol building, glowing as if in a fresh coat of stark white paint, stood majestically against the deep cobalt blue sky. Wooden benches, carefully arranged on the east side of the complex, were being packed with invited guests: writers, children, scholars and artists, campaign workers, both foreign and domestic diplomats. Stretched like a white framed welcome mat before the Capital Rotunda, the Washington Mall was a colorful, moving, breathing sea of countless citizens fighting the bitter cold –rocking back and forth, rubbing their hands together trying to stay warm. At the first sound of cheering, those who sought refuge inside parked cars or in office buildings to escape the blistering sting of nature, went scampering back to their place in the crowd. John Fitzgerald Kennedy's family was ecstatically dignified as were the Bouviers who had been reunited as a family for the first time after twelve long years. Bobby Kennedy and his father Joseph were crowned with top-hats. Smiles were as wide as the bridges spanning the Potomac. The press corps was perched high in a custom-built stand on a pedestal twenty feet off the ground, tied to the presidential lectern by four large round microphones; cameras were poised for action, pencils to notepads. All eyes were glued to the approach leading from the Rotunda to the vacant lectern. Something was stirring in the air in addition to the Arctic chill. Something refreshingly dynamic. Something exhilarating. A tangible goodness permeated everything.

Wearing a beige, sable-trimmed, large buttoned cloth coat, and pillbox hat, her delicate hands warming in a matching sable muff, Jacqueline Kennedy arrived on the platform and took her place beside Lady Bird Johnson, Mamie Eisenhower, and Pat Nixon. Beaming a soft and regal radiance, she set the cue as the Marine band signaled the arrival of her husband, the President-elect.

John Fitzgerald Kennedy walked toward the podium in a vigorous, triumphant, and kingly manner–his chestnut hair groomed close to his head; his body warmed by the protection of a choice chesterfield topcoat; his tan face lit by the profound realization that his dream, now a reality, was just beginning.

Richard Cardinal Cushing delivered a long, proud invocation. Marion Anderson sang, and Robert Frost, visually impaired by the glaring sunlight, sadly stumbled through his delivery of a new poem inspired by the occasion, relying instead on one taken from his memory, *"This land was ours before we were the land's . . ."* At nine minutes to one o'clock on November 20, 1961, President Dwight D. Eisenhower relinquished his presidential responsibilities when Chief Justice Earl Warren, using the Fitzgerald family's Dourey Bible, administered the oath of office to John F. Kennedy, thirty-fifth president of the United States of America, the first president to be born in the twentieth century. Victoriously grouped behind Kennedy were his newly appointed administration's braintrust of lawyers, politicians, and other knowledgeable people; all forged from the same metal as he–ambitious, determined, optimistic, and stalwart believers in the intrinsic value of change, yet tempered by the unpredictable climate of civil struggle and international relations.

America was primed for change and pointedly focused on issues of employment, civil rights, and national security. The post war Eisenhower years witnessed the country burgeon and blossom into an envious world power, but it had become economically stagnant and the cold political shadow of communism had become a precarious and menacing issue, the threat of war a push away from reality and total destruction.

Furthermore, the unrest created by unequal opportunities for the Negroes was festering in angry words and public confrontations. Their "back of the bus" stature as American citizens was still the order of the day, but demands for equality had manifested in civil disobedience. The nation needed help and leadership willing to address these explosive issues. Countrymen needed to be unified in purpose–in harmony of spirit and determination. Needs and wants were bound in a ball of racial bigotry. The nation needed to be reminded that the American dream was still achievable and that their government was busy creating needed jobs, but nothing was going to come easy or without sacrifices. People needed to feel secure that the government was attentive in keeping a protective vigil, and strong in its conviction to uphold the principles for which it was founded.

Gleefully panning the massive crowd gathered on the nation's front lawn, the great seal of the office of the President of the United States of America boldly displayed on the baluster in front of him, Kennedy removed his overcoat and acknowledged the delegation surrounding him with a nod of his head and a euphoric smile. He reached inside his coat pocket and pulled out his speech and placed it on the podium directly in front of him. His eyes sparkling—his confidence at full throttle—President Kennedy took a breath and began:

"We observe today not a victory of party but a celebration of freedom—symbolizing an end as well as a beginning—signifying renewal as well as change. For I have sworn before you and Almighty God the same solemn oath our forefathers prescribed nearly a century and three-quarters ago.

"The world is very different now. For man holds in his hands the power to abolish all forms of human poverty and all forms of life. And yet the same revolutionary beliefs for which our forebears fought are still at issue around the globe—the belief that the rights of man come not from the generosity of the state but from the hand of God."

John F. Kennedy punctuated his speech with frozen breath and clenched thrusting fist. Coatless, framed by the aura of his youth, the tone of his voice radiated confidence, and his inflection sparked attention. Kennedy's persona as the newly elected President escalated with each carefully selected word; his education reflected in the high polish of his delivery. His message was rich with simplicity yet keenly focused on the responsibilities and needs of a changing democratic nation.

"We dare not forget today that we are the heirs of that first revolution. Let the word go forth from this time and place to friend and foe alike, that the torch has been passed to a new generation of Americans—born in this century, tempered by war, disciplined by a hard and bitter peace, proud of our ancient heritage—and unwilling to witness or permit the slow undoing of those human rights to which

this nation has always been committed, and to which we are committed today at home and around the world.

"Let every nation know, whether it wishes us well or ill, that we shall pay any price, bear any burden, meet any hardship, support any friend, oppose any foe to assure the survival and the success of liberty.

"This we pledge and much more."

GARLAND, TEXAS

Cradling a hot cup of coffee, Mr. Oliver leaned forward in his chair and focused intently on the small black and white Zenith screen as the new President spoke. His wife listened closely as well, sipping slowly on a glass of iced tea. This was the man they voted into office. They were a little hesitant at first because he was Catholic and they were Protestant; but they followed their intuition, believing that Kennedy was a leader. A righteous man. An honest man. A believer.

The Olivers were plain folk. They enjoyed the status quo and like most Americans, they anxiously feared the growing spread of Communism. Communism was a government they didn't understand. One which operated without caring or listening to the needs of its citizens. The blood red flag with its hammer and sickle symbolically represented an ongoing threat to their freedom, their most sacred right. The Soviet flag with its hammer and sickle had become as loathsome as the Nazi Swastika.

Kennedy was quick to stir the Oliver's patriotism. America's freedom was bought with the blood of a revolution and it's stature as a world power was hardened when it rolled up its sleeves and went to war overseas. A passion for the American way of life was permanently embedded in their pride and Kennedy pumped their appreciation of their heritage until it was full blown.

"To those old allies whose cultural and spiritual origins we share, we pledge the loyalty of faithful friends. United, there is little we cannot do in a host of new cooperative ventures. Divided, there is little we can do—for we dare not meet a powerful challenge at odds and split asunder.

"To those new states whom we welcome to the ranks of the free, we pledge our word that one form of colonial control shall not have passed away merely to be replaced by a far more iron tyranny. We shall not always expect to find them supporting our view. But we shall always hope to find them strongly supporting their own freedom—and to remember that, in the past, those who foolishly sought power by riding the back of the tiger ended up inside.

"To those people in huts and villages of half the globe struggling to break the bonds of mass misery, we pledge our best efforts to help them help themselves, for whatever period is required—not because the Communists may be doing it, not because we seek their votes, but because it is right. If a free society cannot help the many who are poor, it cannot save the few who are rich."

Mrs. Oliver glanced over at her husband then back at the television. Freedom was easy to understand and stopping communism was too. But where, and how? It was difficult to identify with the value of protecting little huts and villages. What did hut dwellers know of freedom and how would they benefit from a democratic government? Would it mean anything to them? Mr. Oliver remained quiet, riveted to every word.

"To our sister republics south of the border, we offer a special pledge—to convert our good words into good deeds—in a new alliance for progress—to assist free men and free governments in casting off the chains of poverty. But this peaceful revolution of hope cannot become the prey of hostile powers. Let all our neighbors know that we shall join them to oppose aggression or subversion anywhere in the Americas. And let every other power know that this hemisphere intends to remain the master of its own house.

"To that world assembly of sovereign states, the United Nations, our last hope in an age where the instruments of war have far outpaced the instruments of peace, we renew our pledge of support—to prevent it from becoming its shield of the new and the weak—and to enlarge the area in which its writ may run.

"Finally to those nations who would make themselves our adversaries, we offer not a pledge but a request: that both sides begin anew the quest for peace, before the dark powers of destruction unleashed by science engulf all humanity in planned or accidental self-destruction.

"We dare not tempt them with weakness. For only when our arms are sufficient beyond doubt can we be certain that they will never be employed."

"Scary. Don't you think? The push of a button." Mr. Oliver commented. The shadow of the bomb was a horrible reality, even in Garland, Texas. Especially late at night and early in the morning when everything was quiet and sleeping peacefully. Residential bomb shelters were everywhere, even if they were called storm shelters like the one in the Oliver's backyard. Schools religiously practiced the art of running for cover: hurricanes, tornadoes, earthquakes! While tornadoes were always a serious threat in Texas, all the kids knew why they were practicing–they wanted to be ready for "the bomb." Mr. Oliver thought it was good that the new President understood the importance of keeping an eye out for America's neighbors. Peace–is it possible?

Beverly, the Oliver's fourteen-year-old daughter, was rehearsing a new song in the back bedroom. Mr. Oliver leaned backward, turning an ear toward Beverly. Children–that's what peace was all about: keeping them and their children safe from harm, and guaranteeing them their God given liberties, he thought. He loved listening to Beverly sing–what a special gift.

"But neither can two great and powerful groups of nations take comfort from our present course–both sides overburdened by the cost of modern weapons, both rightly alarmed by the steady spread of the deadly atom, yet both racing to alter that uncertain balance of terror that stays the hand of mankind's final war.

"So let us begin anew–remembering on both sides that civility is not a sign of weakness, and sincerity is always subject to proof. Let us never negotiate out of fear. But let us never fear to negotiate.

"Let both sides explore what problems unite us instead of belaboring those problems which divide us.

"Let both sides, for the first time, formulate serious and precise proposals for the inspection and control of arms–and bring the absolute power to destroy other nations under the absolute control of all nations.

"Let both sides seek to invoke the wonders of science instead of its terrors. Together let us explore the stars, conquer the deserts, eradicate disease, tap the ocean depths and encourage the arts and commerce.

"Let both sides unite to heed in all corners of the earth the command of Isaiah–to 'undo the heavy burdens . . . (and) let the oppressed go free.'

"And if a beachhead of cooperation may push back the jungles of suspicion, let both sides join in creating a new endeavor–not a new balance of power, but a new world of law, where the strong are just and the weak secure and the peace preserved."

The temperature made Washington, D.C. a frigid host for the inauguration. Kennedy was surrounded by bitter cold but kept warm by his infinite enthusiasm. Elected to his new responsibility by a slim margin, Kennedy was accepting the reigns from Eisenhower in full stride with a new map for the future and the muscle of a new generation. There was a new frontier to explore and it was going to require all the strength and resources the President could mobilize.

"All this will not be finished in the first 100 days. Nor will it be finished in the first 1,000 days, nor in the life of this administration, nor perhaps in our lifetime on this planet. But let us begin.

"In your hands, my fellow citizens, more than mine, will rest the final success or failure of our course. Since this country was founded, each generation of Americans has been summoned to give testimony to its national loyalty. The graves of young Americans who answered the call to service surround the globe.

"Now the trumpet summons us again—not as a call to battle, though embattled we are—but a call to bear the burden of a long twilight struggle year in and year out, 'rejoicing in hope, patient in tribulation'—a struggle against the common enemies of man: tyranny, poverty, disease and war itself.

"Can we forge against these enemies a grand and global alliance, north and south, east and west, that can assure a more fruitful life for all mankind? Will you join in that historic effort?

"In the long history of the world, only a few generations have been granted the role of defending freedom in its hour of maximum danger. I do not shrink from this responsibility—I welcome it. I do not believe that any of us would change places with any other people or any other generation. The energy, the faith, the devotion which we bring to this endeavor will light our country and all who serve it—and the glow from that fire can truly light the world."

Kennedy's magnetism was in full gale. His words were eloquently honed and his vision was crystal clear. The Olivers were encouraged by what they were hearing and rejuvenated by his rhetoric. The contrast between Kennedy and Eisenhower was refreshing. His charismatic charm was undeniable. His youth, which some people thought was not in his favor during his campaign, was his best ally. It represented hope and change, and personified new beginnings.

"And so, my fellow Americans: ask not what your country can do for you—ask what you can do for your country.

"My fellow citizens of the world: ask not what America will do for you, but what together we can do for the freedom of man.

"Finally, whether you are citizens of America or citizens of the world, ask of us here the same high standards of strength and sacrifice which we ask of you.

With a good conscience our only sure reward, with history the final judge of our deeds, let us go forth to lead the land we love, asking His blessing and His help, but knowing that here on earth God's work must truly be our own."

Mr. Oliver could relate to "God's work" and was glad the new president had his priorities in order and wished the best for his administration. He turned the television off and went back to work.

After the speech and before the official parade, Kennedy retreated to the White House, already burdened with his inheritance—a nation in crisis. His "passing of the torch" meeting with Eisenhower apprised him of the international military strategy which was rapidly moving forward, with or without his blessing. Military advisors were pressing for America's intervention in Laos (the first domino to Thailand, Cambodia, and South Vietnam) to mightily convince Russia that the United States would defend it's sovereignty at all costs—on all shores. Kennedy was also briefed about the nation's deteriorating monetary system and the erosion of its gold position. And just the day before, the President-elect was informed that the CIA was backing a political takeover in Cuba, by training and financing anti-Castro guerrilla forces. They already had forces being trained in Guatemala.

Putting aside his worrisome thoughts for a moment, President John F. Kennedy gallantly entered the Oval Office to sit at his new desk. In front of him were two telephones, two pens, an ink blotter, a desk pad, and the problems of a nation.

CHAPTER TWO

Dallas

In 1839 when John Neely Bryan searched for a place to settle, he picked a spot with little promise and few resources other than the water flowing from one of the three muddy forks of the Trinity River. The land was flat, punctuated only by a few scattered hills. It was hot, windy, dry, humid, all at the same time it seemed, and a long wagon ride from the coast where prosperity and growth usually began.

But Dallas didn't wait on anything or anybody; it provided its own resources, starting with Bryan himself. Bryan knew people needed to cross the river so he provided a ferry where they could cross safely. In 1872 a group of ex-confederate officers, who referred to each other as "Colonel," found that the Houston & Texas Central Railroad was going to skirt town by nine miles so they raised a quick $5,000 and cleverly packaged it with a free right of way to make sure the tracks passed through the city. A year later they influenced yet another railway to swing through town, the Pacific Railway. This time they sent a group to Austin where they successfully managed to attach a small-print amendment to the railway's right-of-way bill requiring that the railway tracks pass a watering station called Browder Springs. It sounded reasonable and no one bothered to question where Browder Springs was. Little did they realize, it was in Dallas. In 1936, Houston, San Antonio, and Fort Worth were all vying with Dallas to land the Texas Centennial celebration. As historical as the other cities were to the legacy of the Lone Star State, Dallas won the award after flashing a cool $3.5 million money roll. Ironically, Dallas wasn't even a city when Texas won its independence; but, Dallas had drive, ambition, and capital. It knew how to promote and had become preoccupied with winning.

Second generation promoters became resourceful too. Dallas found herself strategically close to the rich oil fields of east Texas and, like it did with commerce from the cotton belt, it made sure that the oil business was funneled through town. Texans needed money to fuel their search, drill their wells, and refine their crude, and Dallas had plenty of it. Financing the industry and banking its royalties caused even bigger things to happen, in Big "D." The banking and insurance industries developed powerfully influential men who became as resourceful as necessary to perpetuate their interests and secure Dallas' future as a thriving financial center. Many service related industries developed, further propelling the boom; and with them came jobs, housing, and more jobs. Business men fanned the country with incentives for industry to move to the Big D. Money, networking, legislation–Dallas used all available resources to create a twentieth century boom town–and it worked. Other than New York City, Dallas had more new office space under construction than any city since the end of World War II. Nine new buildings were shooting skyward–two over fifty stories tall. Two-hundred eighty-eight square miles and spreading. The 1960 census credited Dallas as the sixteenth largest city in the country with over one and a quarter million people in the greater area; 125,000 of Negro decent and 25,000 of Mexican decent, but any Dallasite would have told you 1961 was pushing Big D even bigger.

Dallas was also a city of churches; not great spiraled gothic wonders, but hundreds of community churches where people mixed prayer with service and good food with fellowship. Dallasites didn't parade their Deity but they promoted His goodwill and harmony as part of their daily routine. Spiritual character helped the city move forward by providing stability and maturity. Boundaries between religious sectors were practically nonexistent. Catholics were helping Protestants, and vice-versa, and Jews were busy working with everyone.

To say Dallas was a city on the move is an understatement. Decisions were made with a handshake and swiftly implemented. Dallas was flourishing and it looked like there was no stopping. Politically, Dallas was a mercantile oligarchy. Banks and the merchants ran the city. Deposits in Dallas banks were three billion. Money was available to fund any well thought out plan that had potential and looked to be well-managed. Dallas was still the top international cotton market, plucking over a half-billion dollars in annual revenue. Dallas was: 2,700 wholesale distributors pumping four-billion dollars into the economy. It had one-hundred twelve oil-related businesses in the city, each earning a net worth of over one million dollars–more than any other city. Dallas was a transportation hub served by eight airlines, nine mainline railroads, thirty-seven truck lines. It was a leading fashion center and well-known for its attractive women. Dallas was diversity.

Understanding the money dynamics of diversity and its direct relationship to the quality and speed of decision making, Dallas wanted a new way to politically ensure its interests were coordinated and aggressively promoted by a consensus of leaders ready to act at the drop of a hat. What was an easy routine for the *Colonels* became impractical for third generation entrepreneurs. There were too many decision-makers to meet on someone's front porch. Robert L. Thorton, president of Mercantile National Bank, developed a political model in line with the desires of city leaders. His plan was accepted and the Dallas Citizens' Council was born.

The Dallas Citizens Council went to task. The council of executive directors were in general accord with many of the city's priorities. They carefully outlined goals for the city to insure that appropriate attention to detail was implemented to maximize the city's resources for future opportunities. Being successful businessmen and serving as the city's visionaries, they wanted more respect and demanded attention for Dallas in a big way. Competing with New York City, Chicago, and Los Angeles, city image was becoming more important and Dallas had to dress and act more cosmopolitan. Void of the significant components promoting cultural arts which made a city truly great, the council was quick to correct the issue. A new art museum, a symphony orchestra, an opera company, a new library, became council priorities and materialized in grand fashion. Knowing the growing importance of the aerospace industry, the council raised five-million dollars to launch a research center to attract engineers and their families, simultaneously promoting Dallas as a city of the future.

The Citizens Council may have run Dallas, but there were a few select men who were thought to run the Citizens Council: Karl Hobilitzell and Robert Thorton, James Aston, C.A. Tatum, Lester Potter, Stanley Marcus, and Erik Jonsson. While there were many wealthy oil men in town, the power in Dallas belonged to bankers and executives. And when they hooked up with the oilmen, anything could happen. Since business tended to operate conservatively, and the city was brimming with a horde of conservative white-collar managers, that was the political direction of Dallas' leadership. Unlike Houston, where blue-collar roustabouts had strong pull, Dallas wasn't influenced by unions. And, there was no pressing desire to organize the labor market.

Dallas was an open-shop city where most employees were productive, well paid, and content with their status.

Poverty in Dallas was kept confined to well-defined pockets. There were few clapboard houses and unpaved streets. Dallas approached neediness by providing self-help solutions to depressed areas. Just north of downtown an area called Little Mexico was a shining example: income was poor but neighborhood pride was contagious. Property was cared for and residents were proud to be part of the project. Negro-white relations were stable only because segregation lines between the *have* and the *have-nots* were still well-delineated and generally accepted. The civil unrest causing problems in other cities was swallowed by a prosperous business climate that provided a little something for everyone.

Downtown Dallas was blessed with a magnificent and readily recognizable skyline which shot up from the flat land like cattails on a vast lake. The flying red horse atop the Magnolia Building, the blue Southland Life Towers, the rocketing Republic National Bank spire, and the circular architecture of Dallas Memorial Auditorium combined to create a unique postcard appearance in its design. For those people who had never been east of the Mississippi, Dallas looked like a big time-big city.

When the Texas sun closed shop on the Dallas working day, people rushed away from the hustle of downtown to a patchwork of bedroom communities sewn to the city in a circular pattern: executives cruised north to the Park Cities, managers drove to far north Dallas and scattered pockets of shaded neighborhoods in Oak Cliff and Lakewood. Laborers bussed themselves south. There was no housing downtown. No ball parks or concrete courts—only a few movie theaters: the Majestic, The Palace, the Capri. They catered generally to people enjoying extended lunch hours or tripping downtown on the weekend. However, on Commerce Street, within short walking distance to the Adolphus and Baker Hotels, were night clubs feeding off conventioneers and a growing legion of late night regulars.

Weekends though were different when the clubs were infiltrated by an intriguing fusion of vacationers, leftover conventioneers, and Texans on wheels. Since towns like Palestine, Paris, Ponder, and Waco didn't have burlesque and frowned on drinking, downtown sucked in rebel rousers from hundreds of miles around.

Right in the middle of the Bible belt, Dallas honored strict liquor laws and enforced the Bring Your Own Liquor (B.Y.O.B.) policies. Clubs were allowed to only sell setups, beer, and champagne. Brown bags were stylish, champagne was expensive, and interestingly enough—beer was generally ignored. The drinking age was twenty-one but youngsters were still allowed into the clubs to spend money on cokes. Behind the buzz of the general audience was a small local infrastructure, an after-hours community, comprised of attorneys, show girls, executives, policemen, businessmen, politicians, mobsters, and bankers, you name them. At one time or another, for one reason or another, most everyone rubbed elbows with one another. As divergent as the mix was, whether they wanted to or not, they became a close knit community.

The downtown burlesque scene was comprised of three clubs. Barney Weinstein owned the *Theater Lounge,* his brother Abe Weinstein owned the *Colony Club,* and a Chicago transplant named Jack Ruby owned the *Carousel Club.* The Colony and the Carousel were located across the street from the Adolphus Hotel and separated by a parking lot serving patrons of both clubs. The Theater Lounge was located on Jackson Street, a five minute walk south.

The Weinsteins and Ruby didn't always see eye-to-eye and had inadvertently developed a relationship similar to feuding stepsisters. Even if the feuding was mostly one sided. The clubs operated by the same rules, shared the same crowds, were visited by the same police, were governed by the same entertainment guild, and sometimes shared dancers. However, it was uphill for Ruby, trying to play catch up with the Weinsteins who had been anchored in Dallas long before him. Ruby first opened his club on Commerce Street as the *Sovereign Club* offering private memberships which allowed members the privilege and convenience of being served mixed drinks. But it didn't work. B.Y.O.B. was uniformly preferred. So with a little ink and a new look, the Sovereign Club became the Carousel Club.

The burlesque scene kept downtown breathing at night. Amid the hustle of its entertainment, a strange brew of personalities and ambition, public policy and hidden agendas, bubbled to a steady boil.

President Kennedy was pleased with the changes he made in the Oval Office. He brightened the office by having the green walls painted white and covering two red sofas with white fabric to match, then by taking down the beige curtains to allow the scenery of the Rose Garden to walk through the windows. He decorated the room with miniature ships; the walls with naval battle scenes. And he replaced the desk with one his wife had found. It was being used as a television stand in the White House basement. The desk was hand-carved from the timbers of a British sailing ship and had been presented to President Rutherford B. Hayes by the British government as a token of friendship when the ship was scrapped. (The ship had been found abandoned and drifting at sea years earlier by Americans. It was returned to England and presented to Queen Victoria.)

Behind the desk two flags stood at attention, Old Glory and the Presidential Standard. On his desk, President Kennedy had placed the treasured coconut from his PT109 boat episode, a crystal ashtray, a small sheathed dagger, and a set of bookends bracing a select volume of texts including the world almanac and the Bible.

Once settled in his new position, President Kennedy went to work by issuing Executive Order No. 1 ordering the Secretary of Agriculture to double the rations of surplus foods provided to some four-million needy Americans. Next, not wanting anyone standing between himself and his aides, Kennedy abolished the top level Operations Coordinating Board set up by Eisenhower and then dispensed with seventeen interdepartmental agencies. The new President wanted everyone to know who was in control and when deadlines weren't met or goals weren't accomplished they had to report to him. Everyone was quick to learn that everything the President requested was due "yesterday." Lights in the Executive office buildings burned late into the night.

CHAPTER THREE

The Search For Tomorrow

The bus from Garland to Dallas transits down Garland Road, up Gaston, then cuts over to Jackson Street, rolling inconspicuously through downtown, leaving only a trail of diesel fumes. The thirty-eight minute trek is highlighted only by the random thoughts of riders as they travel at the speed of telephone poles.

Beverly couldn't relax on the ride downtown. She was mentally rehearsing her dance routine, trying to remember specifics about how the other girls performed during Amateur Night. She finally decided to march out on stage as if she owned the place, nothing too cute or prissy, just a sensual strut. Beverly wanted to win her friend's dare, but she was also extremely curious as to just how good she would be at expressing herself in dance. Beneath it all though was Beverly's passion for the stage—being in front of everyone, all eyes and all ears focused on her, watching with pleasure as smiles lit up the room. She was only three-years-old when she realized how special the feeling was, when she stood tall on the altar, held tight by the preacher so she wouldn't fall, singing a song about a man who loved all the little children in the world.

When the preacher asked little Beverly what she wanted to be when she grew up, she didn't hesitate. "I want to be a saloon singer!" Endless afternoons spent watching old westerns provided her with her first ambition. Saloon girls were special, she thought. They could sing and shake the dusty trail out of the cowboys and fill their hearts with a bit of cheer.

Beverly's guest appearances at church led to her first real opportunity when her parents, realizing how important singing was to her, arranged for an audition on the Ted Mack Amateur Hour. She made the audition and soon became the blond-haired darling of many western halls. Performing in front of an appreciative crowd made Beverly's blood rush and opened her senses to pleasures she ordinarily wasn't able to experience. Driving the country music circuit pushed Beverly into a fast lane, or so it was called. She spent quite a bit of time with adults and was beginning to think like them. It also led her to want to experience more from life, quicker and sooner than everyone else.

Knowing they wouldn't check up on her because the Petersons didn't have a telephone, let alone suspect that she was going downtown to dance at an amateur burlesque show, Beverly bent the truth, and told her mother she was spending the night with her friend, Mary Noel. It was a perfect arrangement; she packed an overnight bag, got a ride to the bus station, and caught the 4:30 to Dallas. She planned a return on the 12:30, at which time she would take a cab from the bus station back to Mary Noel's where a window would be left open. *Simple.*

The previous weekend Beverly and several of her Garland High School friends had made their first visit to the Theater Club. She was infatuated by the entire experience. It was Amateur Night and the place was rocking. It was hard for Beverly to see a stage and not want to be on it. Watching many of the girls parade around in simple, uninspired, routines, then receive roaring ovations, made Beverly wonder how they'd respond if she was on stage.

"I can do better than that." Beverly said confidently.

No sooner had the words tumbled out of Beverly's mouth when she was challenged by one of her friends. "Well, if you think that way —let's see you do it ."

Beverly wanted to accept the dare then and there, but decided that it would have to wait. Jumping in front of an audience of that nature required a little preparation. Besides, she didn't have a bikini, nor was she about to risk being seen by someone who might know and tell her parents. They'd drown in despair.

As the night went on, Beverly became further challenged by the dare, and began thinking about how she could pull it off. *It's not like anyone hasn't seen me in a bikini before.* Beverly was never shy; just the opposite. She was proud of her body, confident the crowd would approve, and curious to experience what it felt like.

"I'm going to do it." Beverly declared. "Next week. Just wait and see."

That was it. Beverly accepted the challenge publicly. There was no going back.

As she stepped down from the bus a smile ripped across her face. The anticipation of the evening exhilarated her. She liked being downtown. It was a concrete playground: alive, awake, and open all night. It intoxicated her and she wanted the feeling to last forever. Downtown was adult; news stands, blinking lights, and exhaust. Walk–Don't Walk. Towering buildings. Everywhere she looked were people she didn't know, people she wanted to know, some she felt she had to know.

Beverly had called the Theater Club earlier to ask about dancing that night and was asked by Barney Weinstein to come in early for an interview, and to bring a bikini. Mr. Weinstein was an amicable man who loved the pleasure of women and enjoyed judging "talent" for his Amateur Nights. His interviews were short and simple. "Can you dance?" "Are you eighteen?" "Let me see your legs."

True to his routine, Mr. Weinstein asked his questions, watched Beverly dance a few steps, and admired her as she flashed a little leg.

"Very good. I can tell you're going to do well; everyone is going to like you. Please be here on time at seven o'clock. Seven o'clock."

Beverly thanked him, shook his hand, and as she turned to walk away, she remembered something extremely important. "Oh, and one thing, Mr. Weinstein. It's important . . . I mean, I can't let anybody recognize me."

"Why not?"

"Well . . . my parents are old fashioned and easily offended. It would hurt them if they somehow found out. And I wouldn't want to hurt them."

Barney understood. He thought for a moment then snickered to himself. "You can wear a mask and we'll call you the *Masked Débutante.* What do you think of that?"

Beverly smiled, "Great! The Masked Débutante it is. See you at seven."

Beverly's ambition to be a professional singer never changed and she couldn't help but think about the possibility of performing at one of the clubs. She was growing tired of twanging out country songs and wanted to explore the rapture of jazz and the slippery melodies of tender love songs. Candlelight, tablecloth, and piano notes. But that ambition would have to wait, Beverly thought, as she walked down the stairs, tugging upward on her bikini strap. *Let's get through Amateur Night first.*

A few blocks from the club Beverly found a drug store and bought what she needed to make her mask. Using a man's black silk handkerchief and a piece of elastic, she made a modest but effective veil. Her bikini was white with a small flowered lace ruffle.

The house was packed as usual and noisy with money. Soft drink or setup; it required an I.D. to make the difference. The crowd was an odd mixture of young and old, men and women, wild and crazy. Downstairs, upstairs, stairway, table, and aisle—it was standing room only. Beverly waited in a small cramped room with the other girls; some overly anxious, some well-practiced; she was a little of both. Beverly didn't have the stage fright experienced by several of the girls, but other than in her mind's eye, she wasn't practiced. Waiting her turn, bobbing her head to the music, Beverly thought about how fast she should pull down the zipper to her dress. Occasionally, she reached beneath her dress to adjust her bikini.

Before long, it was time for the *Masked Débutante* to make her debut; four-inch heels and a lot of leg led the way. Beverly took long swift steps, scanning the audience from right to left. The lights were so bright and the platform so tall, that it made it impossible to see how many people were out there. However, she could tell from the wolf whistles and hand clapping that they were pleased. As Beverly strutted brashly about the stage, she reached for her zipper and slowly pulled it down, letting her dress drop to the floor. With a well-placed kick, Beverly's dress flew in the air, into her hands, and whipped over her shoulder. Planting her left foot center-stage, lifting her back leg in a tuck, she twirled in a graceful sweeping motion until she was dizzy.

Hearing all the racket made Beverly feel appreciated and powerful. The mask had worked, Beverly felt anonymous. The bikini worked too, she wasn't embarrassed. The dare was behind her, but the thrill lingered. With her last wave, Beverly decided to return the next weekend. Right before she exited, she took another spin, stooped down, placing her left hand on her knee and her right hand to her lips, she floated a kiss into the audience.

Beverly returned the next weekend for another Amateur Night and decided she wanted to dance again. To break the routine and add a bit of variety, Barney asked Beverly if she would dance at his brother Abe's place, The Colony Club, on Saturday night. The practice of staggering Amateur nights and show times provided the Weinsteins with the flexibility of sharing dancers. Not every girl in town wanted to be an exotic dancer or was brave enough to at least give it a stroll. There wasn't a ready pool of volunteers from which to choose.

Abe was a gentleman, just like his brother, and Beverly took an immediate liking to him. He was kind, intuitive, and developed a quick rapport with people; she was no exception. Abe knew how to listen and Beverly knew how to talk. They both felt comfortable with each other and after her performance that Saturday night, Beverly realized she liked the Colony Club better, and Abe was a big part of it. It wasn't something she tried to analyze, it was something she experienced. He made a few suggestions, and changed her black veiled disguise to a glittery Mardi Gras mask which suited her better. She was still uneasy about her parents finding out.

Nighttime Dallas was concentrated in a couple of small areas downtown and they were well patrolled, so Beverly felt safe walking to the bus station. Lingering a little too long after her second performance at Abe's, Beverly zipped out the door and down the street to catch the 12:30 back to Mary Noel's. Rushing by the Baker Hotel Drug Store, Beverly heard a man calling, "Hey! What's a pretty little girl like you doing down here this late?"

Beverly turned around, keeping her pace in full stride, not knowing if she was the one being spoken to. He repeated himself, she then paused . . . and took a closer look. He looked familiar. She thought she had seen him once or twice at one of the clubs.

Beverly continued walking. "Why, I have a bus to catch." Her reply didn't answer his question but she felt it provided her with an excuse to keep walking. However on second thought, he seemed warm, friendly, and unthreatening, so she stopped for a moment.

The man had a full face and a fast-forward character, marked by his rapid fire mouth. His hair was jet black and slicked neatly back. His eyes were coal black; they could be piercing or vacant, and sometimes both. "Hey, thanks for stopping. I didn't know if you would or not. But you did, and I'm glad that you did. I'm Jack Ruby," he said reaching out his hand. "I own the Carousel Club. What's your name? I know you have one. Everybody does."

Beverly dropped her alarm and waited for him to stop talking. *What do you know—the Carousel Club.* "I'm Bixie Bonham. It's nice to meet you," she interjected.

"Hey, I saw you dance over at the other club. You were good. You know, I was thinking of having my own amateur night. Think maybe you'd like to come dance at my place?"

Beverly was flattered and wondered how he recognized her without the mask. She figured, since he owned a club, he probably made a point finding out that kind of information. However, she wasn't ready to commit to anything, in fact, she had about decided to "retire." Each time she took the stage she worried a bit more about her parents finding out. She couldn't fathom the emotional consequences if they learned of her nocturnal routines. Besides,

Beverly was a singer—not a dancer, and it was time to get back where she belonged.

"Thanks for the offer. But I believe my brief career as a dancer is over. You can't be an amateur forever, and I certainly can't be a professional. If my mamma and my daddy ever caught me down here, they'd kill me."

"I understand. It's a big decision. Not everyone has the talent or the fortitude to do it. Well Bixie, if you change your mind let me be the first to know. You'd like my club. Have you been to my club? If you haven't—be my guest; it's a nice club; it's got class. I like class; you have class; I can tell—I know all about it. You either have it or you don't. It takes hard work for some people and others just have it. Know what I mean?"

Beverly knew what he meant, but he seemed to be confusing people and things. "Thanks. I haven't been to your club but I've heard about it and I've walked by it many times. Maybe some night. Do you know Barney and Abe Weinstein?"

"Yeah, I know them. Maybe too well. Maybe not enough. I don't know sometimes. They're always stealing my ideas. Sometimes, my girls. They tried to anyway. How much did they pay you?"

"They didn't pay me. It was Amateur night." Beverly didn't understand the question. Only *professionals* get paid.

"Oh, I thought they paid some of the girls? Those girls that keep coming back anyway. You know who I mean. They do don't they?" Ruby was fishing for the answer he wanted. He was angry that the Weinsteins could pull off something so ingenious as packing the house to the rafters with spenders and the stage with women they didn't have to pay. If they were paying them, it would be a violation of AGVA, the resident artist's guild, and he could register a formal complaint.

"No, they didn't offer me a dime. I wasn't expecting anything either. I did it on a dare." Beverly looked at her watch. She wanted to talk longer but needed to hurry, the bus didn't wait on anybody. "Listen, I enjoyed meeting you but I'm going to miss my bus if I don't hurry. Maybe we can talk again sometime."

"Yeah. I'd like that. Here's my card. Take it and come see me if you change your mind. You're a very pretty girl. Hey, take care."

"Thanks, but keep your card. I know where to find you. I wouldn't want my parents finding it."

"Sure. Hey, can I walk you to the bus station? It'd make me feel better knowing you weren't walking alone. Know what I mean?"

Beverly agreed she would like the company, so Jack continued talking and she kept walking.

During the bus ride back to Garland, Beverly thought about change. She used to think the days passed too quickly; then weeks started flying by, and then the months dropped from the calendar before she could pick up the paper from the last. She was soon to be fifteen-years-old and wondered how much her life would change by sixteen. Sixteen was supposed to be a special birthday for girls; an initiation into "nearly adulthood." A time when girls developed opinions. A time for more responsibility and better makeup. However, Beverly had been playing the part for years. Riding the country singing circuit pumped her full of opinions and she had been buying her make-up at Nieman's for some time.

The "new generation" had the reigns of the nation and the new President wanted to be in full control. He wanted to know everything. Most decisions he saw as his alone; his new cabinet didn't convene as often as previous administrations and were primarily delegated to fact finding and report generating, two–three times a day. Kennedy liked politics; it was the way a president gets things done, he was quoted. To further his cause and to keep everyone on his toes, he kept a file in the White House profiling every Senator and Representative: his family, his education, his tenure, his voting record. If Kennedy wasn't discussing policy with them in his office, he was with them on the phone. He knew what they needed. They knew what he wanted. John Kennedy was everywhere in the political machinery which ran the country. He had his hands on everything. Decisions were based on solid advice which he combed from people on all levels of government. He tried to kick-start things which weren't working or he rearranged things so that they would. He rewired agencies which were smoldering and he yanked those that were dead. His energy seemed limitless. He remarked, "Under our system of government, either the President is everything or he is nothing."

John Kennedy always kept his door open to his staff should they need to see him. The best time to approach him, they learned, was near 7:00 PM when his workday was winding down and he was beginning to think about going upstairs.

Galloping at full stride, President Kennedy hit a wall on April 17 at Red Beach Bay and Blue Beach on the southern shores of Cuba. The covert military operation against Fidel Castro, which the President inherited from the previous administration and driven by the Pentagon, had disintegrated into a shameful fiasco for which the President accepted full responsibility as the country's Commander-in-Chief. Caught in the middle of a battle he didn't authorize, Kennedy was faced with the dilemma of whether or not to order an airstrike to protect a brigade of stranded American soldiers, thereby overtly endorsing the attack and risking the wrath of Russia at the wrong time.

Later, as the night faded to morning, President Kennedy was seen alone outside his office, his shoulders slumped, his hands buried deep in his pockets, his eyes close to tears.

Recovering from the political and public backlash of the Cuban derailment, John Kennedy, in a special second State of the Union message, launched a program which epitomized the indelible spirit and muscle of the young President's thinking and recaptured the public's appreciation for his youth. With an awe inspiring speech, President Kennedy proclaimed that America had "tossed its cap over the wall of space" and was going to put a man on the moon by 1970. He later addressed the students and faculty at Rice University in Houston and expounded:

"Those who came before us made certain that this country rode the first waves of the industrial revolution, the first waves of modern invention, and the first wave of nuclear power, and this generation does not intend to flounder in the backwash of the coming age of space. We mean to be a part of it. We mean to lead it, for the eyes of the world now look into space, to the moon and the planets beyond; and we have vowed that we shall not see it governed by a hostile flag of consent, but a banner of freedom and peace. We have vowed that we shall not see space filled with weapons of mass destruction, but with instruments of knowledge and understanding."

The thrill of the space program and its first manned spacecraft orbit provided the President with the springboard he needed; however, his glee was quickly diverted to what lay ahead. Just around the corner in June, were face-to-face meetings with a stubborn French President Charles DeGaulle in Paris and an uncompromising Nikita Khrushchev in Vienna. His visit at 10 Downing Street with Harold Macmillan in London afterwards though, did not carry a worry. Berlin, nuclear weapons control, Laos . . . there was a lot to talk about.

Like her celebrity husband the President, Mrs. Kennedy was receiving quite a bit of adulation. Attractive, cosmopolitan chic, and always regally outfitted, she quickly captured the fascination of women, the ink of newsprint and the focus of cameras all across America. Similar to the feelings of great expectations from the office of the President, the office of the First Lady was also being looked to for something refreshingly different, and she wasn't letting anyone down.

The First Lady had the opportunity to display her diplomatic charm when she was invited by her husband to accompany him to Europe. He was beginning to realize how valuable she was becoming in his crusade to break down the barriers of communication.

Arriving in Paris was a homecoming of sorts for the young Bouvier–an American of French descent, and it was a test. The French, always peculiarly observant and frank, would acknowledge the President's arrival, but would have their attention trained on the President's wife and her European debut. Europeans could not help but keep an eye on America; their present freedom was irrevocably tied to America's strength and her strength was indirectly dictated by the fire and fortitude of its leadership. The special television tour of the White House the Kennedy's prepared to be aired two days before their arrival heightened their expectations. The young President's wife walked through the mansion with the grace and beauty of a movie star, her French rolling from her tongue to perfection. At the end of the tour, her husband, the President of the United States, spoke to the French audience in their native language as well. What more could they want?

Jacqueline Bouvier Kennedy's choice of clothes for arrival at Orly airport in Paris was a simple wool coat and a pillbox hat. It was raining, but hundreds of thousands of Frenchmen lined the ancient streets to welcome her back. Back to the boulevard Saint-Michel, back to the Sorbonne, the Place de la Concord, and onto the Quai d'Orsay where she and her husband were staying. The Kennedy's were immediately and unpredictably embraced by the French. Americans had been blindly stereotyped as precocious and boisterous –careless and insensitive, however, the new presidential couple changed the stereotype with one waltz through Paris.

Outside the palatial Quai d'Orsay, the Seine River quietly flowed to sea. Inside, chambered in separate ends of the third floor hallway, Jacqueline Kennedy slipped into the comfort of the Chambre de la Reine and bathed in a silver mosaic tub in a mother-of-pearl bathroom used by Queen Elizabeth II. John Kennedy relaxed in a hot bath to ease the pain in his back.

President Kennedy and President Charles DeGaulle were able to keep accord during their official visit as it unfolded over the course of the following days. They didn't agree about America's role in Europe, but they respected one another. Kennedy wanted to provide nuclear weapons to NATO but be involved in any deployment. DeGaulle felt that put America in the drivers seat which was unacceptable. Kennedy tried to impress upon DeGualle the seriousness of Khrushchev's threats to take Berlin. DeGualle thought that if Khrushchev wanted to risk taking Berlin he would have already done so. Kennedy warned that such was not the case. Kennedy tried to get DeGualle to commit his support to help crush communist intrusion in Laos but DeGualle said that France "would in no way dream of military intervention," however, France wouldn't publicly condemn the United States for her doing so. Latin America, Africa, more NATO, Kennedy and DeGualle covered everything but got nowhere. Five separate meetings did not resolve any issues but it served to bring the two countries closer together in respect then ever before. The two leaders in turn, gained first hand knowledge of the other's vision for their country and their personal appointment with history.

With the official meeting between Kennedy and DeGualle in the history books, the last evening was reserved for a grand dinner at the Versailles Palace. Jacqueline Kennedy dazzled everyone. Honoring the French in a way that only they could affectionately understand, the First Lady of America wore a gown designed by a master French artist. Multicolored flowers embroidered in a tapestry of white silk was crafted by Hubert de Givenchy into a bell-shaped skirt and fitted sleeveless top. A matching white silk jacket was draped from her shoulders.

When all was said and done, President Kennedy in retrospect, said in departing Paris, "I am the man who came here with Jacqueline Kennedy."

Kennedy didn't fair as well with Khrushchev as he had with DeGualle. Advised that it was too early in his presidency to attempt to spar with the Soviet leader, Kennedy proceeded anyway to initiate his plan to open the door of communications between the two world powers. Kennedy understood Khrushchev's grand plan; he laid it out in a speech he delivered barely six months prior, "We will beat the United States with small wars of liberation.

We will nibble them to exhaustion all over the globe, in South America, Africa, Southeast Asia."

Armed with a satchel full of advice and a heart aching for peace, Kennedy went head-on with the aging Communist. Kennedy began the meeting by trying to set the stage for a productive session where both men came to a better understanding of common problems and in light of their growing differences how the two countries could work in concert to avoid the prospects of nuclear war. Khruschev retaliated quickly. He was tired of trying to develop relations with the U.S. when they continued to follow a doctrine that pursued the liquidation of communism. Kennedy tried to correct Khruschev. He said the U.S. was not trying to end communism, however, it was adamant that communism stay put in countries that were already practicing such. Khruschev stated that communism was a social inevitability and would triumph in debate not war. He reinforced his belief by stating again, that the Soviet Union desired complete disarmament.

Kennedy responded that communist minorities should not force their will on countries that believe like they do, that the majority should have freedom of choice. Khruschev batted back, questioning if America's intention was to "build a dam against the development of the human mind and conscience" thereby not allowing a natural course of event to take place that would inevitably result in victory for the communist regime.

For two days, Kennedy and Khruschev battled philosophy, questioned intentions of interference and noninterference around the globe, and paraded their own versions of patriotism to a critical and impassable gridlock. Khruschev dominated the talks with bone crushing efficiency and frightening audacity which underscored his feeling that the young American President was weak and could be easily manipulated; using the Bay of Pigs failure as his example. He made threats that tore through Kennedy with cutting calm and great alarm. Kennedy was frightened as to what may lay ahead.

In parting, Kennedy tried one last time to calm Khruschev's brashness before something rash happened in Berlin which could force America to retaliate. Khruschev emphasized he would meet force with force should America or anybody violate its interests or cross its borders in Berlin. War or peace was a U.S. problem!

While President Kennedy displayed great control and poise during the meetings, after all was said and done, he looked visibly dismayed. It was the first time he had spoken with a man of intellect for whom reason was not part of his civil protocol.

On the plane to London, Evelyn Lincoln, the President's secretary, found a small piece of paper on which John Kennedy had scribbled the prophetic words of Abraham Lincoln,

I know there is a God—and I see a storm coming;
If he has a place for me, I believe I am ready.

CHAPTER FOUR

Luwanna Jean

In a surreal way, the night club scene was attractive to Beverly, but too risky for a fourteen-year-old still concerned about pleasing her parents. Reluctantly, she went back to the country; the jamborees, the steel guitars; but, it wasn't long before she felt stagnant again. Even though she walked away from dancing, she couldn't leave the thrill of downtown—it was vibrant, spontaneous, and magnetic. She liked the fast track and everything about it. It drew her back night after night, to watch, to breathe in the magic, and to chat with a growing circle of new exotic friends.

As the tempo was winding down late one evening and the barkeep was drying the rim of another glass, Beverly was trying to talk herself into staying a little longer. She really didn't want to know what time it was, but her intuition told her it was time to leave. After saying her goodnights, she took to the stairs wishing she could just snap her fingers and be home. Catching her heel on one of the steps, Beverly tripped and tumbled down the stairs, smashing what appeared to be every part of her body. She tried to extend her arms to break her plunge, but she was flying too fast. Sprawled face down at the foot of the stairs, Beverly wasn't moving. Someone yelled for help, and within a minute, several people were hovering over her, trying to see if she was alive and breathing. With a little help, she was able to sit up. Holding her hands to her head and chest, she moaned painfully. Shari Angel, one of Abe's dancers, and her husband, Wally Weston, recruited themselves to rush Beverly to the emergency room at Baylor Hospital. In the hospital's admission area when they asked for a name, Beverly replied, "Bixie Bohnam." (She was still keeping a few secrets.)

Dr. Frank White and Dr. Dennis Factor tended to Beverly, taking a close look at every inch of her, touching lightly to determine any obvious bone breaks. Pressing the stethoscope to her back and then her chest, they listened closely to her breathing to make sure she hadn't punctured a lung. The doctors then noticed that Beverly was bleeding between her legs. They were deeply concerned she might have suffered a miscarriage. They listened again and took several X-rays. Beverly still ached all over. She felt like someone had taken a baseball bat to her.

When they reviewed the X-rays the doctors were relieved.

"Ms. Bonham. You took quite a fall, young lady. We were worried at first but there's no need to worry–the baby is doing fine."

"What!"

"Your baby is doing fine. Don't worry yourself any."

"Baby? You said . . . baby?"

"Ms. Bonham, you do know you are pregnant, don't you? In fact you're six months pregnant."

Beverly thought they were joking. She didn't appreciate that kind of humor and thought it was rude of them to try and play with her.

"No way. No way . . . you're crazy."

The doctors glanced at one another, then Dr. Factor said, "You really didn't know?" The two men were surprised but not amazed. Often, fit and trim girls Bixie's age, naively move through early pregnancy unaware they are a few months away from being a mother. Bixie's face confirmed she hadn't a clue she was pregnant. Immediately, the doctors changed their approach, and counseled her about what to do next and offered to serve as her doctors. Beverly tried to listen, but was awe struck, realizing that there was another heart beating inside her. A tiny heart.

Beverly thought back to the only time conception could have happened and was transmogrified. Her emotions overloaded and she felt faint. Joy battled anger–reason wrestled with her feelings.

"Here, listen for yourself." Dr. White said, handing her the stethoscope and placing it to her abdomen.

Thump, thump, thump, thump . . . .

Listening to the fast heartbeat pounding inside her almost caused Beverly to cry. She was so confused and felt so alone. What were her parents going to think? How were they going to act? What about the father? But most importantly, what about the baby? Thump, thump, thump, thump . . . .

Beverly's parents were devastated when she explained everything and how it had happened, but they were as supportive as loving parents could be. They told her they would uphold whatever decision she made—after the baby was born. Beverly's sister, Mary Ann, insisted that she keep the baby under any circumstance. "Beverly! God will never forgive you if you give that baby up." Mary Ann knew about the misery of guilt and its relentless torment. Before Beverly was born, Mary Ann was asked to watch her younger brother while her mother was upstairs. In the few short minutes that it took to look away, little two-year-old Lon Harrison Oliver managed to swallow a handful of strychnine, which to his young eyes looked like table salt—something he liked a lot. Ever since her brother's death, Mary Ann carried the bitter guilt that she was personally responsible, even though she wasn't, and that her mother would never forgive her. She loved Beverly and didn't want her to make a decision that would haunt her the rest of her life.

Beverly wasn't going to make up her mind too early about whether to keep the baby or give it up for adoption. She knew who the father was but refused to be pushed into a marriage that wouldn't have a chance of surviving.

"Mother . . . Dad. I don't love him. I'm very angry with him and that will never change. It wouldn't be fair to our child to be caught between us. There's nothing to gain by us getting married." Beverly was being honest. A random, one-time act of youthful thoughtlessness wasn't going to cause her to spend the rest of her life married to someone . . . she didn't even want to think about.

Seventy-million deaths; Berlin was at a breaking point and that was the estimate of American lives lost provided the President if a nuclear war became a reality. Searching his intellect, calling upon prayer, utilizing all available resources, John Kennedy struggled with a horror so inconceivable it defied logic.

Berlin was a city who's people were politically separated between East and West; a city where some people were living free and others forced to live; a city scarred by an invisible wound cutting the city in two. Soviet policy planned Berlin as a stepping stone in neutralizing Germany, then Western Europe, and eventually causing the breakup of NATO. Without NATO, the President knew—Europe was in danger. Possibly, a war over Berlin could mean the end of civilization.

Before President Kennedy's first meeting with Khrushchev, a strategy for Berlin was being charted, but a workable solution was nowhere in sight. Khrushchev's cold-hearted vacuum of wayward reasoning petrified the President and concern for Berlin kept him imprisoned. Trying to understand how to negotiate with Khrushchev was hopeless. Each June day had been a step closer to a showdown. If Kennedy didn't take a step forward with each foot in the dirt Khrushchev took, he risked losing Europe. Kennedy's address to the nation in July was mirrored by Khrushchev in August. Both men spoke about the perils of nuclear war and emphasized the need to sit and reason but offered nothing of resolve.

Germany, France, and Britain joined the United States in a brainstorm session to discuss the feasibility of inviting the Soviet Union to a four nation peace conference, but lack of a solid proposal for peace and France's hostility killed any progress. De Gaulle was adamant that such action would be "construed as a prelude to abandonment . . . and as a notice of surrender."

Berlin was reaching a boiling point and Kennedy knew it, something was going to explode. Over thirty thousand East Germans had fled to the West. A thousand people a day. And, Khrushchev couldn't stop it. He had to do something, Berlin was too valuable.

August 13, 1961. Just past midnight the sound of jackhammers and heavy machinery gave alarm that something was happening. Roadblocks and barbwire sprang up at every crosspoint connecting the two Berlins. Before dawn the flow of Easterners into the Western sector of the city was halted. Anticipating that Khrushchev was going to do something, the Kennedy administration was caught off guard but helpless to do anything since everything was still east of the border. On August 17, a crude gray wall of blocks began to rise stretching the length of freedom. In a tense, bold, scary move, John Kennedy made his decision. Before the ink could dry on his order, the 1st Battle Group of the 8th Infantry, a convoy of 1,500 men and armored vehicles, crossed the Soviet controlled border of East Germany under threat of war, then sped unchallenged the one hundred and four mile autobahn to West Berlin.

What began as a threat challenging the mettle of men . . . what began as a showdown between superpowers . . . what began as the beginning of what could have been the end, dissolved into a stalemate of consequence. The wall, in all its stone cold symbolism, in all its menacing might and functionality . . . became the solution that eased the trigger readiness of two nations breathing words of war.

Khrushchev kept the dignity he needed, Kennedy had the peace he wanted.

Labor was everything Beverly had heard about but different than anything she could have imagined. On February 22, 1962, at about 8:30 PM, Beverly gave birth to a beautiful baby girl. When her baby was placed in her arms, she cried for air and Beverly wanted to comfort her. She wanted her to know that she was safe. Cradling her newborn warmly in the folds of her arms, watching every little breath she took, Beverly whispered the name, Luwanna Jean, and took her tears away. *Luwanna Jean. Luwanna Jean it's your mother.*

Recovering in a blissful daze, letting nothing but motherhood take control, Beverly bonded with her little girl in the quiet of her room. Luwanna was so small and lovely. Delicate and vulnerable. Her hair was dark brown and baby fine, and her blue eyes shouted for attention. Beverly kept playing with her tiny hand, letting Luwanna grab the tip of her finger and hold on tight with a pint-sized squeeze. Beverly felt she could lay there forever touching her baby-soft skin. After they took Luwanna back to the nursery, Beverly plunged into a deep restful sleep. Far into another reality, Beverly experienced a vivid dream—the story of Solomon: two mothers and the one baby. Rather than have the baby killed, each mother getting half, the true mother relinquished her paternal rights to save the precious young life. When Beverly awoke, she asked to see Luwanna. She held her tight—as close as she could. Luwanna was warm and soft, just like before. She had better color than when Beverly first held her, and that was good. Beverly counted her "itsy-bitsy" fingers, her "teensy-weensy" toes, and checked her over gently from head to foot. Luwanna was perfect. Every detail was flawless. She looked again at her tiny fingernails, wondering how they could be so small.

"Please, come take her," Beverly said gently, handing Luwanna to the nurse. As she walked away, Beverly blew Luwanna a kiss.

The papers were signed and Beverly asked to see her baby again, but her request was matter-of-factly refused. She was told that it was not only against better judgment, but against the rules at Hope Cottage.

"Excuse me!" Beverly barked, grabbing the papers she just signed. "If you want to keep me from tearing up these papers then you bring me my daughter, now! I have something I want to say to her."

Beverly held Luwanna once again. Luwanna had to hear from her mother that she loved her and that she would be forever missed. Looking deep into her baby eyes, Beverly poured forth every ounce of love she could muster. "Mamma loves you, my precious. I'll never forget how special it feels to hold you, my little wonder. You will always be in my heart. I love you."

Beverly held Luwanna close as she whispered. She wanted Luwanna to feel the warmth of breath and the softness of her voice as she spoke each word, and to store them somewhere in the back of her mind to keep with her forever.

"Mothers know," Beverly thought. She knew . . . the baby knew. It was good-by.

CHAPTER FIVE

Interlude

Nineteen-sixty-two was turning into a year full of heartaches.

Beverly was sixteen and already feeling used. The trauma of giving birth and then giving up her baby, took a greater toll than she realized. While she was able to keep her thoughts of Luwanna locked in a secret chamber in her mind, her spirit still ached and led to a craving for change. She wanted to do something different, something refreshing. She found it in Arlington.

A new theme park had opened which a school teacher friend, Richard McMahan, told Beverly about. He had worked there the previous summer and thoroughly enjoyed it. When another friend, Joe Poovey (Johnny Dallas) told her they were looking for singers, she decided to try out for the auditions. With her experience she thought the job was in the palm of her hand, and a few minutes into her song and dance, it was.

Beverly stared at herself in the mirror: a red and white polka dot dress, tight at the waist and low from the neck, black opera hose, black high heels, and a big red rose stuck in her hair. *Here I am—a saloon singer at the Crazy Horse Saloon.* Ironically, her prophecy of being a saloon singer was fulfilled.

Six Flags was demanding. Up at seven each morning, Beverly had to be dressed, in make-up, and on stage by 10:00 AM. The show was forty minutes long, there was a twenty-minute breather, then it was show time again. Ten shows later at 10:30 PM, she was able to make the long trip back to Garland, or on occasion, go out on a date.

The singer at the Crazy Horse Saloon was someone to watch—the word got out. With her blond hair, blue eyes, and clear skin, Beverly had that apple pie look. Her bouncy voice, those crazy songs, and that cute costume, were set off by fiery red lipstick and nail polish. And when she smiled, it looked like no one could be having more fun than she. It was tiring, but Beverly enjoyed singing to the crowds packing the saloon. She sang the same songs over and over, but each new face made them fresh again. Each performance Beverly selected a cute little boy to sing to and send his heart fluttering. She winked at quite a few men too.

Beverly had a few dates with Angus (Ango) Wynn III, whose father was the developer and owner of the park. She also dated a man by the name of Larry Ronco, Jr. Larry was from New York and a representative of Eastman Kodak. It was his responsibility to manage the Kodak displays and keep the park stocked with plenty of film. He exposed a lot of film as well; taking pictures of Beverly at every chance he could around the park. The snapshots of Beverly ended up as promotional pictures plastered at every Kodak "Hot Spot." She was also featured in a short Six Flags film advertisement. It was shown constantly and she loved every minute of it.

Larry and Beverly hit it off quickly and soon became close friends. Beverly felt comfortable around him. He approached the relationship in a mature manner and was careful to earn her respect.

During one afternoon performance, Stanley McIlvane, a park executive, stopped by the Crazy Horse to speak with Beverly. After the hall cleared he told her Charlie Meeker wanted to see her in his office right away. Beverly had that gut feeling that something wasn't right. (Meeker reported directly to Angus Wynn.) *Does this have anything to do with my dating Ango?*

Mr. Meeker swirled his chair around and asked Beverly to take a seat. There was no need to beat around the bush, so he fired point blank. "Beverly, I understand that you're a stripper, and frankly, we don't need someone like you representing Six Flags. This is a family park and our employees must epitomize the principles that govern such. Effective immediately you are no longer an employee here. Is that understood?"

Beverly was dumb-struck. She had no idea what he was talking about. "I beg your pardon. That's absurd, Mr. Meeker. I have . . . ."

"What were you doing last night at that party then?" Meeker asked, thinking he had Beverly cornered.

"First of all, what I do at parties and with my personal life should be of no interest to this park. Secondly, if you think for one moment that I stripped at that party, then you're terribly misinformed and out of your mind. I was at a party, but I was asked to sing and I did. Who told you this?"

"That's irrelevant. Besides, I don't believe you. You're fired and you can leave now."

Beverly was insulted and felt victimized. "Well, Mr. Meeker. That's just fine and dandy, if that's the way you want it. But, you better get busy taking down all those wonderful posters around the park with my picture on them. All of them! You never did get my written permission to use them. Oh, and don't forget the promotional film I appear in for this park 'where I'm no longer an employee'."

Beverly left in a huff. Mr. Meeker's bullheadedness made her angry and the thought of loosing her audience to something so asinine made her mad.

It's his loss not mine, he'll soon realize.

Abe was glad to see Beverly again and cheerily agreed to let her sing at the club and see how things turned out. *Bill Bailey, Blues in the Night, Embrace Me*–Beverly cranked out her new repertoire and stole the show. The Colony Club had a new singer.

After explaining to Abe what had happened at Six Flags, Beverly learned what had cost her the job and was surprised that indirectly, Abe had something to do with it. Abe told Beverly that he was visiting a friend, Layfe Phypher, at the park who insisted on taking him over to the Crazy Horse Saloon to listen to a pretty young lady sing. Abe took one look at the singer and smiled. "Sure, I know Beverly, she used to work for me." Naturally, when people thought of girls working for Abe, it wasn't as a singer.

President Kennedy had spent the first half of the year juggling a lifetime of issues, none of them easy to manage. Nuclear disarmament and the banning of nuclear testing was month-in month-out, touch and go issue; the Department of State was being revamped; foreign policy was trying to influence the United Nations while struggling with Laos, the Congo, Angola, Mozambique, Portuguese Guinea, Apartheid, and Vietnam. The CIA was running amok. Economics, racism, foreign aid, food-for-peace, the balance of payments, conservation, and education.

True to his nature, John Kennedy continued to devour everything he could to stay on top of everything and to exert as much control as he could as both a visionary and helmsman. The original reports prepared for him by the State Department he trashed. He had little use of overviews; he wanted detailed information about operations so he could make more informed decisions. He revised protocol, trimming formal diplomacy of its superfluous dress so men could engage men in private conversation and candor. He met with leaders, both celebrated men and minor dignitaries–European, Asian, and African, and he was studied in all their issues. Kennedy's knowledge of small world problems and his desire to keep the breath of democracy flowing freely earned him personal respect and strengthen alliances. He discussed uncertainty and hope; he invited opinion, he spoke openly–he listened intently. He cared. Those who shared with him the dreams and fears of their countrymen walked away with pride but not disillusioned with false promises or great expectations.

A testament to John Kennedy's concern to promote international cooperation and good will toward America was being planted in countries all over the world by young men and women voluntarily serving in the *Peace Corps*, then barely a year old. The Peace Corps's mission was accomplishing more than could be wished for. While it was argued that a few thousand students crusading for economic development was a "handful of sand cast into the vast sea of underdevelopment," the measure of the programs success could only be sampled in the hearts of the volunteers as they shared what they knew with those who didn't know how.

As the summer of 1962 reached midpoint, John Kennedy could look in retrospect and take pride in the distance covered by his administration over diverse, uncharted, and dangerous political terrain, and feel encouraged that with time, prayer, and more work, the new frontier would be peacefully settled.

President Kennedy received an urgent message from the CIA alerting him to strange, suspicious developments in Cuba. Why were 5,000 Soviet specialists in Cuba and what were they helping Castro with? What were they building? And why were more men and supplies coming?

In short order, American technology, utilizing a series of reconnaissance flights, provided the answer. Working like beavers, a vast network of long range missile sites were being covertly constructed by the Soviets and Cubans. Missiles which could be fired at the United States and arrive on selected targets faster than some people could pray.

Strategic defense system or not, nothing was fail-safe.

CHAPTER SIX

Along The Watchtower

John Kennedy sat staring at the future, his hand flexing in front of his face like a barometer of anxiety. The horrific threat of a nuclear holocaust had once again shadowed his presidency and thoughts of children tempered his mind with restraint. His brother Robert sat before him.

Conclusive photographic evidence that the Soviet Union was placing offensive missiles in Cuba laid in a folder face down on his desk. Information which was yet to be made public. President Kennedy felt betrayed, but remained incredibly calm. The Russian Embassy, the Russian Foreign Minister, and even Khrushchev, denied that they were, or would, place nuclear weapons on foreign soil. But the pictures didn't lie, and he wondered why they denied it. This evidence of a covert plan to position destructive warheads within range of every North American city was proof that what flared in Berlin had silently steamrolled underground into an aggressive plan to checkmate the United States of America. It had been four days since the first photographs were handed to the President on October 15, and a decision on how to react had been secretly contemplated with persistant attention and keen focus. Kennedy was quick to pull together the resources of reasoning he needed to analyze every detail, scrutinize every alternative, and design a plausible solution. He permitted his executive committee to control their own roundtable, periodically entering the room to take their temperature. He understood that his continued presence in the meeting would be a distraction and impede the creative process. It was paramount that the boundaries of applied reasoning were stretched in search of the right decision. A decision that would halt and reverse the actions of a hard-line tyrant without pressuring the man to the point of madness. Kennedy wholeheartedly believed that backing an opponent into a corner was dangerous and that it was critical to swallow self-righteousness and humbly assist the adversary in saving face to his countrymen.

Before he made a decision about Cuba, Kennedy wanted to know everything there was to know. In addition to listening to his counselors, he studied his own intelligence reports which bypassed normal channels of information, including the CIA and the Pentagon. But, all the midnight brainstorming with his advisors, all the reports, resulted in only two alternatives and "not doing anything" was not one of them. The decision to impose a Naval blockade around the island and confront any ship carrying missiles or other military machinery was met head-on with plans to invade Cuba and destroy not only the strategic missile sites, but its airports and military airpower as well. Supporters of a bombing strike against Cuba insisted it would quickly remove the immediate threat and send a powerful statement to Moscow that the U.S. was deadly serious. Supporters of the blockade thought that a raid on Cuba and the killing of innocent civilians would jeopardized long term peace plans with other small countries struggling with independence; furthermore, the deaths of Russian soldiers and engineers assisting with the buildup could possibly lead to nuclear retaliation. A blockade was viewed by the warhawks as too weak–an ineffective stance which could not stop progress on the missile sites and immediately lead to a blockade of Berlin. Robert Kennedy was adamant about not bombing and stuck by his guns. He declared that sneak attacks on small nations was not in America's tradition. He vigorously insisted that such an act was not ethical and would constitute "a betrayal of our heritage and out ideals," akin to the unprovoked bombing of Pearl Harbor. Whatever the President should decide, a decision had to be made before the sensitive situation was presented to the public and the situation was at hand.

The debate about Cuba was finally put to a vote but Kennedy didn't want anyone to bear the burden of guilt if their vote was cast on a plan which failed; instead he stepped forward and cast the only vote that mattered and ordered everyone to begin preparations for a quarantine. The term *quarantine* was chosen to describe the nation's actions instead of *blockade* in hopes that it wouldn't equate as an act of war. Those who were in favor of a military strike seemed pacified that such an action didn't negate the possibility of launching a military strike if the quarantine didn't produce results.

At 7:00 PM on October 22, President Kennedy stood before the nation and alerted its citizens that the United States had been betrayed by the Soviet Union and that nuclear missiles were being delivered, positioned, and manned in Cuba; missiles capable of reaching destinations as far north as Canada and as far away as Mexico City. He explained the quarantine in simple purpose and asked for understanding, "But the greatest danger of all would be to do nothing . . .

Our goal is not victory of might, but the vindication of right . . . not peace at the expense of freedom, but both peace and freedom, here in this hemisphere, and, we hope, around the world. God willing, that goal will be achieved."

Global reaction to Kennedy's quarantine was met with varied approval and skepticism, and in some quarters—outright fear. Some countries questioned if there actually were missiles in Cuba, or if it was a CIA ploy to justify an invasion. If there were missiles, some thinking went, the U.S. should just permit them; after all, America had missiles in Europe close to Russia. Regardless how the debate was being battled, Russian ships with nuclear cargo were crossing the Pacific and bulldozers were plowing new ground in Cuba to await their arrival. In Florida, over 150,000 U.S. military troops were poised for combat.

Khrushchev retaliated by dispatching a letter to Kennedy saying everything in Cuba was complete, that all the missiles were defensive in nature, and that if the United States didn't withdraw its quarantine, the Soviet Union might be forced to take necessary measures of its own. However, if the quarantine was called off and a guarantee not to invade Cuba was insured by the United States and that it guard against other transgressors, then it "would change everything immediately."

Kennedy had not even had time to respond to the Khrushchev letter when a second letter arrived. This letter was ominous. It propositioned the United States to remove its missiles in Turkey and agree to a non–aggression pact toward the country in exchange for the missiles being withdrawn from Cuba. Kennedy had no sooner rejected the notion to his advisors than word came that an American reconnaissance plane was presumably shot down over Cuba. Then another American reconnaissance plane was monitored flying over Russian territory near Alaska, presumably off course, spawning fear that the Soviets might think that such a bold act was premeditated as a final preparation for invasion. Something had to give. Kennedy was careful not to be too reactionary but he had to make a move to keep Khrushchev from making the wrong move. In the maddening rush to resolve the tense situation, Robert Kennedy suggested that Khrushchev's second letter be ignored and a reply given to the first letter.

A response to Khrushchev's first letter was quickly prepared and hand delivered to the Soviet Ambassador on October 17. Its contents welcomed a swift resolution by halting work on the missile bases and neutralizing all warheads under supervision of the United Nations. A demand for a reply was attached threatening military action if assurances weren't received within twenty-four hours. President Kennedy, Robert Kennedy, and everyone involved, waited in the quiet of not knowing what would happen. Time crawled at the speed of impatience as dark took the sky.

Victory can be difficult to measure when history's yardstick is perpetually lengthened. But early the next moring as Khrushchev's reply slowly spelled adherence to America's plan for resolution, the somber days of October were quieted and victory was measured in the faces of children everywhere.

On the eve of the holiday season, in the cold of December, on the Ellipse in the nation's capitol, President Kennedy expressed his deepest desire after the struggles of 1962.

"The old year is coming to an end. It has been a long year, a troubled year, a year of anxiety and trial and danger. Yet it is a year which, I deeply believe, has brought the world closer to mankind's abiding vision of peace.

"As we light this tree, as trees are lit across our land and across the earth, let the spirit of Christmas rise freely within ourselves . . . and, in that divine illumination, let us drive bitterness and hate and cruelty from the souls of men. As Christ knew, this is the hardest, the most unending fight of all . . . but it was in that fight He found His glory. Our highest hope is to follow humbly in His path. In the words of John Greenleaf Whitter:

"Blow, bugles of battle, the marches of peace;
East, west, north, and south, let the long quarrel cease;
Sing the song of great joy that the angels began,
Sing the glory of God and of goodwill to man!"

II

The Carousel Club
Jack Ruby—In Search Of Class
1963
The Day Before
November 22, 1963
The Mourning After

CHAPTER SEVEN

The Carousel Club

When Beverly returned to the Colony Club, Shari wasted no time taking her under wing, teaching her the ropes, and making sure she was protected from the older girls' vices. Shari was the only one at the club who had known Beverly was only fourteen when she first came to the club and that she was still underage. Even though Beverly was a singer, Shari told her about the rules dancers had to follow: two girls could not be on the stage at the same time, no flesh-colored G-strings, and no aureoles showing around the pasties. No pubic hair–at all. No touching one's own breasts. No crotch grabbing. No tips.

Beverly's new style of singing blended well with the decor and clientele of the Colony Club, more so than the Theater Lounge. The decor was refined in subtle ways catering to more polished tastes. Black, white, and gold applications gave the main room a dressed-up look.

The club was conveniently located at 1322½ Commerce Street across the street from the Adolphus Hotel. The ½ in the address meant there were stairs involved. The staircase leading up to the club was covered with a thick plush red carpet interrupted by a small landing. At the top of the stairway was a semicircle-shaped counter, tightly covered in black leather and accented with band of silver. Patrons having tackled the stairs were pleasantly greeted by a lovely lady perched behind the counter, who quietly collected the two-dollar cover charge. Commanding the attention of anyone who entered the grand club room was the performance stage. Whether it was occupied or not, the room was framed to accent the stage. Suspended from the ceiling in a graceful presentation of horizontal arcs was the stage lighting supported by two poles dressed in art nouveau. Likewise, the walls bordering the stage were accented with strong nouveau lines.

Measuring about twenty-five by thirty feet, the stage was elevated from the floor, doubling between shows as the dance floor. Wrapped around it was a shiny black, knee-high, metal rail which served as a reminder to any lustful man to keep his hands to himself. Beverly often sat on the rail as she serenaded someone. As Beverly moved closer and he moved closer, then she, then him, to the point where he believed he was just a kiss away . . . she would bounce up and walk away to sing to someone else, looking back over her shoulder to wink with a curious "maybe later" glance.

Joe Garcia's orchestra played behind a net drape separating the musicians from the performers in a simple dreamscape. Music jazzed around the room like smoke or sprang from table-to-table in up-beat chaos. Black leather chairs, white linen table cloths, plush carpeting, and flickering candlelight together created a sensuous atmosphere. In the back corner of the room, opposite the stage, was an inconspicuous door leading to where it all really happened. Behind the door was another stairway leading to Abe's private club where he entertained his select clientele. Most people frequenting the Colony Club were unaware of its existence. Cast in soft blue lighting and unusually framed in dark blue mirrors, softened further with the delicate feel of velvet, the secluded room served its guests in whispered elegance.

The third floor also accommodated the dressing rooms and a shower. There was one community dressing room for all the dancers. Beverly, Wally, and Chris Colt, had private dressing rooms. A narrow back staircase led to the holding room for the stage.

Everyone relished their favorite dancers but Chris Colt and her "forty-fives" brought the men in by the truckloads, and they weren't talking about the guns on her hips. Chris favored short western suits, white boots, and even standing still, she had a flair for getting everyone's attention. She was well-sculpured. There wasn't a blemish on her entire body.

Bubbles Cash, another blond bombshell, drew crowds from clear across Texas. She was so gorgeous men did double takes to insure she wasn't a mirage. Toi Rebel. Spice and nice. A delicate, saucy, and tempered young woman; she was a stick of dynamite who every man wanted to pick up, and take home. Black hair. Black eyes. Pretty beaded gowns. Her appearance flaunted an elegance which almost seemed incongruous with a striptease act.

Toni Turner danced with live snakes for awhile, but switched to something less slithery and more in accord with her personality, a long handled powder-puff. During her routine Toni would dip the powder-puff in a box of Gardenia-scented powder and hand it to a male customer, allowing him the pleasure of powdering her long legs. After the first leg was dusted, he would hand it back to Toni for more powder so that he could continue with her other leg. Looking him seductively in the eye, Toni would load the puff with excess powder and promptly dust the gentleman with enough powder to make it impossible for him to explain to his wife or girlfriend what he was really doing late after work.

The girls were fortunate to have a teddy bear for a bouncer, one who knew his job. Bob Larkin knew how to flex his attitude and deliver a tenacious message to anyone even contemplating touching one of the girls. He was a likable person whose face usually was tattooed with a huge white toothy smile. Fortunately, unlike the Carousel Club, there were very few altercations.

Other than with Shari and Chris, Beverly spoke with most of the girls only on a casual basis. She drew an imaginary social line between them and actively kept her private life separate from her nightlife, and they knew it—even if they didn't fully understand it. Truthfully though, Beverly was still playing the tiresome game of hiding the burlesque scene from her parents, and as much as she wanted to tell them what she was doing, she couldn't. Besides, she was younger, a singer, and was paid more than most of the dancers. This became a sore spot with those who knew, causing tempers to sometimes flare in spontaneous fights of will and fingernail. One evening after laughing with some of the girls in their dressing room, Beverly turned to leave when Toi, who for some reason had become greatly perturbed, grabbed a green water bottle and struck Beverly hard on the back of her head. Beverly reacted quickly, pouncing on Toi with speed and vengeance. She jerked Toi onto the middle of the floor and proceeded to beat the tar out of her. Beverly was fuming and couldn't stop banging Toi's head against the floor. She soon became covered in Toi's blood. Bob Larkin heard the commotion and raced to the dressing room in time to break up the fight before things got nastier. Toi was dragged off in one direction and Beverly the other. Beverly was taken to the emergency room in Garland where her doctor, Dr. Speegle, resided. When he saw Beverly splattered with blood he was worried. But, once the dry blood was scrubbed off, Beverly only had a black eye and a couple of bite marks. The blood was all Toi's.

The next day, Abe was furious with Toi, and demanded that she continue to work—busted teeth and all. He gave Beverly the week off—with pay.

A few months later, Toi was at it again. Beverly and Carri Castle, another dancer, were chatting when Toi intruded. "Carri, where's my money? You better give me that money back, or I'll wipe-up this floor with you." Toi demanded. When it came to losing money, nostrils flared easily. Toi and Carri had earned some money together earlier that week and were paid with a check. Toi had given Carri her share in cash, which she promptly spent, but when the check bounced, Toi wanted her money back.

Beverly promptly stepped between the two girls as Toi tried to close the gap. Carri was extremely petite, even younger than Beverly, and didn't stand a chance against Toi's wrath or right hook.

"Excuse me, Toi!" Beverly, said. "If you seriously want to do that, you gotta walk through me before you get to her. And I don't think you really want to do that again. Do you?"

Needless to say, Toi didn't. Teeth were expensive.

Beverly knew how to scrap with the girls, but she also knew how to joke with them as well. As she spent more time at the club with everyone, she became a prankster and enjoyed playing games with some of the them. Bubbles in particular. When Bubbles came to town she introduced a new grind to the burlesque stage. She started seducing the floor, the wall, the post. It was a new era for the Colony Club and Beverly thought Bubble's act was too raunchy and didn't belong in Dallas. Furthermore, Beverly's performance had to follow Bubbles' routine and Beverly couldn't stand it; especially since Beverly performed with all her clothes on.

Jokingly, Beverly couldn't help but try to take a little air out of Bubbles' act and divert the audience's attention. With all its studded beads, Bubbles' bra weighed nearly five pounds. During her striptease she would take it off, swing it around high over her head, let it fly from her hand and slide on the stage floor underneath the curtain. Waiting mischievously behind the curtain, Beverly would take Bubbles' bra and sling it back across the stage. Bubbles would toss it back underneath the curtain. Beverly would sling it back.

The Texas-Oklahoma University weekend pep rally always brought the largest crowds downtown. Traffic outside on Commerce Street and inside the Colony Club was bumper to bumper. The standing-room-only crowd kept the cash registers overflowed, but to the chagrin of the girls, they could not take the night off to party under any circumstances. It was strictly forbidden. Furthermore, anyone wanting to get dressed in time for the first show needed to leave home an hour or two earlier than usual. The girls knew that a "hospital stay" was the only excuse Abe would accept for any absence. That, or laying lifeless in a morgue somewhere. Abe wanted all his girls at the club on Texas-OU night because of self-preservation. Crowds were so rowdy and volatile that if the particular girl they came to see wasn't on stage, the walls could come down. It wasn't worth the risk. Texas-OU weekend netted more arrests for drunkenness and disorderly conduct than most months combined and Abe wasn't going to let the Colony Club become a boxing ring.

The girls felt left out of the Texas-OU bash. It was party time out on the streets and they had to work. One Friday night, before the big Cotton Bowl showdown, the girls still had quite a bit of time before curtain call and were impatiently bored. And a bored Beverly was critically dangerous. Reaching into her makeup kit, Beverly grabbed a couple of boxes of sidewalk poppers left over from the Fourth of July—just the cure for the boredom. Beverly coerced Chris and Carri to climb out on the third floor fire escape to watch and titillate the crowd. Pop-pop! Pop! People below were bewildered. At first they would look all around wondering where the noise was coming from, but it wasn't long before the girls caught everyone's attention. Pop-pop!

Abe was going about his routine of preparing the club for a blow out when Hal Hood, the Dallas County Fire Chief, marched into the club and confronted Abe. "Abe, those girls of yours are causing quite a ruckus out on your balcony. They're throwing firecrackers into the crowd and I'm afraid someone might get hurt. You wouldn't want that would you?"

Abe didn't believe Chief Hood. "Not my girls. They're professionals. They're showgirls. They must be Jack Ruby's girls."

"No Abe. They are 'your' girls on 'your' fire escape. I'm right, go look for yourself. I have no reason to fool you."

Abe insisted that Chief Hood follow him upstairs to the dressing rooms to see for himself. Abe was confident that his girls were minding their own business and getting dressed. Not his girls. Professionals.

Abe's jaw dropped when he looked outside and saw Beverly and the girls just as Mr. Hood had said—his girls on his fire escape, throwing crackerballs into the crowd below. Adding insult to injury, the girls were clothed only in their dressing robes with their hair still in rollers. And not a single one of them had on any make-up.

Abe was shamed. The look on his face cut to the bone and the girls knew he was sincerely embarrassed by what they were doing. He didn't need to say anything. His eyes pierced straight through them. His gaping mouth suggested that he was speechless. The three "professional" entertainers left the balcony with their "tails" tucked tightly between their legs. Beverly knew—that Abe knew whose bright idea it was to disturb the peace, and it took a long time for her to get back in his good graces.

Jack benefited that year from a falling out that Wally Weston had with Abe Weinstein. Wally grabbed his jacket and Shari and left the Colony Club for Jack's place He welcomed them with open arms. Wally was replaced by comedian Artie Brooks. Always dressed in a black tuxedo, Artie ran the show with panache. He was a riot and kept Beverly and everyone within ear shot in complete hysterics.

With Shari next door at the Carousel, Beverly found herself going over there more and more often to visit.

CHAPTER EIGHT

Jack Ruby: In Search Of Class

It was late. Beverly and Jack were sitting at a table enjoying random conversation, hot coffee, and the fluorescent ambiance of the bus station diner: luggage, newspapers, and smashed cigarettes. Beverly finally had a car so she was no longer constrained by the 12:15 bus to Garland, but she was tiring. She knew Jack could talk all night–she would soon need to head home. He had told her he usually stayed up until breakfast, grabbing some eggs at Denny's over by Love Field, the Dobb's House on Cedar Springs, or at Lucas B&B on Oak Lawn and then grabbed a little early morning shut-eye at his apartment or on the cot in the back room of his club.

Beverly was fascinated by Jack. He was proud yet humble. As rough as he could be, he knew how to be a gentleman.

"Beverly, tell me when you started singing. How'd that happen? I hear you used to sing at the Big D Jamboree. Boy, I bet that was a lot different than the Colony."

Beverly relished telling her story of singing from the altar and pocketing a few dollars from the little old men who thought she was so cute. Jack said he admired her spunk. When he was about eight, he started hustling a little change himself by selling Christmas shopping bags for a few pennies. He told her he liked Christmas and enjoyed giving, especially to the orphanage: big Teddy Bears, new footballs, dolls with floating eyes. Every year, he went shopping for kids without parents, he prided himself. He told her that on most Sundays, Wally, Shari, he, and a few others, would visit the Veterans Hospital and perform a little act to cheer everyone up.

When Beverly and Jack visited, he did most of the talking, often repeating himself and using misplaced words. He kept her laughing. He liked to tell jokes, often racist, sometimes sexist, however he felt different when someone told a Jew joke. Leroy and Rasses were his favorites. "Hey Leroy. Why did you tell those folks down at the feed store I was a low down rotten scoundrel?" "I didn't, Rasses, I don't know how they found out." Jack chortled. When he told a joke his face would light up and for that split second you could see right through him. He wasn't laughing at Leroy and Rasses, he was poking fun at himself and how insane everything was.

Beverly made a point to remember Jack's jokes; Abe always enjoyed a good razz. He remembered every joke he heard, or so he prided himself.

Working on a hot refill, Jack's joke still bouncing around in her mind, Beverly watched as a young boy trooped by with a busted lip and a bruised eye, treading three feet behind his dad, his eyes painfully fixed on the floor. "Look at that poor little boy; he must have taken a terrible fall." Beverly remarked. It hurt just looking at him; his eye was purple and near swollen shut.

"Yeah," said Jack. "He probably took one like the kind I always took." He paused for a moment watching the boy fade into his thoughts of his childhood. "You know I never had a chance when I was growing up. Everybody needs a little stroking once in awhile and the only stroking I got was with a baseball bat. I once had a broken leg and instead of feeling sorry for me–my dad beat me. Yeah, he said it was my fault and it was going to put him out, you know. Broken bones weren't cheap. It seemed that everything that went wrong was my fault. That made it easy for him. Hard on me–easy for him."

Jack Ruby's childhood was tough. Some children were fortunate for the opportunity just to get to be a kid; he was not so lucky. His dad, a Russian immigrant carpenter, took to heavy drinking and frequent rages making family life miserable. It became so rough that when Ruby was twelve he was ordered to a foster home after his dad left and his mother went mentally overboard. During the next few years he saw several homes. It was there in the stale and vacant recesses of his mind that he adopted an admiration for the wrong lifestyle by associating with a group of known gangsters. Jack wanted to make things happen for himself and knew it took money; gangsters knew how to make it. He vowed he wouldn't be like his dad, beaten by his own cruelty, dependent on alcohol to boost his depleted confidence, quick to push his fists around. After running a few errands for some local hoods, Ruby became an errand boy for the members of the Al Capone mob, including the cigar-smoking icon himself. He also made a little money selling pennants, parking cars, and scalping tickets. A dollar here, a dollar there.

Beverly didn't know what to say and felt pity for him. She always thought Jack didn't drink because it would interfere with managing the club. Her parents were so polite and thoughtful, it was hard to think that any parent would want to hurt someone they brought into the world. She sat there while he played out the rest of the story in his head.

"What about you as a kid? Tell me something I don't know." Jack's attention came back to the table.

"What would you like to know?"

"What about your parents? I bet they treated you with kid gloves. Brothers? Sisters?"

Beverly wasn't ready to share her family history with him because she had been so secretive with everyone about her age. Instead, she just covered a few highlights. "You've heard me talk about my older brother, Eugene; however, I have an older sister, Mary Ann, and a younger sister Glenda. We get along pretty well. Eugene's my protector; he's always watching out for me. I love my parents, but sometimes I feel their marriage is too centered around all us kids. They seem to have lost the spark that set them afire years ago. My dad is a sweetheart; he doesn't have a mean bone in his body. He doesn't even know how to use a mean word. He's soft-spoken and works hard. He would always spare the rod when we misbehaved, but we certainly knew where he stood and how disappointed he was with us. My mother . . . sometimes my mother is hard to get close to; I don't know why. I love her with all my heart and soul but don't feel she returns it. Oh, I know she love's me, but it's her intensity—something is missing. I wish she would talk to me like a friend sometimes—I think she hurts inside. I wonder sometimes how different their lives would have been if they hadn't had us kids to provide for."

The conversation had turned to a sad note. Jack looked at Beverly, his dark eyes blacker than the night painted on the flip side of the window. Loneliness has a way of loitering around bus terminals and it eventually pulled up a chair.

Class. Above everything else, "class" was what Jack wanted for his club, for himself, for everything around him. At times that's all that seemed to matter to him; his biggest fear was not having it. It was his mission in life and the remedy for dealing with the sour impressions of his childhood. Jack thought he'd suffered enough so it was his time to live a little, or live a lot! He defined class as "money and prestige" and without class—life was a failure. The club raked in a lot of cash but it was never enough. He knew a lot of people, had a lot of friends, but it was never enough. And through his embattled tempera-ment, his lack of creativity, and most importantly disrespect for advice, he occasionally lost both.

Jack thought his club looked classy and was the first to brag, "woe be" to anyone who disagreed. However, walking up the tight single flight of stairs to the Carousel, through the gaudy front doors, and into the club, it was evident that "class" had been misrepresented, especially if you'd just come from one of the Weinstein's clubs. Patrons were greeted by a bill of fair highlighted by wanton photographs of his show girls, beckoning them to pay the $2 cover for a peek inside. The party room was square and somewhat gaudy, measuring about 50 feet by 50 feet and lined up against the walls were large dark booths covered in slick black plastic. The floor was covered in dark red carpeting dusted with cigarette ash and wet from spilled champagne. The stage area was wooden and large enough for a five piece band to crowd in the corner and tap a beat for the girls to strip. Advertised as the southwest's only runway stage bar, the Carousel offered more ringside seats than any other club in Dallas. Three runways paraded the girls into the audience, often causing the ruckus of which Jack inevitably found himself in the middle. (It often became too tempting for some young whippersnapper to keep from trying to grab at the girls.) To the left of the stage along the entire wall was the bar; its gold-padded plastic counter was always cluttered with brown paper sacks and setups; its barstools tended by B-girls ready to pump anyone and everyone for tips. Hanging from the ceiling were gold crowns–there were crowns everywhere, and a huge fleur-de -lis flanking each side of the stage. Jack's crowning glory was a giant three dimensional painting of a gold stallion which he displayed on an easel.

However, since first arriving in Dallas, Jack did achieve some success in upgrading his visual image. Once known as the Chicago Cowboy, he was frequently seen outfitted in elaborate western outfits, grabbing a microphone for a rehearsed impromptu monologue at the old Plantation House on Industrial. At the Carousel he dropped the cowboy suit for wide-brimmed hats and high-collared shirts and was always grabbing the mike to raffle off razor blades, turkeys, or on whatever he scored a deal.

Jack was a joker and a fighter. Profanity rolled off his tongue in rapid fire, and many of those who crossed his imaginary boundary, by not measuring up to his definition of class, were lashed with insults and occasionally thrown down the stairs. Jack didn't hunt for fights though–they found him. He was so volatile, it took just a rub in the wrong direction at the right time before he erupted and took care of business with his knuckles. He practiced the art of being first to the punch. That was his advantage; he wasn't going to give the other guy a chance to think, leading to many situations which could have been avoided. But who was keeping count? One moment he was talking to someone, the next moment he was jerking some creep next to him by the collar and dragging him to the top of the stairs. It was a show. Some people came just to see Jack do his thing. On stage–off stage. To them, he was the show. The girls were only an added attraction.

When Jack was in the club everyone knew it. When he wasn't, he was out on the street hustling for more customers. He was a go-getter, always pushing something, and promoting his club at the same time. Newspapers, radio stations, handbills, free passes, Jack did everything he could think of to make his club more successful. He knew all the doormen at the hotels and encouraged them to send out-of-towners to the Carousel. When he would find crowds standing in line at the Colony Club, waiting to see a show, Jack would raid it, baiting Abe's customer's with free tickets for the "Best Show in Dallas."

As one columnist wrote about Ruby, "Jack knew no emotional plateaus. He was usually blazingly furious or naively blissful. He reduced his emotional upsets into personality conflicts." Yet, Jack prided himself by being surrounded with friends. In fact, he measured his prestige by the number of names he could mention as friends. Since Jack didn't gamble or drink much, he got his thrills by being with people. He was always talking, shooting the breeze, dropping names. "Hey, I was at the Cabana last night and ran into the Mayor." He wouldn't say that he was the one who initiated the conversation or that they really didn't know each other. He would simply imply that they were good friends. Being associated with people of power gave people power, Jack thought. And power–was class. Beverly often cautioned him, "Jack, you use the word 'friend' too loosely. In your whole life, if you can count the number of friends you have on your two hands, then consider yourself a blessed man."

Ruby's "class" stigma applied to women as well. They either had class or they were not worth his time. He would upgrade a girl to one "with class" only when she merited it by changing her appearance. It was a shallow assessment; but he graded on the curve.

Jack had a big heart for his "friends." He was often walking one of his regulars down the stairs to a cab with specific instructions, in the form of wadded-up dollar bills, for the driver to take care of them. Once, Jack even advised a customer that he was spending too much money on one of the girls and was being taken as a fool. This was right after the customer had put a down payment on a car for her. It was no news to the customer, however. He just liked being near her, smelling her perfume, gazing at her body, feeling her warm breath on his cheeks. Then, he considered the money he spent worth every penny.

Jack also had a soft spot and a hard bed for drifters. He often took someone in who was down on his luck. He'd then give him a few bucks and some chores to do. He often cussed at them for being lazy, and banged them around. But he got the satisfaction he wanted and they got the hot meal they needed. Jack fed others, too. He liked feeding people: the guys at the cleaners, the parking lot attendants, the newspaper staff and the police. Neither would he let anyone pick up a food tab when he dined out; that was classy he thought.

Sometimes the dancers chipped in to buy Jack a girl to sleep with. This kept him honest, they believed. However, to Beverly's knowledge, Jack didn't sleep with any of his girls.

Even though Jack carried a bundle of cash and remained uncomfortably behind in income taxes, he delighted in loaning his girls money. He always answered a request for an advance with back-talk. "Why if I were you, I'd save my money for emergencies. Looks like you'd learn by now to spend your money wiser and make it last all week long." Inside though, he was tickled to death to help the "pretty little things." Jack knew if he just handed them the money it would make him a softie. He didn't want that.

Jack never had the money that Abe did, and he failed to learn that it didn't take money to be respected. He equated the two together. Therefore, he was always trying to get more of it.

Jack kept a gun inside his money bag. Whenever he made a trip to the bank or ran any errands he stuck the gun in his right coat pocket. He usually kept his money in a paper sack cleverly hidden inside the kitchen oven. He didn't want all his money moving through a bank account.

As far as Beverly knew, Jack didn't pimp. While he frequently arranged for his girls to "party" with someone, he didn't take money for it. "Take care of him for me," Beverly would hear Jack say. It was his opinion that if any of his girls made extra money, great for her—she needed it. The fact that he could arrange something pleasurable and profitable for two people was all he wanted. After all, he was in show business, and it was girls they came to see and dream about getting close to. If touching was involved, it took place elsewhere.

Fortunately for Jack, a man by the name of Andy Armstrong wandered into the Carousel looking for a job. After a few off-color remarks spiced with a little Ruby humor, and a short interview about experience, expectations, and rules, Jack offered Andy a job. He also used Andy as a good excuse to fire his present barkeep, Bob, who always had his hand in the till. No sooner had Andy walked out of the office than Jack picked up the phone and told Bob to get lost.

Jack was impressed with Andy after his first night tending the bar. Jack gave him advice about how to control the girls and made sure that Andy understood that the business of paying for drinks the girls ordered for customers was his responsibility.

Andy was an honest, hard-working man for Jack. He knew the boundaries and worked within them. He knew how to pay attention and when not to; he engaged patrons in casual conversation and knew not to be contesting. Whatever the girls said, he kept confidential. "Call Jack, Mr. Ruby," they warned. Jack told Andy to call him Jack, but he still called him "Mr. Ruby." Andy refused the many drinks that were offered to him. Something which Jack admired even more about him. When someone came to the bar who looked like money, Andy would whistle Dixie to one of the girls. She would then shanty on up to the targeted victim and engage him in the champagne game. No sooner would a bottle of champagne be ordered than it would be turned upside down on the floor and another one would have to be ordered . . . then another, and another. A bottle of champagne cost Ruby only a few bucks but customers shelled out near twenty. The girls earned a commission on each bottle.

Andy made a few extra bucks taking pictures of people dancing with the girls. Occasionally, he ran into trouble when someone thought he was being set up for some "bad" publicity.

Andy ran a lot of errands, for the girls and for Jack. He was a maintenance man, too—stage lights, plumbing. There was always something to do and Andy was always doing it.

It was sometimes Andy's responsibility to walk Sheba, Jack's dog. Once, Sheba ran off down Commerce and Andy nearly lost his job over it when he returned without the dog. Sheba and Jack's other dogs were his children and he pampered them with baby talk and often chauffeured them around town.

Jack's bouncer was Corky Crawford. Jack took a strong liking to him, probably because he saw a lot of himself in Corky. Corky had a serious demeanor and, like Jack, he enjoyed providing free flying lessons down the Carousel stairs. Between the two flight instructors, they launched quite a few careers.

On the spur of the moment, Jack asked Beverly to fly down to Galveston. He had a meeting and he'd wanted her to tag along. Jack thought it was important to be seen with a good-looking gal hanging on his shoulder, and Beverly fit the bill. It made him look more important.

Abe didn't mind his girls taking some personal time off so long as it wasn't on the weekend and someone performed in their place. Because the Colony Club and the Theater Lounge were within five walking minutes of each other, many other girls performed at both clubs, "doubling," they called it. Abe and Barney staggered the shows so they could maximize their talent. Dallas was a big city but there still weren't many girls in town wanting to be an exotic dancer. Some dancers weren't allowed to double. Nikki Joy at the Theater Lounge and Chris Colt at the Colony. Beverly was to stay put as well.

Sue Bailey from the Theater Lounge agreed to double in Beverly's place while she was away with Jack. A few extra bucks was all it took.

Beverly and Jack flew out of town in the early morning on a private plane and arrived safely about 10:00 AM. Jack didn't say whose plane it was but took delight in pretending that it was at his disposal. After they had checked into separate rooms at a motel, Beverly didn't waste any time slipping into her suit and heading to the beach. Jack joined her surfside for about an hour then left for his meeting, saying he had to meet with an attorney, some other man, and a dame. He didn't say what the meeting was about, and she didn't care to know. The Texas sun was brilliant, the breeze blowing off the Gulf of Mexico was cool, and the beach had its fair share of good-looking people. A meeting was the last thing she wanted to go to.

Beverly got an early start on sunbathing and Margaritas. The sound of the waves was relaxing, the smell of the salt water stimulating, and the feel of her beach towel was soft and warm from the sand. Another Margarita and it was time to roll over. Off in the distance, Beverly noticed three guys trying to surf in the small waves rolling to shore, and since no one was watching, Beverly thought it would be a good time to learn to surf herself. She downed her drink and scurried off. She was correct about no one watching but wrong about the learning part. After successfully flirting her way into a private lesson, Beverly only mastered the art of slipping off the board. In the shallow training ground, she fell off the board no sooner than she got on it, face first into the sand. Not once. Not twice, but too many times. The grainy sand finally took a toll on her nose, skinning it badly from the bridge down to her lip. *How am I going to go on stage looking like this? Abe's going to skin me alive. All except my nose, that is.*

Beverly tended to her injury with a little antiseptic cream and then got dressed to join Jack and his friends for dinner. However, life as a beach bunny wasn't easy and, since she wanted to make sure she had some energy to hop back on stage the following night, she decided to crash early. Jack dropped her off at the motel and went back out for coffee.

The next morning Beverly discovered she had to pay another price for playing outdoors. Her tender skin was "fried to a lobster red." Gingerly, she struggled out of bed and painfully looked in the mirror. "If Abe doesn't shoot me, I'll do it myself." She felt miserable. That "dad-blasted breeze" had her fooled into thinking she wasn't getting much sun. *Right.*

Jack took one look at her, squinched his face and shook his head, "Beverly, look at you. I'm so sorry. How's that nose?"

The pilot was late. Very late. Beverly and Jack were irate when he arrived over two hours after they were supposed to leave. She was worried enough about what Abe would say about her face being so banged up, let alone what he might say if she was late. But she made it on time. As customary, Abe wandered out of his office to watch Beverly sing. She knew she would get a berating.

Sure enough, Abe was standing at the top of the stairs waiting for her. "Beverly, what in the world have you gone and done to yourself? You know better than that! You're a show girl. A professional. You're supposed to take better care of yourself than that. You should be ashamed. Why you're brighter than a fire truck and have more bruises than most of those boxers who come in here."

Abe's reaming was the last thing Beverly needed. Insult on top of pain. *It wasn't my fault.* However, she could now add surfing to her list of life's little accomplishments.

Friday and Saturday were amateur nights at the Theater Lounge and the Colony Club respectively and both clubs filled the rafters with big spenders, young and old—it would drive Ruby nuts. It wasn't fair, he thought. They were going against the union by not paying the "amateurs." Some of them were professional amateurs, he complained. Jack really wanted his own amateur night, but he didn't want to settle for a week night. He didn't want to share Fridays or Saturdays with the Weinsteins. Beverly suggested that if he staggered his shows right, the crowds that came downtown would migrate between the two stages. After all, the Weinstein's staggered shows at their clubs on week nights to get mileage out of the girls. Why couldn't he?

But Jack wouldn't listen. Instead, he continued to wrestle with AGVA to have the brothers legally reprimanded. No luck. He irked a number of newspaper writers, complaining they favored the Weinsteins. He saved clippings to show them how they were discriminating about his club. He wouldn't sit still.

Ruby made friends with the Dallas police. He made a point to remember their names and encourage them to stop by. He told his staff not to charge them. When he had a chance, he'd run a sack full of sandwiches over to the police station. Police visited all the clubs downtown though, not just Jack's. Abe, Barney, everyone made a point to encourage the cops to stop by and spend some time. Jack Ruby just made a bigger production out of it. He wanted to be somebody important and treating the police like celebrities helped. He ordered his waitstaff to refuse taking any money from the men in blue.

It was a great cost-effective security measure for the club owners to have a few authorized guns standing guard, and in turn, it was a great place for the police to drink coffee. Free security—free coffee. Free peeks. On any given night there would be no less than four uniforms cradling a hot cup of coffee and "checking it out." After hours—off duty and out of uniform, it was more than coffee, but they kept drinking to their own hang-outs.

The coming year was going to be good for Jack, he boasted. He was bragging and looking forward to bringing the necessary resources together to launch a ritzy nightclub he wanted to open over on Turtle Creek. It would be luxurious, catering to everyone that was someone, springboarding him over the Weinsteins onto the top of entertainment hill.

When Christmas finally rolled around, Beverly joined Jack, Shari, Wally and the others for the pilgrimage out to the orphan home. Bringing happiness and smiles to abandoned little faces brought a rich joy to Beverly. She then knew why Jack made it such a priority every year and why he spoke so affectionately about the experience.

CHAPTER NINE

1963

Nineteen-Sixty-Three brought the White House a list of high priority issues demanding serious scrutiny. Great Britain, Europe, Asia, Russia, the American ghetto, college campuses, domestic and foreign economics; conditions at home and around the world were changing and conflict was the order of the time. Something needed to be done quickly.

Setting aside the ideological, historical, and common differences between themselves so they could progress constructively, Great Britain and Europe were still trying to design a "grand plan" to organize their resources into a strategic financial and military alliance. In January however, French Premier Charles de Gaulle slowed the progress of implementing the "grand design" by refusing to endorse the direction the plan was taking. While he respected American might and supported her during the Cuban missile crisis, once Russia crawled back across the Atlantic with its tail in tuck, he became publicly adamant that the U.S. stay on the its side of the ocean, that Britain stay out of the Common Market, and that France defend herself, leaving Germany caught in the crossfire.

While the European alliance went back to the drawing table, President Kennedy and his advisors struggled with strategy in the jungles of Asian diplomacy. People were beginning to question the nation's intervention in the Vietnam war with the mood varying from indifferent to overboard—from withdrawal to full throttle war. Dyed-in-the-wool patriots insisted that the U.S., as the hammerhead of democracy, honor its big brother obligations by halting communism on whatever soil it took root. The Monroe Doctrine's decree for America to protect the sovereignty of its Western Hemisphere neighbors had developed over the past thirty years into a global cause. The imaginary boundaries of America had been stretched further than the range of a Polaris missile.

President Kennedy felt government should not run contrary to the basic wishes of her people and that democracy was the best form of government to satisfy the most inherent need of people everywhere—the desire to be free and independent. And, he felt that capitalism was the infrastructure required to make it all happen. Democracy and capitalism were geared for a world at peace because they put faith in their people, yet, they were vulnerable to nations geared for war. While in the long run, a system based on respect for the rights of the individual would prevail, the perils of the past had demonstrated that a dictatorship had the advantage in mobilizing forces and focusing military direction under the deceiving veil of propaganda. Kennedy was not intimidated by the terror of war but knew that precautionary measures had to be instituted and battles had to be fought. American heritage was a perpetual testimony that men are not afraid to die for a life worth living, that free men could not be frightened by threats and that aggression would meet its own response.

Understanding America's province, respecting her obligation as a powerful nation to lead the charge for peace and freedom for any threatened nation, President Kennedy began to reevaluate the boundaries of that responsibility, and the situation in Vietnam challenged his thinking. He felt that since the world's problems were man—made, they could be solved by man; that, "No problem of human destiny is beyond human beings." The nation's original role in the Vietnam war as that of an advisor nation was being jeopardized by adversaries campaigning for complete military involvement and pushing for the deployment of U.S. soldiers. Kennedy stood firm and opposed them, insisting that a political solution—not a military solution, provide the answer in Vietnam. He studied the situation carefully, he listened closely to his advisors, and he treaded cautiously, concerned about the cost of American lives in a jungle war that might never be won. Knowing well what could be lost—Kennedy wanted to know what would be gained?

Beverly and Larry Ronco continued seeing each other, almost nightly. She was attracted to his maturity and he to her spontaneity. They enjoyed being together and grew close.

Not wanting to disillusion Beverly, but wanting to be honest about his feelings for her, Larry had confessed that he was married to a woman back in New York but that their marriage had soured and that he was moving forward with a divorce so he could marry her. He told Beverly that it was she he loved and to pledge his commitment, he presented Beverly with an engagement ring. Beverly had mixed emotions about Larry's revelation. She was glad Larry was honest. She suspected he might have been involved with someone else–but not married. Her first reaction was one of dejection and to refuse to accept his ring. The entire scenario developed like a television script and she didn't want to play the part of the fool. Larry was sincere and romantic. He encouraged her that the divorce would happen soon. Spring was just around the corner, if she could wait that long.

Beverly wanted to believe Larry. She believed he cared for her but questioned if he was really prepared to sever the relationship with his wife. *People change. Why not Larry?* She had just turned seventeen and wondered if she was too young to marry. But Larry was strong, he was real, and she loved him. Beverly accepted the ring with his promise to make things happen quickly.

As the year moved midterm, President Kennedy thought more and more about the importance of world peace and it became the central topic of his speeches. In an inspirational commencement address to students at American University in Washington, President Kennedy spoke to the world. His heart was pumping, his spirit intense, Kennedy opened his soul:

" 'There are few earthly things more beautiful than a university,' wrote John Masefield, in his tribute to English universities–and his words are equally true today. He did not refer to spires and towers or to campus greens and ivied walls. He admired the splendid beauty of the university, he said, because it was 'a place where those who hate ignorance may strive to know, where those who perceive truth may strive to make others see.'

"I have chosen this time and place to discuss a topic on which ignorance too often abounds and the truth is too rarely perceived–yet it is the most important topic on earth: world peace.

"What kind of peace do I mean? What kind of peace do we seek? Not a Pax Americana enforced on the world by American weapons of war. Not the peace of the grave or the security of the slave. I am talking about genuine peace, the kind that makes life on earth worth living, the kind that enables men and nations to grow and to hope and to build a better life for their children–not merely peace for our time but peace for all times.

"I speak of peace because of the new face of war. Total war makes no sense in an age when great powers can maintain large and relatively invulnerable nuclear forces and refuse to surrender without resort to those forces. It makes no sense in an age when a single nuclear weapon contains almost ten times the explosive force delivered by all of the allied air forces in the Second World War. It makes no sense in an age when the deadly poisons produced by a nuclear exchange would be carried by wind and water and soil and seed to the far corners of the globe and to generations yet unborn.

"Today the expenditures of billions of dollars every year on weapons acquired for the purpose of making sure we never need to use them is essential to keeping the peace. But surely the acquisition of such idle stockpiles–which can only destroy and never create–is the only, much less the most efficient, means of assuring the peace.

"I speak of peace, therefore, as the necessary rational end of rational man. I realize that the pursuit of peace is not as dramatic as the pursuit of war–and frequently the words of the pursuer fall on deaf ears. But we have no more urgent task.

"Some say that it is useless to speak of world peace or world law or world disarmament–and that it will be useless until the leaders of the Soviet Union adopt a more enlightened attitude. I hope they do. I believe we can help them do it. But I also believe that we must reexamine our own attitude–as individuals and as a nation–for our attitude is as essential as theirs. And every graduate of this school, every thoughtful citizen who despairs of war and wishes to bring peace, should begin by looking inward–by examining his own attitude toward the possibilities of peace, toward the Soviet Union, toward the course of the cold war and toward freedom and peace here at home.

"First: Let us examine our attitude toward peace itself. Too many of us think it is impossible. Too many think it is unreal. But that is a dangerous, defeatist belief. It leads to the conclusion that war is inevitable–that mankind is doomed–that we are gripped by forces we cannot control.

"We need not accept that view. Our problems are manmade–therefore, they can be solved by man. And man can be as big as he wants. No problem of human destiny is beyond human beings. Man's reason and spirit have often solved the seemingly unsolvable–and we believe they can do it again.

"I am not referring to the absolute, infinite concept of universal peace and good will of which some fanatics dream. I do not deny the value of hopes and dreams but merely invite discouragement and incredulity by making that our only and immediate goal.

"Let us focus on a more practical, more attainable peace–based not on a sudden revolution in human nature but on a gradual evolution in human institutions–on a series of concrete actions and effective agreements which are in the interest of all concerned. There is no single, simple key to this peace–no grand or magic formula to be adopted by one or two powers. Genuine peace must be a product of many nations, the sum of many acts. It must be dynamic, not static, changing to meet the challenge of each new generation. For peace is a process—a way of solving problems.

"With such a peace, there will still be quarrels and conflicting interests, as there are within families and nations. World peace, like community peace, does not require only that they live together in mutual tolerance, submitting their disputes to a just and peaceful settlement. And history teaches us that enmities between nations, as individuals, do not last forever. However fixed our likes and dislikes may seem, the tide of time and events will often bring surprising changes in the relations between nations and neighbors.

"So let us persevere. Peace need not be impractical, and war need not be inevitable. By defining our goal more clearly, by making it seem more manageable and less remote, we can help all peoples to see it, to draw hope from it, and to move irresistibly toward it.

"Second: Let us re-examine our attitude toward the Soviet Union. It is discouraging to think that their leaders may actually believe what their propagandists write. It is discouraging to read a recent authoritative Soviet text on Military Strategy and find, on page after page, wholly baseless and incredible claims—such as the allegations that 'American imperialist circles are preparing to unleash different types of wars. . . that there is a very real threat of a preventive war being unleashed by American imperialists against the Soviet Union . . . (and that) the political aims of the American imperialists are to enslave economically and politically the European and other capitalist countries . . . (and) to achieve world domination . . . by means of aggressive wars.'

"Truly, as it was written long ago, 'The wicked flee when no man pursueth.' Yet it is sad to read these Soviet statements—to realize the extent of the gulf between us. But it is also a warning—a warning to the American people not to fall into the same trap as the Soviets, not to only see the conflict as inevitable, accommodation as impossible, and communication as nothing more than an exchange of these.

"No government or social system is so civil that its people must be considered as lacking in virtue. As Americans, we find communism profoundly repugnant as a negation of personal freedom and dignity. But we can still hail the Russian people for their many achievements—in science and space, in economics and industrial growth, in culture and in acts of courage.

"Among the many traits the people of our two countries have in common, none is stronger than our mutual abhorrence of war. Almost unique, among the major world powers, we have never been at war with each other. And no nation in the history of battle ever suffered more that the Soviet Union suffered in the course of the Second World War. At least twenty million lost their lives. Countless millions of homes and farms were burned or sacked. A third of its industrial base, was turned into a wasteland—a loss equivalent to the devastation of this county east of Chicago.

"Today, should war break out again—no matter how—our two countries would become the primary targets. It is an ironic but accurate fact that the two strongest powers are the two in the most danger of devastation. All we have built, all we have worked for, would be destroyed in the first 24 hours. And even in the cold war, which brings burdens and dangers to so many countries, including this Nation's closest allies—our two countries bear the heaviest burdens. For we are both devoting massive sums of money to weapons that could be better devoted to combating ignorance, poverty, and disease. We are both caught up in a vicious cycle in which suspicion on the one side breeds suspicion on the other, and new weapons beget counterweapons.

"In short, both the United States and its allies, and the Soviet Union have a mutually deep interest in a just and genuine peace and in halting the arms race. Agreements to this end are in the interests of the Soviet Union as well as ours—and even the most hostile nations can be relied upon to accept and keep those treaty obligations, and only those treaty obligations, which are in their best interests.

"So let us not be blind to our differences—but let us also direct attention to our common interests and to the means by which those differences can be resolved. And if we cannot end our differences now, at least we can help make the world a safe for diversity. For, in this final analysis, our most basic common link is that we all inhabit this small planet. We breath the same air. We all cherish our children's future. And we are all mortal.

"Third. Let us re-examine our attitude towards the cold war, remembering that we are not engaged in a debate, seeking to pile up debating points. We must deal with the world as it is, not as it might have been had the history of the last eighteen years been different.

"We must, therefore, persevere in the search for peace in the hope that constructive changes within the Communist bloc might bring within reach solutions which now seen beyond us. We must conduct our affairs in such a way that it becomes in the Communist's interests to agree on a genuine peace. Above all, while defending our own vital interests, nuclear powers must avert those confrontations which bring an adversary to a choice of either a humiliating retreat or a nuclear war. To adopt that kind of course in the nuclear age would be evidence only of the bankruptcy of our policy—or of a collective death-wish for the world.

"To secure these ends, America's weapons are non- provocative, carefully controlled, designed to deter, and capable of selective use. Our military forces are committed to peace and disciplined in self-restraint. Our diplomats are instructed to avoid unnecessary irritants and purely rhetorical hostility.

"For we seek a relaxation of tensions without relaxing our guard. And, for our part, we do not need to use threats to prove that we are resolute. We do not need to jam foreign broadcasts out of fear our faith will be eroded. We are unwilling to impose out system on any unwilling people—but we are willing and able to engage in peaceful competition with any people on earth.

"Meanwhile, we seek to strengthen the United Nations, to help solve its financial problems, to make it a more effective instrument for peace, to develop it into a genuine world security system—a system capable of resolving disputes on the basis of law, of insuring the security of the large and the small, and of creating conditions under which arms can finally be abolished.

"At the same time we seek to keep peace inside the non-Communists world, where many nations, all of them our friends, are divided over issues which weaken Western unity, which invite Communist intervention or which threatens to erupt in war. Our efforts in West Guinea, in the Congo, in the Middle East, and in the Indian subcontinent, have been persistent and patient despite criticism from both sides. We have also tried to set an example for others—by seeking to adjust small but significant differences with our closest neighbors in Mexico and Canada.

"Speaking of other nations, I wish to make one point clear. We are bound to many nations by alliances. Those alliances exist because our concern and theirs substantially overlap. Our commitment to defend Western Europe and West Berlin, for example, stands undiminished because of the expense of other nations and other peoples, not merely because they are our partner, but also because their interests and ours converge.

"Our interests converge, however, not only in defending the frontiers of freedom, but in pursuing the paths of peace. It is our hope—and the purpose of allied politics—to convince the Soviet Union that she, too, should let each nation choose its own future, so long as that choice does not interfere with the choice of others. The Communist drive to impose their political and economic system on others is the primary cause of world tension today. For there can be no doubt that, if all nations could refrain from interfering in the self-determination of others, the peace would be much more assured.

"This will require a new effort to achieve world law—a new context for world discussions. It will require increased understanding between the Soviets and ourselves. And increased understanding will require increased contact and communication. One step in this direction is the proposed arrangement for a direct line between Moscow and Washington to avoid on each side the dangerous delays, misunderstandings, and misreading of the other's actions which might occur at a time of crisis.

"We have been talking in Geneva about our first step measures of arms control, designed to limit the intensity of the arms race and to reduce the risks of accidental war. Our primary long-range interest in Geneva, however, is general and complete disarmament—designed to take place by stages, permitting parallel political developments to build the new institutions of peace which would take the place of arms. The pursuit of disarmament has been the effort of this Government since the 1920's. It has been urgently sought by the past three administrations. And however dim the prospects may be today, we intend to continue this effort—to continue it in order that all countries, including our own, can better grasp what the problems and the possibilities of disarmament are.

"The one area of these negotiations where the end is in sight, yet where a fresh start is badly needed, is in a treaty to outlaw nuclear tests. The conclusion of such a treaty, so near and yet so far, would check the spiraling arms race in one of its most dangerous areas. It would place the nuclear powers in a position to deal more effectively with one of the greatest hazards which man faces in 1963, the further spread of nuclear arms. It would increase our security—it would decrease the possibilities of war. Surely this goal is sufficiently important to require our steady pursuit, yielding neither to the temptation to give up the whole effort nor the temptation to give up our insistence on vital and responsible safeguards.

"I am taking this opportunity, therefore, to announce two important decisions in this regard.

"First: Chairman Khrushchev, Prime Minister Macmillan and I have agreed that high-level discussions will shortly begin in Moscow looking toward early agreement on a comprehensive test ban treaty. Our hopes must be tempered with the caution of history—but with our hopes go the hopes of all mankind.

"Second: To make clear our good faith and solemn convictions on the matter, I now declare that the United States does not propose to conduct nuclear tests in the atmosphere so long as the other states do not do so. We will not be the first to resume. Such a declaration is no substitute for a formal binding treaty, but I hope it will help us achieve one. Nor would such a treaty be a substitute for disarmament, but I hope it will help us achieve it.

"Finally, my fellow Americans, let us examine our attitude toward peace and freedom here at home. Then quality and spirit of our own society must justify and support our efforts abroad. We must show it in the dedication of our own lives—as many of you who are graduating today will have a unique opportunity to do, by serving without pay in the Peace Corps abroad or in the proposed national Service Corps here at home.

"But whatever we are, we must be tall, in our daily lives, live up to the age old faith that freedom and peace walk together. In too many of our cities today, the peace is not secure because freedom is incomplete.

"It is the responsibility of the executive branch at all levels of government—local, State, and National—to provide and protect that freedom for all our citizens by all means within their authority. It is the responsibility of all citizens of all sections of this country to respect the rights of all others and to respect the law of the land.

"All this is not unrelated to world peace. 'When a man's ways please the Lord,' the Scriptures tell us, 'he maketh even his enemies to be at peace with him.' And is not peace, in the last analysis, basically a matter of human rights—the right to live out our lives without fear of devastation—the right to breath air as nature provided it—the right of future generations to a healthy existence?

"While we proceed to safeguard our national interests, let us also safeguard our human interests. And the elimination of war and arms is clearly in the interest of both. No treaty, however tightly it may be worded, can provide absolute security against the risks of deception and evasion. But it can—if it is sufficiently in the interest of its signers—offer far more security and far fewer risks than unabated, uncontrolled, unpredictable arms race.

"The United States, as the world knows, will never start a war. We do not want a war. We do not now expect a war. This generation of Americans has already had enough—more than enough—of war and hate and oppression. We shall be prepared if others wish it. We shall be alert to try and stop it. But we shall also do our part to build a world of peace where the weak are safe and the strong are just. We are not helpless before that task or hopeless of its success. Confident and unafraid, we labor on, not toward a strategy of annihilation but toward a strategy of peace."

Jack Ruby needed a change of pace—a new headline dancer. Someone who could pull customers away from the Weinsteins. New Orleans was the place to look. One of the performers he had in mind was a woman called Jada, Janet Conferto, who was dancing at a club called the Sho-Bar. She was billed as the *hottest exotic* and that was just what he felt he needed. Jack called Harold Tannenbaum, Jada's agent, and arranged for a meeting.

Jack told Beverly he was taking off for New Orleans to book a new act and asked if she'd like to go with him—she agreed, and shortly thereafter, they were checking into a hotel on Bourbon Street, in the middle of the French Quarter. After they set things in their rooms, Jack told Beverly that he had some business to take care of so she wandered around the shops in the hot June afternoon then relaxed at the hotel.

Arriving at the Sho-Bar, Ruby met with Nick Graffanini who shuffled him over to another club at 500 Bourbon Street. When he got there he spoke to the club's night manager, Cleeve Dugas, who told him that there weren't any dancers available and suggested he go over to the Sho-Bar and check out the hottest stripper in town—Jada. When Ruby made it back to the Sho-Bar he did meet-up with Tannenbaum and they discussed booking Jada to perform at the Carousel Club.

That night Beverly and Jack sat in the audience to watch Jada perform. They were impressed. Jada was a rare, provocative dancer. Bright, flowing red hair framed her sculptured face—hair which she often fanned high in the air, letting it cascade back upon her shoulders. Contrived to excite, her eyebrows would dance up and down while her mouth would pucker to a beautiful fullness then spread into a large, moist, sensuous invitation of wantonness, milking the attention of every man in the audience. Ballerina hands, raw energy, animal magnetism—Jada was always moving, parading around the stage, swinging her arms, wiggling her wiggle, bumping, grinding. She used every part of her body to "tell her story." She understood the importance of rhythm, eye contact, and the power of sexuality. Anatomy in motion and, oh, what a mouth!

Jada was the act Jack Ruby was looking for, even though Beverly thought it might be too nasty for a Dallas crowd. Arrangements were made and soon after Jada finished her contract at the Sho-Bar, she would be headed to the Carousel Club.

The first part of the year had challenged the President on all fronts and he steered through the controversy and the challenge with admirable calm and steadfast authority. Kennedy's popularity, which rose with the high tide as Khrushchev's boats were turned back after the missile crisis, had suffered through civil rights issues. Congress was in a gridlock and unable to move forward with administrative proposals designed to help level the playing field for minorities, reduce taxes, and appropriate foreign aid. And placed before Congress was a historical treaty waiting for ratification. A treaty endorsing a ban on worldwide nuclear testing. Every day had its own priorities, pitfalls, and progress, but Mrs. Kennedy was soon expecting a child, and the joy of expectation brought the First Family some fresh air.

Shortly before noon on August 7th, as the President stopped by his office to collect his mail, his secretary, Evelyn Lincoln, told him that Mrs. Kennedy was on her way to Otis Air Force Base Hospital. John Kennedy immediately ordered the helicopters to escort him to Andrews Air Force Base and a waiting jet.

Less than two hours after the President left the White House, Patrick Bouvier Kennedy was born weighing four pounds and ten and one-half ounces, nearly five weeks ahead of schedule. Mrs. Lincoln, who had accompanied the President, watched him follow his wife down the hall of the hospital as she was being taken to her room. She looked at him and said, "Congratulations, Mr. President." He looked at her, a broad smile beaming his delight.

Hours later, the baby's condition worsened and preparations were made to move young Patrick Kennedy to Boston's Children Hospital. The President's son was born with respiratory complications. The baby's lungs were smothered by a thin membrane making it difficult to exchange oxygen for carbon dioxide in the blood. A condition which claimed tens of thousands of infant lives every year.

Dressed in a white surgical gown, watching his son struggle to breathe from the porthole of a pressurized chamber, the President was informed that the antibiotics weren't working and that the only hope was for Patrick's own defense systems to work a miracle. After his son's condition stabilized, the President took a short rest but was soon back at Patrick's side. Patrick's breathing soon became more labored and he struggled for air. It was time. Thirty-nine hours after Patrick Bouvier Kennedy made his first noise, he took his last breath. President Kennedy, still holding his son's hand, was told by the nurse, "He's gone." Tears fell from the President's eyes in a passionate moment that crushed everyone around. No one had seen him cry before.

August closed with an avalanche of condolences from all over the world, and the days of September began with a quiet retreat to Newport, Rhode Island for a tenth wedding anniversary. And then, the Senate ratified the test ban treaty, springboarding the President into the public again. Wanting to feel the pulse of America, wanting to establish a personal and better rapport with the people who hadn't voted for him, and wanting to move forward with his campaign for peace and equality, President Kennedy left Newport and headed west.

The theme of Kennedy's trip through the west became decisively focused on world peace. He emphasized that "the competition with communism would dominate the rest of our lives, but we should not let it become a competition in a nuclear violence." He understood how science and technology was unstoppable, how near impossible it was to bring accord between all people within a single citizenship, and how fickle alliances could prove to be. Kennedy pounded home his belief that the world had turned the corner toward world peace. "The most striking thing about our world in 1963 is the extent to which the tide of history has begun to flow in the direction of freedom. To renounce the world of freedom now, to abandon those who share our commitment, and retire into the lonely and not so splendid isolation, would be to give communism the one hope which, in this twilight of disappointment for them, might repair their divisions and rekindle their hope."

Upon his return from a trip back to New York, Larry immediately called Beverly, wanting to meet her for lunch. He had a present and was excited about giving it to her. And since he had business with Jack at the Carousel, he suggested they meet there. He told her how much he missed her and how much he was looking forward to seeing her. When she arrived, Larry and Jack were busy talking. Larry had something in his hand that Jack kept trying to take from him, but Larry was trying to explain something and wanted his full attention. Moving closer, she noticed Larry was holding a movie camera. Larry eventually handed it to Jack and he started admiring it.

"Larry, how much do you want for this camera? What do you say? How much?"

"Jack, I told you this camera is a present for Beverly. Like I said, if I could get my hands on another one I would be happy to give it to you, but it's not even on the market yet. I was fortunate in getting this one while I was in New York. Beverly wanted a new movie camera that was easy to operate and this . . . ."

"Is that the camera you got me, Larry?" Beverly interrupted, as she threw an arm around his waist. He gave her a strong hug back and a kiss on the cheek.

"Yes. I was trying to show Jack how simple it was to operate. Look, all you need to do in loading it, is to drop a film magazine like this into the side of the camera. And if Jack will let go of the camera, I'll demonstrate."

Jack reluctantly handed Beverly the camera.

"Jack, I'll do what I can to get you one. I promise."

"Yeah. You do that. As soon as you can. You can use my phone . . . ."

"I'll do what I can." Larry then showed Beverly how to load the cartridge and operate the buttons. The camera was made by Yashica, Larry said. "The hard part will be waiting for the film to be developed. Until the camera is widely distributed, you'll have to send it back to Rochester for developing."

Beverly could care less where she had to send it. She was thrilled to have a new camera with film to boot, a camera others didn't have at that time. She held the viewfinder up to her eye and panned the room, pretending to film. She wondered what she would film first.

Larry and Beverly left to go to lunch and Jack tagged along. "Larry, don't forget you promised me a camera like that. You won't, will you? You're my friend, so treat me right. Like I said, you can call . . . ." Larry and Beverly looked at one another wondering who had invited Jack.

Beverly was hoping that Larry had other good news about his divorce.

Beverly timed her trip to Nieman's during lunch, thinking Jack would like to break and grab a bite to eat, but as she walked into the club, she quickly noticed her plans were out the window. Jack was sitting at a table with David Ferrie rummaging through a lunch sack stuffed with sandwiches, cream cheese, and bagels from the deli.

"Beverly, help us with this good food." Jack offered as she approached the table. Ferrie stood up, grinned, and pulled out a chair for her. She had seen Ferrie at the club so often she thought he was an assistant manager who Jack had hired. Jack had never formally introduced him to her as the manager, but the way Ferrie pushed his way around while he was there, made her think he was.

David Ferrie was creepy looking, Beverly thought. The silly toupee he wore, his dark black, hand-painted eyebrows, when coupled with his paranoia, gave him the semblance of a cartoon character. His Orleans's accent was soft and he spoke fast like Jack. She thought he looked like a little buzzard. And, compared to most men in Dallas, he dressed offbeat—wearing a dark brown sport coat with his white short sleeve shirt opened at the collar and flared over his lapels. With mouths full of food, the two men began playing a game of one up-manship about their life's small accomplishments. Ferrie rambled through a display of his multilingual talent. French, Spanish, German. Ruby countered with the fact that he could last longer in the sack with someone. Ferrie said he could fly a plane. Jack said he could fly everything but a plane.

Beverly took off the jacket to her sundress and giggled, "I bet you men can't do this" and shimmied from her waist up. Ferrie turned to Jack, "I think she's got us there, Jack," a wide grin cracked his animated face.

Ferrie was shifty-eyed and had a hard time looking her straight in the eye when he spoke. However, he showed signs of extreme intelligence and as the conversation wandered from one subject to the other Beverly became impressed by the little man. Jokingly, Ferrie started speaking Russian as if he thought she could understand him. He then launched into German, and as he had done earlier with Jack, he rambled through an exposé of several other languages: French, Italian, Spanish. He claimed he could write all them as well, and started scribbling on a napkin. Beverly didn't know if he was pulling her leg or not, but whatever he was writing looked like that which he was speaking. Ferrie's concentration was intense, but his mind wandered randomly, as if he had other things on his mind.

"Jada, oh Jada. Jada-Jada-jing jing jing."
With this jangling introduction, Jada glided slowly out onto the Carousel stage. Her thick, flaming-red hair was set off by her fire-engine red lipstick and long curved nails. Within moments, she made eye contact with nearly every man in the room. Tightly wrapped in an expensive beaded gown, Jada was constantly moving her 5'7" frame around the stage. Her performance was explosive–and oozed sex appeal. She liked to take the tip of her finger and stroke the side of her body, pretending it was hot to the touch. She enjoyed crawling on the floor with her leopard rug. Everyone in the audience wanted to be that leopard.

Off stage it was the same way for Jada. She was the sexiest woman Beverly had ever seen; pretty, but not beautiful. They soon became friends. At the club Beverly would wander over between shows. Jada and Beverly played a game when they walked together downtown. Whoever turned the most heads won, and on most days, Jada did. Beverly thought Jada was more educated than the other girls, even though she didn't speak English very well. She also didn't cuss. Jada told Beverly she was from Brazil. But Beverly wasn't sure if it was true or not.

Jada was staying at the Alamo Court Motel on Fort Worth Avenue and was usually found lying around the pool during the day, soaking every ounce of sun that was measurable, turning her skin a dark baked brown, confusing some people into thinking she was Negroid, or so she told Beverly. Jada's act on the Carousel stage became as hot as the Texas sun. Jack Ruby had his headline act and the crowds were definitely showing up. However, the more comfortable she became with the audience, the more chances she took.

Since her friend Shari had moved her act over to the Theater Lounge while Jada was in town, Beverly would see her when she visited with Jack, between shows. (There was always something going on at Jack's.)

Late one evening, when Beverly was at the Carousel, she saw Shari's husband Wally, who in the middle of his comic routine, walk across the stage to a noisy group of men seated at the end of the runway who were rudely interrupting his show. He asked them to tone it down. Reacting brashly, one of the men reached into his coat pocket and shouted, "You stupid fool, I'll tone you down." He pulled out a gun just as two policemen walked up. "The cops are here!" Someone shouted.

Beverly heard the gun hit and skid across the floor after it was kicked away. Beverly recognized the two officers who came into the club as Geneva White's husband and Patrick Dean. She had seen them both several times before and was glad they showed up when they did. Geneva was a hostess who Jack had hired to help people find a place to sit. She relied on her husband to pick her up after work.

A few nights later, Beverly had laid the microphone in its cradle and took a deep breath. Singing in front of a responsive crowd always gave her a rush of excitement. Exhaling deeply before she left the stage allowed her to take it all in and carry it with her. Having a little time between shows, Beverly wandered next door to catch Jada and maybe visit with Jack or Larry, who had quit his job with Kodak after Six Flags closed for the season and was hanging around the club quite often. Kodak wanted him back in New York but he wanted to stay in Dallas. Besides, he told Beverly, he wanted to stay near her, even though he was having problems getting the divorce finalized.

Stairs. Beverly was tired of climbing stairs and tried to wish them away. Abe's place–Jack's place, up-down, up-down. Her heels made it twice as cumbersome. As she opened the door into the Carousel, smoke swirled out into the stair well as if it had been waiting by the door to be let out. Smoke was another thing she tried to wish away. Beverly looked around then noticed Jada sitting with Jack and another man at a table near the runway. Beverly made her way over and Jack rose from his chair, motioning to her as if she wasn't already walking his way. Jada smiled.

"Beverly. This is my friend Lee Oswald. He's with the CIA." Jack said, nodding his head toward the man on his left, who was sitting at the table in his own cloud of detachment. Beverly tried to extend a simple hello to acknowledge Jack's friend but he seemed as if he could care less about meeting anyone. She quickly assessed that he wasn't worth the bother—to her anyway. He was a "dark" person. When Beverly met people she saw them as having either light or dark personalities, and this man disturbed her. Not that he said anything to warrant that impression, it was an unsolicited gut-feeling she had. Oswald was dressed in casual drab; he was slouched in his chair, his arms folded defiantly across his chest. His eyes were narrow and fixed on Jack as though he was not pleased. Jack, however, was spirited when he introduced Oswald as if he was proud to know someone with the CIA. Beverly didn't know what the CIA was but she thought it must be important or Jack wouldn't have brought it up. She wondered if Lee Oswald really was a friend, or if Jack was once again a little loose with his terminology.

Days later, Beverly had finished her routine and said goodnight to Abe. Then she walked over to the Carousel with her brother Eugene to see Jada. When they arrived, Wally was on stage hamming his way through another skit when he became engaged in yet another confrontation. Trying to cause a disturbance, a man stood up in the middle of the club and yelled at Wally, "I think you're a filthy Commie!" Wally immediately stopped his act. He was furious. Hecklers were part of the show and often they became the butt-end of one of his jokes, but having been accused of being a communist was something to fight about. Wally clinched his fist and shouted back, "What did you say?"

"I said that you're a filthy Commie!"

Wally tossed his microphone to the floor and leaped off the stage. In the blink of an eye he sent a fist smacking the heckler in the mouth. Stunned, the man fell backwards. Jack flew across the room and jerked the man towards him, his black eyes blazing, "I told you little creep—don't ever come back to my club again." Furiously, Jack ushered him out of the club by his jacket sleeve and shoved him toward the top of the stairs.

Beverly recognized the man as Lee Oswald, the man she'd met a few nights before. *Jack, Jack, Jack–introducing someone as a friend one week then throwing him down the stairs the next.*

Things settled down when Jada took the stage and cranked up her gyrations and soon the magic hour finally arrived and the after hours crowd took over. Whisky started flowing more freely and so did tempers. Wally however, was still disturbed about the encounter with Oswald and soon left. Eugene left too, but Jack asked Beverly to stay and help serve drinks. Just as Beverly was leaving, Wally came back to the club to get his jacket which he had left, but Ferrie refused to let him back in, speaking to him through a crack in the door. He told Wally that there was private business going on and he couldn't come in. Beverly walked around Ferrie to make her exit. She looked back at the crowd beginning to huddle together and wondered if it would get any crazier. Wally left without his jacket.

Larry and Beverly were still dating but it was tapering off. The divorce was always just around the corner and Beverly was growing tired of hearing the same excuses. Beverly didn't know where Wally went but Larry volunteered to take his place until they found someone else. Larry had never entertained before, but he knew where he could get some great material. Right next door at the Colony Club from Artie Brooks.

After one of Larry's "stolen" routines, Beverly coerced Larry to the back staircase to get a breath of fresh air. Sitting on the steps, Larry was toiling with something he wasn't sure he wanted to share with Beverly and, Beverly too, had something she wanted to share with him, but didn't know how to approach the subject. Beverly wanted to tell Larry that stealing Artie's material was cruel and she was angry with him. He was so blatant about it, that many people became disgusted with Larry. No sooner would customers leave the Carousel Club in time for Artie's show when they would hear the same jokes they heard minutes before.

"Beverly, you're never going to believe what happened." Larry spoke first. "That guy Ferrie offered me $50,000 to go kill Castro in Cuba."

"Oh, get out of here. You're full of it." Beverly said, still thinking about how to tell Larry to change his act.

"No, he was serious. At least I think he was. He ranted and raved about how dangerously close the Communists were to America and that if Castro was taken out, it would be easy to get Cuba back. Especially the gambling!"

Beverly didn't know what to say. That little Ferrie guy might not be so smart after all, she thought.

The next week, on Monday, November 18, Beverly agreed to help Jack host another after-hours party—serving the drinks. Jack had a strange new assortment of friends at the party that night, most of whom she had never seen. While Beverly made the rounds with her tray, Jack was busy talking "ninety-miles-an-hour" with everyone around. One man she met was a guy who introduced himself as Roberto Guzman. He had dark hair, square shoulders, an angular chiseled face, and spoke with a throaty accent. He stood about 5'6". Later that evening when Beverly was standing near his table, she saw him take his fountain pen from his coat pocket and start writing "*RG*" over and over on a cocktail napkin, as if he was trying to remember who he was.

"What would you like to drink?" Beverly asked him.

"A Cuba Libra." he replied. That was the first rum drink anyone ordered. Everybody else wanted whisky and Coke, except a great big man who asked for scotch and soda.

It was a night on edge and everyone was on a short fuse. Something static in the air had charged the place with heated words and it didn't take long before a confrontation erupted. After a short volley of name-calling, David Ferrie jumped out of his seat, yanked a gun out of nowhere, and pointed it across the table at someone, his finger wrapped around the trigger.

Jack reacted quickly. Grabbing David by his arm, he thrust it upwards, nearly lifting Ferrie off his feet, while someone else restrained his intended victim. Jack was ticked at Ferrie. "You little sawed-off SOB. One of these days someone is going to shove that gun of yours where the sun don't shine."

Ferrie was getting in the bad habit of enforcing his opinion with a waving gun. Jack was lucky this time. It wouldn't be long he felt that Ferrie would squeeze his small little finger and send a bullet through someone.

Beverly became uncomfortable and got Jack's attention for a moment. "Jack, I don't like this at all. I'm sorry, but I'm out of here. This is getting too hot for this little blond!"

"Yeah. I understand," Jack said, still fuming, trying to figure out what to do with the situation. Ferrie was the situation. Guns were to be kept under wraps at his club. Those were the house rules! Under the table, in your pants—your pocket, anywhere but out in the open. "The little jerk." Jack mumbled.

During that week, entertainer Bill DeMar, a ventriloquist, magician, and memory expert, was featured at the club for a five week engagement. Part of his act was a memory retention exercise. He would have upwards to twenty people, scattered all over the room, stand up and then call out the name of an object, one by one as fast as they could. Then randomly, DeMar would repeat what each person had called out, not missing a beat. Beverly was amazed. This was the third time DeMar played the Carousel. The first time, Jack told him to pack his bags after three nights–his act had too much class. DeMar added a little ballyhoo to it and Jack changed his mind.

November was nearing its end, and Beverly took a short inventory of her life. Her affair with Larry was running on fumes. Jada was spending too much time chumming up to people she didn't know or care about, and her two closest friends had become shadows. Jada was disturbed about something she didn't want to talk about and Shari was quiet about Wally.

The only bright spot Beverly could look forward to, was using her new camera to film President Kennedy when he came to Dallas. It wouldn't be long. Friday, November 22, was circled in her mind.

CHAPTER TEN

The Day Before

EARLY MORNING

President Kennedy had a full mental agenda to juggle: his family, raising money for his re-election campaign, LBJ, Connally and Senator Yarborough, the Bobby Baker scandal, civil rights, education funding, John Crone, his new appointment as head of the CIA, and Vietnam. Despite pleas from concerned friends and constituents, despite death threats, despite the unsettled feeling he was experiencing himself, John F. Kennedy decided to proceed with his trip to Texas that afternoon. Adlai Stevenson, fresh from a bruising visit to Dallas where he was thumped over the head by a not-so-well wisher, as well as Evelyn Lincoln, were among those advising him not to go to the right-wing hotbed. However, Texas votes were critical and Kennedy didn't want the Democratic Party to self-destruct through its own political pettiness. The idea of dumping Johnson as his running mate probably played a hand as well in making the trip necessary. He needed Texas.

After signing a series of directives and dictating several letters, telling the children he was going out of town for a few days, and after speaking with Mrs. Lincoln about the delivery of some red curtains and rugs to adorn the White House, Kennedy met with Ted Sorrenson to review the speeches he was going to deliver in Texas. Sitting at his desk in the Oval Office, turning his attention to the speech he was to give in Dallas at the Trade Mart, he asked Ted if there were any appropriate Texas jokes he could use. While it was important to him that the audience get a clear message, he didn't want them to be too intimidated by the inferences made to the casual way Texans play political poker.

Texas politics was ruled by oil interests and defense contracts, both industries butting heads with the direction that Kennedy envisioned for America. His Oil Depletion Tax was a slap in the face to the oil barons and was receiving strong opposition. His recent agreements with Khrushchev stood to monkey-wrench the future of the cold war and the millions of dollars pouring into Texas firms. The Cuban missile crisis woke him up to how dangerous the world had become and to the insanity of a nuclear age where countries had the awesome power to decimate one another. He thought that "where nature makes natural allies of us all, we can demonstrate that beneficial relations are possible even with those that we most deeply disagree –and this must someday be the basis of world law."

After the ink had dried on the Nuclear Test Ban Treaty, while Russia was concentrating on agriculture and struggling with its economy, Kennedy was trying to resolve a situation in which the United States had become entrenched while expanding and stretching the boundary and the definition of the Monroe Doctrine and its provincial responsibility to curb the tide of communism. Kennedy was not interested in the country being involved in a war which could not be won nor did he want to back down from his inaugural promise to bear any burden.

Kennedy inquired about the weather in Texas and when told how hot it would be, he realized that they had packed the wrong clothes, and frowned at the thought of Jackie sweltering in the heavy pink suit selected for her to wear the next day. The President's back was bothering him again so he was wearing his back brace for extra support.

Air Force One, fresh, polished, and mechanically prepared, was waiting on the Tarmac at Andrews Air Force Base. The Secret Service armored Cadillac and the dark blue Presidential limousine were already in the Lone Star State, resting in the dark hold of a C-1 Cargo plane, its flags asleep on the front of each wheel fender. Making the rounds in Houston, San Antonio, Austin, Fort Worth, and Dallas, the President's front men were preparing for his arrival. So were many others.

Jack Kennedy sat in one of three helicopters poised on the White House lawn outside the Rose Garden, waiting for Jackie. Little John was close by his side, dressed comfortably in his London Fog coat. Outside it was cold and drizzly wet.

Kennedy asked Secret Service man Clint Hill, who was assigned to Mrs. Kennedy, to round her up.

Finally, Jackie was spirited across the grass toward the choppers dressed in a white wool *bouclé* dress and coat, soon to weigh heavy on her in the Texas warmth; San Antonio was a short three hours away. In a whirling spin the Presidential entourage lifted from the safe hold of the nation's house and flew southwest as several well-wishers watched. The wind followed the wake of the metal birds, spinning in small invisible swirls. The sound of rotors was followed by an eerie quiet as if the White House knew what lay ahead.

At Andrews Air Force Base, after he was hugged first by his mother, then by his father, both telling him for the last time he couldn't go, John John burst into tears. It didn't seem fair, he thought. He wanted to go. Sitting forlorn in the helicopter, absently listening to animal stories told by Mr. Foster, John John's eyes were fixed on the great white plane he wanted to be on.

Curled on her right side, Beverly was still fast asleep, lost in her dreams, a short sleep away from waking. Her day was planned from sunup to sundown to sunup. The sun which filtered through the window was trying to tell her, "Good morning."

EARLY AFTERNOON

Nestled in the back of the plane, Clint Hill was flipping through magazines. Jack Kennedy, his bulging black alligator briefcase by his side, studied cables, intelligence reports, and briefing books, and was already concerned if his wife was enjoying herself. This was the first opportunity in awhile in which Jackie had accompanied her husband on a trip. But after the success of the European tour, he became extremely aware how important an asset she was in his ongoing campaign. Europe embraced the young couple as one of their own and Jackie had a lot to do with it. When the trip was over, the Kennedy's were given high marks for exhibiting old world class, a different and welcomed image for Americans. John Kennedy needed Texas and he needed her. *"Viva Jacqui!"*

Mrs. Kennedy's day necessitated changing into the proper clothes, then maintaining her hair and the black beret she wore. Over 125,000 people were lining the streets of San Antonio, and 175,000 were stirring in Houston.

The press was ready. Cameras were in place and moving through a series of checks. Newsmen were visualizing the evening headlines.

Senator Ralph Yarborough was thinking about how to deal with the political darts that Vice President Johnson and Governor Connally were throwing his way. Connally was the former Secretary of the Navy and represented the conservative Democrats of Texas, the oil industry, rural conservatives, and the growing suburban businessman. Yarborough repre-sented the liberal Democrats whose interests reflected the old populist tradition with the new force of organized labor, New Frontier liberalism. First, there was no chance that he was going to ride in the same car with his adversaries. Secondly, how should he deal with the political snub of not being invited to the party that night being hosted by the Governor.

Lyndon Johnson was at the airport getting his hair trimmed. Ladybird was smiling and preparing to receive the First Family to Texas. John Connally was temporarily out of town, hustling to get back in time to join the Presidential party.

Communications channels across the great state were in place. Phone companies had been working overtime to get phone lines installed and working for the press and the temporary White Houses in each of the cities. Reporters, photographers, and television teams were primed to cover the President's movements, speeches, handshakes, and whatever else might happen. Facilitating the coverage and allowing reporters to experience first-hand the intensity and disposition of the sweltering crowds gathered to welcome the Kennedy's, the press would be riding in the motorcade in a bus, four cars behind the President's limousine.

Kelly Air Field, San Antonio. Lyndon Johnson was taking time to line up a reception for the President. Ladybird was gossiping with an old friend she saw standing in the wings of the crowd. Running late after a giving a speech in Austin, John Connally was trying to land in a borrowed plane just ahead of the President's. Nellie Connally was anxiously waiting for her husband, using her necklace like worry beads.

The Chamber of Commerce was ready with the red carpet while the Mayor of San Antonio was being chastised by the Secret Service for not carrying any identification after they accosted him taking pictures of the limousine. In a chorus of goodwill San Antonio greeted the President and his wife, who had changed into a white dress accented by a black leather belt.

Waking to the sound of silence, Beverly stretched her arms out above her head playing with the stillness of the late morning. Sleep was wonderful she thought, full of wishes, hopes, woven in the changing fabric of her dreams. Sleep was a return to primal innocence. A time she could become childlike again. Sometimes, sleep was a time for answers. Answers to prayers, answers to things that were bothering her. In the few moments that trail after sleep, yet dissipate before critical thought takes control, Beverly sometimes felt the burn of truth. *"Am I doing what I should be doing? Am I doing what I think I'm doing? Can I be happier? Are my parents right? What about life after death?"*

Beverly lay in bed for a few minutes longer, trying to focus on her day's agenda, but still concerned about the questions which visited her moments before. Breakfast would be quick; she wouldn't have any. As always, the hairdresser would be next. Bath, yes, no, yes? Usually, the hard part of her morning exercise was deciding what to wear that evening, even though she had little to choose from. Even though it was the last thing she decided on the night before, she had to reconsider her choice in the morning. That morning however, her decision was easy—the green and white polka-dot dress which Jack had given her to wear to the party that night. It was silk. It had come gift-wrapped in beautiful paper and an embossed foil that said Margo's LaMode. It was one of the nicest dresses she owned and the only present Jack had ever had wrapped for her. Beverly had arranged for the night off. Her plans called for an evening of all night parties, and in the morning—she was going to see President Kennedy as he drove through downtown Dallas. There would not be time to change. *What will Jackie be wearing? I wonder if the President will see me?*

The weather report called for increasing cloudiness in the evening with scattered showers likely across north Texas through the morning.

AFTERNOON

Other than being concerned that the wind was blowing her hair and that the warm Texas air was wrapped around her like the smothering hug of some unwanted acquaintance, the President's wife was doing marvelously. She looked convincingly bewildered at their popularity and how inspired people became in their presence. San Antonio turned out for the President's sweep through town in a torrent of hand lettered signs, waving flags and streaming confetti. Children, nuns, firemen, blue collar, white collar—people were every-where. They were smiling. They were cheering. The crowds were lathered and roaring ecstatically. Jack Kennedy was grinning ear to ear. He wasn't going to be denied the pleasure of delicious spontaneity.

Brooks Medical Center was going to receive the President and benefit from a speech he was going to deliver in dedication of the facility. They weren't quite ready to receive the extra twenty-thousand people that showed up. There had been only nine thousand chairs unfolded.

After a short security frenzy of people moving too close to the President and his wife, order was restored, and Kennedy began to address the crowds. The wind blew stronger, making it hard to hear, carrying much of the President's speech away before his audience could applaud his commitment to direct America forward to a New Frontier, or respond to his plea for pathfinders and pioneers willing to blaze a trail through crisis and opportunity. Many people missed his inspired allegory as he dramatized again how America had "tossed its cap over the wall of space" and was ready to continue with great speed and safety to "explore the wonders on the other side."

Although Beverly wore her hair in a stylish bob, the weather was "baking" hot. Sitting patiently underneath the sweltering hum of a blowing hairdryer, her blond hair wound tightly around large plastic pink curlers, Beverly focused her attention on new song sheets. From time to time she would sing a stanza or two . . . or three or four. Her smile was beginning to warm up as well. For Beverly, having her hair done and visiting with Barbara Perkins was an everyday ritual which she looked forward to with unmitigated pleasure. Barbara was more than Beverly's hairdresser; she was one of Beverly's most cherished friends and confidants. The grooming protocol also helped bring Beverly back down to earth, bringing everything that happened the night before back into innocent perspective. Nighttime could get so crazy with the company she kept. Everyone was so busy hustling, drinking, gambling, smoking, loving, planning, that even for someone who didn't drink, mornings could be a dizzy hangover affair. *Being a singer is different than being a stripper . . . even though I sing at a burlesque club. Isn't it? Of course it is.*

Embrace me, my sweet embraceable you. Embrace me my irreplaceable you. Just one look at you . . . .[1] Beverly set her song sheets down and thought. Was she drawn to the burlesque scene because it was . . . like wearing red shoes to church and was it her way of rebelling? Or, did it just feel right, and was that reason enough? Yeah, she thought. That was reason enough. Beverly had many new friends and was having more fun than she ever had before. *When will I meet someone special? What is he doing now? Where will I meet him? Will I know if he's the right one? What if I don't. Do I really want to be tied down?*

Grab your coat—and get your hat, leave your worries on the doorstep. Life can be so sweet, on the sunny side of the street.[2]

Beverly's effervescence was contagious. Ladies, who were stationed beside her, could not help but feel warm inside and smile themselves, mentally picking up the chorus, *The sunny side of the street.*

LATE AFTERNOON

San Antonio was conquered. Houston was next. Mr. and Mrs. Jack Kennedy, flattered with adoration, spirited by hope, exhausted yet still buzzing, withdrew to their cabin bedroom for the short flight to the oil capital of Texas. Maybe a few minutes alone would renew them. Already pressing hard against the fences at the airport and lining the streets and skyscraper canyons of Houston were upwards to 200,000 people.

Like San Antonio, Houston staged a magnificent welcome for the President. But many people had turned out to see Mrs. President as well. Regally poised in her trademark coiffeur, she beamed a bewitching charm that mesmerized everyone around her. Her large brown eyes, set off by dark manicured eyebrows, became a beacon of goodwill for many people. Her smile formed into a curious fusion of sensuality and character. Her posture was a salute to her self-respect.

Beverly was dressed and feeling vibrant. "Baths are wonderful," she thought. "They make clothes feel so much better." Standing in front of a full-length mirror, she was delighted with the way the silk dress draped from her shoulder and hung from her tight waist in the soft unmistakable fold of silk. The dress was buttoned up the front, flaring outward at the collar in a classic lapel. The sleeves bloused from the shoulders and cuffed tightly at her wrists, fastened in tiny simulated pearl buttons. The feel of the dress was light and delicate. It was soft, slick and–therapeutic.

Around her neck Beverly placed a single strand of white pearls. Then, she played with her wigs. First, she picked up a red wig, then threw it back, opting for a dark one which she folded then stuffed in her make-up kit for later. Beverly had a reputation for wearing wigs and for good reason. Her picture was often in the paper as the "beautiful and talented singer at the Colony Club" and she simply didn't want to be recognized. After all, she was only seventeen and still cared how her new career might confuse her parents. Besides, wearing wigs was easy. On stage, off stage, this party that party, off the stage, on the stage, long sweaty hours, short notice. Red hair, black hair, blond hair. It was fun! She then took off her pearls. They seemed to distract from the eloquent simplicity of the dress and the way it framed her face.

Beverly wrapped her head in a babushka scarf, grabbed her makeup-kit, pulled a light tan all-weather coat from the closet, and headed out the door.

EARLY EVENING

The hotel room furnished for the first family was recently redecorated in Mrs. Kennedy's style. The bar had been stocked with Heineken, the President's favorite beer; the chafing dishes were filled with warm food, daily newspapers were close at hand and the hotel staff was on their best behavior, everything was at attention.

While the President was busy reading and dealing with the comings and goings of his aides, the First Lady was busy getting dressed. A classical black cut-velvet suit, matching shoes, a double strand of delicate pearls, brilliant diamond earrings, and as always, her simple wedding band.

Beverly parked her car and walked next door to the Carousel. It was around 7:45 PM. Entering the club, she saw Jack Ruby standing near the bar, talking intently with friends. Evidently he was not ready to go, so she went back to the dressing room to see Jada.

"Hello, pretty lady," Beverly said. Jada looked up as she was busy struggling with a loose sequin which was hanging down from her costume.

"Don't you look great. Your dress is very pretty," Jada said . . . "I'm glad you're here. I need help with my G-string. I have a sequin that's about to fall off."

Beverly pulled a pair of cuticle scissors from her bag and clipped, then carefully tied the string, saving another outfit from falling victim to frustration and unneeded unraveling. Jada spent a lot of money on her stage clothes. This piece was no different. It was white satin, studded with white bugle beads and silver sequins all over the bra, G-string and panels–all hand-beaded. "A work of art for a work of art," Beverly thought.

"So what's up, gal?" Jada inquired, now relaxed. " Let me guess. You and Jack have plans. Right?" Jada didn't understand how Jack and Beverly could be such close friends; she didn't really like him.

Beverly nodded. The look in Jada's eyes was deceiving. She was saying one thing but seemed to be thinking another. Beverly knew that Jack had been concerned about Jada getting a little wilder on stage and that she was flagrantly flashing several of the customers. Beverly figured that Jada was eager to know if Jack was going to be gone for the evening. The previous night, he had actually turned off the stage light out of embarrassment. She didn't see why. Dallas wasn't New Orleans. But Jada was just having fun. She liked stripping. Unsnapping her G-string, pulling it quickly away then back again to get a charge from watching men crane their necks for a peek underneath. After all, it was a show, and she knew how to entertain. When Jada performed, people got their money's worth. Jack Ruby, nonetheless, didn't want her on-stage shenanigans to be the cause of the Carousel having its curtain pulled by the authorities.

Jack looked at his watch, then zipped across the room like a pinball, bouncing off friends with handshakes and hello's while making his way to the back room to find Beverly.

"Hi, gal. Are you ready?" Jack said, looking very pensive. He was easy to read, yet difficult to predict. Something about Beverly bothered him. She could tell.

"Jack. Don't you look nice." Beverly said waiting for him to say something, but he didn't. Beverly told Jada that she'd see her later, then facetiously asked her not to do anything *she* wouldn't do. Smiling cautiously, Jada told them to have a good time. Jack beamed a hard look at Jada. He knew that she knew what he meant. On the way out, Jack told the girl at the front that he'd be back, thinking that such a comment would help to keep things at the club in line. Jack parked in the lot next to his club. While they were waiting for the attendant to drive it back Beverly became a little concerned that Jack was not being himself.

"We've got ten minutes to get there," Jack said as he opened the car door for Beverly, "I told Larry we'd meet him at nine."

"That's plenty of time, Jack. We just have to drive down the street and hang a right."

"Are you still going to Fort Worth tonight?" Jack asked.

"Sure. You know me–the original party person."

"Then I guess you changed your mind about going to the presidential parade tomorrow?"

"Of course not. It won't be the first time I've partied all night and played all day."

"What are you going to wear?"

"Well Jack, I won't have time to change, so I planned on wearing this beautiful dress."

"You mean you're going to wear the dress I bought you down to see that S.O.B.?"

Silence. For the first time Jack was upset with Beverly, so she wasn't going to push the subject. She didn't want Jack to get into one of his moods and foul everything up before the good time he'd promised her that night.

Jack shook his head. Jack Ruby did not like John F. Kennedy –period. He didn't like his brother Robert, and especially his pompous father, Joe Kennedy.

From what she had overheard, the Kennedy's were trying to squash many of Jack's friends.

The conversation didn't make sense to Beverly. Was he really angry with her for wearing the dress in front of Kennedy? After all, he did buy the dress specifically for her to wear to the party—knowing full well that she would be partying all night. When would she have had time to change? He knew her better than that. Why was he so tensely irritable? His anger did not wear well on Beverly. She was hurt, but Jack had to get over himself. Nothing was going to get in the way of Beverly's good time.

Somewhere, someone was probably polishing the wooden stock on their rifle, cleaning and oiling the long barrel, looking through its telescopic scope, thinking about the next day, and the rest of their lives. Wasn't money and power wonderful? Like an aphrodisiac, wasn't it? You always wanted a little more to help you enjoy the experience of life.

EVENING

The temperature Thursday evening began to drop as a storm front moved across Colorado, New Mexico, the Texas Panhandle, and slipped into North Texas. The sky was lighted by a series of static confrontations and bellowed a low rumble of thunder as the tour group landed at Carswell Air Force Base shortly after 11:00 PM. Fort Worth was still awake and welcomed the motorcade enthusiastically as it made its way downtown along the freeway toward the Texas Hotel.

Throughout North Texas people were finalizing their plans to listen to the President speak in Fort Worth, while others were planning to watch the motorcade in Dallas. Everyone was hoping the weather was going to change.

Sitting on Stemmons Freeway the mint green and white Cabana Hotel was within shouting distance of Dealey Plaza. At 9:00 PM, its parking lot was fairly full. There were several parties being hosted, including one by Pepsi Cola for its bottle distributors which Richard Nixon had come to Dallas to address.

Jack didn't tell Beverly what the meeting was about. But she felt it was important because he was concerned about being late—which was unusual. Jack and Beverly took the elevator to the Mezzanine. Walking through the crowd, and holding Jack by the arm, Beverly noticed how well-dressed everyone was and how glad she was that Jack was thoughtful enough to buy her the dress. Jack spotted the man he was to meet. The man was busy talking to an attractive lady wearing a sparkling blue sequined evening dress. Jack walked up to the man and shook his hand. The man then told the woman that he'd be back later. As they walked away, Jack introduced him to Beverly as Mr. Larry Meyers. Beverly wondered why they didn't introduce her to the girl.

At first Beverly thought they might be headed back toward the elevator—but there was someone waiting for Jack in the *Bon Vivant* Room. When Beverly saw him she recognized him as someone she had seen from the club—Donny Lance. Jack picked a table by the dance floor and everyone took a seat. Beverly sat next to Donny and directly opposite Jack. Mr. Meyers was on her right. Jack ordered coffee for the three men and a champagne cocktail for Beverly.

"Larry get the twinkle out of your eye." Jack cautioned Mr. Meyers. "She's just seventeen."

Meyers did a double take. He couldn't believe it. Jack suggested that Beverly dance with his friend so that he and Meyers could have some privacy.

"I know who you are. Are you married?" Donny inquired of Beverly.

"No."

"What's your name?" Beverly responded.

"Donny."

"What's your last name?"

"Are you Jack's woman?" Donny inquired, changing the subject.

"No. I'm just a friend."

"So, then you date other people?"

"I said, I don't date Jack, we're just friends." Beverly emphasized.

"Would you like to go out with me sometime?" Donny suggested.

"I might."

Beverly thought Donny was attractive. He asked for her phone number but she said that she didn't give out her number to people she'd just met and suggested that perhaps if she saw him at the club sometime they could have a few drinks and get to know each other. Besides, she was staying with her parents and it wouldn't be appropriate. They danced two songs then walked back to the table. Jack was gone when they got back; Mr. Meyers said he went to make a phone call. When Jack came back to the table, Mr. Meyers said he was very hungry, so Jack suggested they leave and get something to eat.

"Why don't we eat here?" Beverly suggested, not wanting to bother with having to get in and out of the car again.

"No I want a Campisi's steak." Jack insisted, as he stood up to get the show on the road.

"Are you going with us?" Beverly asked Donny.

"No I've got an appointment."

"Are you going to tell me what your last name is?" She tried once more.

"It's Donny Lance. Donny Allen Lance." Jack threw in for Beverly's sake.

"Well, Donny Allen Lance, thanks for the dances. I enjoyed it."

Mr. Meyers paid the tab and everyone left.

While the valet was getting the car Mr. Meyers forewarned Jack, "These steaks better be worth the drive."

"Yeah," Jack said, practically licking his lips, "There're the best steaks you're ever going to eat."

The car pulled up and Jack opened the front door for Beverly. But she said she wouldn't need as much leg room as Mr. Meyers, so she sat in the back. (She didn't know why Jack thought those steaks were so good.)

LATE EVENING

The Cellar Club was Fort Worth's downtown burlesque club, and it was humming. Pretty girls were everywhere. So were many of the nation's Secret Service agents. For some reason, perhaps rooted only in the crotch of their pants, they neglected the value of their duties, ignoring the charter of their responsibilities as they indulged in their own selfishness. On the night of November 21, 1963, and into the wee hours of the morning, they went AWOL. Left on guard at the Texas Hotel to protect the President of the United States of America were a contingency of men from the Fort Worth Fire Department.

If a man could have a restaurant as a good friend, it was the Campisi's Egyptian Lounge. It was there that he could take a date, dine alone, or visit with friends, enjoy a great casual meal, then rest easy that his wallet would still be intact. The Egyptian was inconspicuously nestled in the middle of a small cluster of retail stores on Mockingbird Lane, across the street from the Dr. Pepper Bottling Plant. A landmark restaurant, the Egyptian served hot Italian dishes to a unique cross-section of who's who and who's not in Dallas. Crowds, always spilling out of the small sheltered entrance onto the sidewalk outside, wondered who the "regulars" were who would step past them to a waiting table in the back room. Most everyone knew the Egyptian was a gathering-place for the Mob, or so the rumor was whispered. Most people didn't know how the rumor actually got started or if it was really true, but whatever, it added to the atmosphere. There weren't many dining places in Dallas that were—different, the Egyptian was clearly an exception.

The covered foyer to the restaurant was brick, painted in the colors of Italy. The dining areas were served by two red doors separated by a brick column. The door on the left was the main entrance, it having a handle; the door on the right was an exit for some or a one-way private entrance for others, requiring the dexterity to pry it open with the strength of one's fingertips. But you'd better have a reason for doing so. A select few had backdoor privileges. The inside of the restaurant decor was cozy: black linoleum floor, black Formica table-tops trimmed in aluminum. As you walked in, there were seven booths on the right, another four booths were lined against the wall on the left and six tables spaced tightly in between. A full service bar, with seven barstools, operated at full speed in the left corner, across from another large booth. Each booth had an individual jukebox hugging the wall. A lot of change clanked to the bottom of the coin boxes by people mistakenly thinking they were going to hear the words to the music.

Three-quarters of the way down the right inside wall of the restaurant, just before the last booth, was the entryway to the back dining lounge. It was actually a side dining area, but was referred to as the backroom. The short hallway leading back toward the front door to the other dining room was littered with black-framed pictures arranged in a casual gallery which over the years has spilled out into the dining area. Joe Campisi was liked by a lot of people. The pictures were his testament. Joe and Don Meredith, Joe and Lee Trevino, Joe and R.D. Matthews, Joe and Jerry Lewis, Joe and Tony Zoppi.

The threesome arrived at the restaurant a little after 10:00 PM. It was late by Dallas dining standards, so Jack was able to park right in front. Pushing through the front door they were greeted by the smell of fresh garlic, olive oil and oregano.

Jack greeted several people around the room with pats on the back then pointed to a table in the far northwest corner. Jack ordered steak for everyone. "I guess you're going to eat yours raw like you always do?" he said to Beverly with a grin. "Hey, why don't you just lead it in here on a rope. That would be just fine with her," he joked to the waitress, always looking for a laugh. Beverly wondered how many more times she would hear that same old wise crack. Jack ordered his steak medium-well, and Mr. Meyer–medium. Jack ordered Beverly another cocktail, but she declined. Two had been enough. Jack ordered two coffees.

While they waited for the coffee, Joe Campisi brought over a pizza and set it down in front of Jack. "It's on the house," Joe said. Beverly figured it was a pizza that was made by mistake. She wasn't a big pizza eater, but the smell of the fresh baked crust drove her crazy. Joe and Jack were good friends and visited whenever they came in the restaurant. Joe owned Campisi's and played host there like Jack played at his club.

"So Jack, how's business?" Campisi asked.

"You know how it is, Joe. Nothing changes and if it did, you'd know before me. What about you Joe, you doing OK?"

"Yeah, Jack. What's this I hear about Jada? I heard you had to turn the lights out on her a couple of times. What's the matter, she getting too hot for some of your customers? They getting more than their money's worth, you think?"

"She's just unruly! She won't listen to me, Joe. She must think the place is hers or something. I don't know what it is with her—the wench!" Jack fired back. Jada was a touchy subject and talking about her made him uneasy.

"Jack, don't call her that. She's my friend. You just don't understand her." Beverly never did like Jack to cuss and was successful in blocking it out, but she took offense to his statement about Jada. Beverly appreciated Jada's talent and thought her flashing was what the men really wanted, even if she didn't understand the jeopardy her act might have on Jack's licensing.

Joe had to take a phone call and left before Jack became too fired up about Jada. Beverly quickly changed the subject. Jack nervously tapped his spoon on the table until the steaks arrived. Conversation was casual. Jack was not rushed nor preoccupied with anything. His conversation with Meyers was boring and she didn't pay much attention. She thought Meyers was somewhat arrogant; besides, men-talk was boring. All men usually wanted to talk about were guns and other women, neither of which she had any interest in. After Jack ordered a refill and a cup of coffee for Beverly, he asked for "the damage." Beverly then left to freshen up after dinner. When she returned to the table, Jack pulled out her chair and said, "Larry, let's go make that phone call in Joe's office. Beverly, we'll be back in a minute."

Beverly sat pretty, wondering just how long it took to make a phone call. Two refills later they returned. Jack looked over his check and told the waitress to put it on his tab. Meyers paid the tip. Beverly waved good-by to Joe. Jack put on his hat and they walked out into the cool Dallas night. It smelled a little like rain. Beverly thought about the parade the next day, wondering if she might have to wear her raincoat which she had left in the back seat of her car.

Jack opened the car door for Beverly and gave her a subtle smile. She assumed he was feeling better about her dress. He slipped behind the steering wheel and started the old green car.

"Jack what happened to that pilot who used to fly you down to Galveston?" Meyers asked.

"You mean—Buddy? He's moved back up east and I don't have access to his plane anymore."

It seemed to Beverly that they were finishing a conversation they started earlier but Jack was quick to change the subject.

"Beverly, what do you think about that club that I want to open over on Turtle Creek? Think it's a good idea? Maybe you could come sing for me over there. You know it'll be 'the' place in town. I'm going to have the best. What do you think?"

"Jack, like I've told you before, you should do it; it'll make you real happy. But with you being so far from the Colony Club I might not get to see you as often." That was Beverly's way of telling Jack that he shouldn't count on her to come sing for him. She wouldn't have left Abe for anything.

Jack squinched his face. He liked dreaming, planning, and talking about his elegant new club, the one that was going to be the best—a cut above all the others and elevate his position in Dallas' entertainment business. If he could just get the IRS off his back. Jack headed west down Mockingbird, turned south on Central Expressway, cut across town on Elm Street, then north on Industrial Boulevard, right to the service road and then back south toward the Cabana Hotel.

When they pulled in front of the hotel they realized that the valet was closed. This angered Jack. He didn't want to park the car himself. Beverly and Larry waited on the steps for Jack, and no sooner had he driven off, when Beverly noticed that she had left her make-up kit on the floor of Jack's car. Jack gave her a long hard look when he had to go back for it.

"Do you always carry a purse that big?" Meyers asked.

"This isn't a purse," Beverly quipped back, "It's a make-up kit. I need every bit of help I can get."

"I bet your as pretty in the morning when you get up as you are right now." Larry complimented.

"I bet you tell all the girls that."

Jack gave Beverly a hug and she hugged him back, telling him that she had a good time. "Do you have time to go back upstairs?" he asked.

"No. I've got to go get dressed."

"I thought you were dressed."

"Jack, I've got to go put my hair on and change my make-up."

Beverly said good-bye to Mr. Meyers and that it was nice to have met him. She then left to go to the ladies room while Jack and Larry walked toward the elevator. Beverly stepped into the ladies room, put on a dark wig, changed her lipstick, and straightened her mascara. Within a few minutes, she went from being a vivacious blond to a sensual brunette.

Beverly sat in the lobby and waited until 1:00 AM for her escort. He breezed by the Cabana on time then drove her to a party in Fort Worth that would last until the early morning. Her green and white silk polka-dot dress was holding up well. And thanks to a diet-pill, so was she.

1. *Embraceable You,* words by Ira Gershwin, music by George Gershwin
   Copyright 1930 (renewed), W. B. Music Corporation,.

2. *On The Sunny Side of The Street,*
   Copyright 1930 (renewed), Shapiro, Berntein & Co., Inc., New York.

CHAPTER ELEVEN

November 22, 1963

Fort Worth was experiencing a light blowing drizzle, while Dallas was warming to a breaking sun. On the eighth floor, in room 850 of the Texas Hotel in Fort Worth, President Kennedy breakfasted on two soft-boiled eggs, bacon, toast, orange marmalade, orange juice, and a hot pot of coffee. He was dressed in a white shirt with a broad blue pinstripe, a simple blue silk tie, and a plain gray-blue suit. In his pockets were his Massachusetts's Drivers License, six dollars in change, and a Saint Christopher Medal. Already, the President had made a few executive decisions; he first told the Secret Service to leave the bubble top off the limousine, and that without question, Senator Yarborough was riding in the car with Vice President Johnson.

Mrs. Kennedy walked into the room in her bathrobe complaining to her husband that her maid was never around when she needed her. She was ready to dress and needed help. The new pink suit she was going to wear was still hanging in the closet. Her husband said he would speak to her about it, then pointed across the street to the people down below already waiting in the rain for the speech he was going to give that morning. The crowds greeting them in the other Texas cities had overwhelmed him and he was hoping that Fort Worth, and particularly Dallas, would be equally represented. He mentioned to her that the Chamber of Commerce breakfast was scheduled for nine and that she should have plenty of time to get ready.

Picking up the morning paper, the President brought to her attention the headlines which angered him. The rift in Houston between Yarborough and Connally commanded the front-page, reporting that the split between the Democratic factions was widening contrary to the intent of the President's trip to Texas. There was also a full page ad trimmed in a heavy black boarder with the headline reading, "Welcome Mr. Kennedy to Dallas." It asked the President twelve questions indirectly condemning his international policies. He threw the paper down and jokingly commented, "We must really be in nut country now."

Mrs. Kennedy went back to her room. It would take her a while to get ready for Dallas, she wasn't planning on going to the breakfast.

Minutes later, Kennedy stood by the window speaking with Larry O'Brian, an old friend and his Presidential aide. He was fascinated by how fast the crowd was growing. What started out to be a sprinkling of people had now grown into several thousand. They looked out across the street to the parking lot where workers were building bleachers for the crowd. From the high vantage point he had in the hotel window, Kennedy turned to his friend and commented, "If someone wanted to get you, it wouldn't be very difficult would it?"

The President had two phone calls to make. He called Mrs. J. Lee Johnston to thank her for her thoughtfulness. She had taken the initiative to have two paintings from her private collection hung in the suite for them to enjoy. His next call was to former Vice President John Nance Garner to wish him a happy birthday; he was ninety-five.

Mrs. Lincoln stopped by the President's room to ask if she could introduce him to a few of her Texas friends. He agreed and said he'd have the Secret Service alert her when he was ready to leave so she could have them in the hall.

By 8:00 AM it was time to venture across the street. Mrs. Belew, the wife of an important Fort Worth lawyer, had arrived with Representative Jim Wright to escort Mrs. Kennedy across the street for the speech, but the President had to tell them that the First Lady was still working with her hair and wasn't ready. He decided to join them for the walk over. As he left his suite, Kennedy greeted Mrs. Lincoln's friends cordiality with the charm of the boy next door. Once again he took a peek out the window. The crowd had grown to near 5,000 and he was noticeably excited.

Downstairs, Kennedy smiled and nodded at everyone in the hotel lobby as he passed by. He danced down the steps outside the hotel to the cheers of "Here he is. Here's the President."

It was drizzling and Kennedy was coatless, but when he jumped up on the platform truck and began to speak, the sun broke through the clouds and brought sunshine in an irony that wasn't missed by anyone. It was clear by the shouts of, "Where's Jackie?" that the President was part of a team. He politely said, "Mrs. Kennedy is organizing herself. It takes longer but of course, she looks better than we do when she does it. But we appreciate your welcome."

"This city," he began, "has been a great Western City, the defense of the west, cattle, oil, and all the rest. It has believed in strength in this city, and in strength in this state, and strength in this country." Kennedy paid respect to the city of Fort Worth and its role in the country's defense by building fighter planes. He reminded them about the value of exploring new environments –the sea and space. He spoke about the importance of keeping the economy moving forward and he ended by underlining the importance of Americans accepting the burden of world leadership. The cheers flowing from the people of Fort Worth made him feel good. Unlike the crowd waiting in the dry banquet room of the hotel, the parking lot crowd related to Kennedy. They were working class people who were concerned about jobs, and they were hearing what they wanted. These were the people of Fort Worth who had voted for him and when he finished speaking the applause wouldn't stop.

Kennedy jumped down from the truck into a sea of handshakes and glaring eyes, greeting as many people as he could. On his way back to the hotel he stopped by to shake hands with members of the Fort Worth Sheriff's mounted-pose.

Beverly was tired as she slipped out of Fort Worth; the night went fast. Her mind was already thinking about the parade and where she might find a place to watch. She looked down at her dress. *Yeah, when would I have had a chance to change?* She laid her head back on the seat and closed her eyes as the taxi driver skillfully made his way toward Dallas.

The Fort Worth Chamber of Commerce had arranged for its members and other businessmen, a breakfast fund-raiser at the hotel for the Presidential entourage, and it was sold out. The President's entrance was well-received, but not with the fanfare that Mrs. Kennedy had when she arrived. Diverted from her original game plan of going straight to the plane, Clint Hill directed her into the dining area. The President, faced with another, "Where's Jackie?" situation rising, had called upstairs making it clear that he needed his wife by his side; the people of Fort Worth would hang him from the nearest tree if she didn't show up.

Escorted by Clint Hill, Mrs. Kennedy was greeted by a healthy roar and loud whistling as she walked into the room and took a seat beside her husband. She was wearing a nubby pink wool suit; flaring open into double-breasted dark blue purple lapels; a matching pill box hat was set back on her head at a slight tilt.

As customary for visiting dignitaries in Texas, the Kennedys were presented with traditional western gifts. Mrs. Kennedy was given a hand-tooled pair of cowgirl boots, and the President received a fawn-colored cowboy hat.

Mrs. Kennedy smiled as big as she could in appreciation, everyone knowing the chances of her pulling them on was slim. However, the crowd expected the President to at least don his hat for a few pictures, but he didn't. Kennedy thought that presidents should avoid goofy-looking pictures, and a Harvard man in a cowboy hat was just that.

"Put it on Jack." "Put it on," came the response from everyone.

The President grinned from ear to ear. "I will put this on Monday in my office at the White House. I hope you can be there to see it."

President Kennedy then sat down for a brief moment before he was introduced and took the podium again.

"I introduced myself in Paris by saying that I was the man who had accompanied Mrs. Kennedy to Paris. I am getting somewhat that same sensation as I travel around Texas. Nobody wonders what Lyndon and I wear." Jackie had stolen the show until then. Taking the podium in both hands, Kennedy launched into a speech that was designed for the world to listen to and Texans to take pride in. Like his speech outdoors, his focus was on defense-spending and how critical it was to secure the United States place as the protector for democracy and the glue that held strategic alliances together.

"The success of our National defense depends on this city in the Western United States, ten-thousand miles from Vietnam, five or six-thousand miles from Berlin, thousands of miles from trouble spots in Latin America and Africa or the Middle East. And yet Fort Worth and what it does and what it produces participates in all these historic events. Texas as a whole and Fort Worth bear particular responsibility for this national defense effort, for military procure-ment in this state totals nearly one and one-quarter billion, fifth highest among all the states of the union."

Kennedy had everyone captivated; even the people who weren't going to vote for him in the next election. Commitment to spending money in Texas was what they wanted. That's what they read between the lines.

"We should realize what a burden and responsibility the people of the United States have borne for so many years. Here, a country that lived in isolation, divided and protected by the Atlantic and the Pacific, uninterested in the struggles of the world around it, in the short span of eighteen years after the second World War, we put ourselves, by our own will and by necessity, into defensive alliances with countries all around the globe.

"Without the United States, South Vietnam would collapse overnight. Without the United States, the Southeast Asia Treaty Organization alliance would collapse overnight. Without the United States, the CENTO alliance would collapse overnight. Without the United States there would be no NATO. And gradually Europe would drift into neutralism and indifference. Without the efforts of the United States in the Alliance for Progress, the Communists advance into the mainland of South America would long ago have taken place.

"I am confident as I look at the future, that our chances for security, our chances for peace, are better than they have been in the past. And with that strength is a determination to not only maintain the peace, but also the vital interests of the United States. To that cause—Texas and the United States are committed. Thank you."

Applause broke out in a rush of admiration defying party boundaries. It felt good to be an American and for that brief shining moment, everyone was family.

Reverend Granville Walker provided the benediction. Using a traditional prayer, he embellished by adding a message about world peace, then graciously asking for the President's health, and that of his family, to be guarded.

After delivering his speech, the President and his wife went back to the room for a few minutes. President Kennedy needed to make a few phone calls and Mrs. Kennedy wanted to freshen up. She was surprised they had an hour before they needed to leave at 10:40 AM. She told her husband she was pleased, and that campaigning while he was President was much easier. He asked if she would join him in California. She smiled in reply, "I'll be there."

The white limousine transporting the President to Carswell Air Force base was swarmed by excited Air Force personnel in a spontaneous show of support. The President boarded the plane. It was thirteen minutes to Dallas.

DALLAS LOVE FIELD

At 11:39 AM, *Air Force One* touched down in a graceful landing setting thousands of hearts racing. Approaching down runway 31, the magnificent white plane glided to a slow-motion standstill. The Presidential insignia emblazoned on the front of the plane verified that something special was about to happen. For many, time stood still in anticipation of seeing the young president and his beautiful wife. Camelot was visiting Dallas. That trademark Kennedy smile, his chestnut hair. Her radiance. In a moment, they would actually see them in person.

Over by the chain link fence, arranged formally in line, were the cars to be driven in the motorcade down Lemmon Avenue, up Cedar Springs, through downtown Dallas, and on to the Dallas Trade Mart. The lead car was cream-yellow.

Next, sitting silently beneath a grand Texas sky, was a dark blue Lincoln Continental limousine bantering the American Flag and the Presidential Standard. The cars to follow the President's limousine were in line too, along with the motorcycles.

The President and his wife emerged from the plane smiling and waved to the cheering crowd. They watched elatedly as the Camelot couple carefully walked down the steps and over to the fence—noticing their surprise at the bright sunlight and the warm feelings flowing from everyone. After a short hand-shaking tour, the young First Family took their seats for the short ride through Dallas. They were 1,307 miles from their children, 7.2 miles from Dealey Plaza. President Kennedy adjusted his tie; his wife adjusted her hat.

It was 66 degrees Farenheit. The sky was bright blue with a few scattered clouds sliding off to the east. The breeze was blowing briskly from the northwest as the motorcade left the airport.

Scores of people lined the two-mile stretch of the Lemmon Avenue motorcade route. From the Coca-Cola Bottling Plant to the grassy green corner of Lee Park, throngs of spirited Dallasites waited to greet the Kennedys. Even though Kennedy lost by a wide margin in the city, the public was beginning to take the Harvard graduate to its heart. Nevermind the oil-depletion tax, nevermind offshore drilling requests, or tax-loophole deletions. Let the wealthy worry about how Kennedy was going to change things; this was a chance to come face-to-face with a celebrity and her husband.

As the motorcade rolled down the street, the roar of the crowd barreled down Lemmon in a wave of patriotic adulation. It was impulsive, genuine, and just what the President wanted to hear.

Some people in Dallas didn't care one way or the other for the 35th president, and some thought he was enforcing too much government control. There were people who felt that with his soft stance on the cancer of communism, Kennedy was dangerous and wanted him out of office.

The limousine cruised past the Dallas shopping strip in a slow deliberate pace. Eagle Lincoln Mercury, Kip's Big Boy, The Cotton Bowling Palace, El Finex, Friendly Chevrolet, The Prince of Hamburgers, The Comet Car Wash. Maybe this wasn't such a bad idea after all, the President might have thought seeing so many cheering people. As the President approached the intersection at Lomo Alto, he responded to a plea to stop and shake hands. He told Bill Greer, his driver, to stop the car. Again and again, to the chagrin of the President's protectors, Greer did as requested.

Beverly reached her car at about 11:10 AM. It was parked on the lower level of the Colony Club parking lot. Sitting in the back-seat of her car, with her legs stretched out the door, Beverly changed her shoes to a pair of comfortable black flats to make it easier to walk. Reaching down to the floorboard, she grabbed her makeup kit, took out the camera that Larry had given her, and checked to make sure that it had film in it. Beverly locked her car, opened her trunk and grabbed her coat. It had been raining in Fort Worth and she wasn't sure if the rain was going to follow her. She put her coat on since she had to carry her movie camera as well. She then noticed the straw summer bag which had been in the trunk since summer and thought it would be a good thing to keep her camera in. She pulled out her bathing suit, tossed it in the trunk, and replaced it with her camera. Beverly then went back to the car and got another magazine of film to put in the bag. She made sure everything was locked up, closed the trunk, then walked out of the garage. She then took a left on Commerce Street, onto the sidewalk, and headed west to a street south of the crowds gathering on Main Street.

Lemmon Avenue at Lomo Alto. Occasionally, the President would notice an unfriendly sign. Not many. Standing back in the crowd, straining his neck, jumping up to catch a glimpse of the President as he drove by, was Father Oscar Huber of Holy Trinity Church. A small patch of chestnut hair was all he saw. The sun was standing at high noon.

The right turn onto Turtle Creek took the President past sparse waving crowds and by Lee Park, a landscaped oasis running the crooked course of a small green creek, five minutes from downtown. An equestrian statue saluting the Texas Confederate War dead caught the President's attention as he drove by. There aren't many statues in Dallas–this was the only one he saw. Mrs. Kennedy wanted to put on her sunglasses, but her husband shook his head. Greer sped up. Mrs. Kennedy grabbed her hat.

The energy downtown was beginning to flow as the time grew near the motorcades planned arrival. The city and its people were charged with excitement. Beverly kept looking down the side streets for a place to stand but everywhere she looked people were standing, three and four deep. Wondering if she was going to find a place, she remembered the grassy place at the end of the parade route, and decided to continue walking in that direction.

Reaching Houston Street at Commerce, she walked north across Commerce Street then west across Houston. There weren't many people in the park. Most of them were scattered along Houston Street. Across the lawn, however, she saw very few people standing near the curb on Elm Street and assumed that was where the motorcade would pass. She was thrilled that it wasn't crowded and felt lucky. She was glad she kept looking.

Walking across the lawn in a deliberate pace, thrilled about how close she was going to be to President Kennedy, Beverly scanned the area, curiously looking at everyone who had come to see him. She selected a spot near a young boy and his father, leaving room in front of her so she could walk up to the curb if she wanted. The boy acted like he couldn't wait until the President drove by. Beverly began looking through the viewfinder, making sure she could operate the movie camera as Larry had instructed. To her left she noticed a lady in a red coat and a girl with a hand camera. Across the street she noticed a man standing on a pillar holding a movie camera to his eye, looking as if he might fall off if he wasn't careful. Fortunately, a woman was bracing him from behind for safety.

The crowd gathered along Harwood Street, enthusiastically welcomed the President to downtown Dallas. But those lined wall-to-curb down Main Street provided the litmus test for the success of the parade. People were hanging out windows, waving flags, screaming good cheer. They were smiling, clapping their hands, calling out to the President and his wife. Every square-inch of standing space was occupied. Dallas was bubbling with controlled hysteria.

"Thank you . . . thank you." President Kennedy repeated over and over. "Thank you."

The ten-block procession down Main Street reached a small open area fronted by a massive, grand old red stone courthouse on the President's left and the cement-colored buildings on his right, blue sky high above, and the Trade Mart ten minutes ahead.

Beverly let down her camera for a moment and turned around. She heard the crowd start clapping and cheering and knew the President was about to turn off Main Street and onto Houston Street. She could hear the rumble of the motorcycles. The roar became louder as the motorcade moved closer.

Once past the courthouse, the limousine made a slow sweeping right turn onto Houston Street. Straight ahead, in perfect view of the President, was the Texas School Book Depository, and someone on the sixth floor waiting for him. The southeast window was half-open. If the President had looked up at the right time, he might have seen a protruding rifle barrel.

Beverly couldn't wait, he was almost there. The people on Houston street were yelling and she knew it was time. She placed the camera back up to her eye and aimed it toward the corner of Houston and Elm. She pressed the shutter button and started filming. Shortly, two motorcycles turned the corner followed by a light colored car and then the flags on President Kennedy's car came into her viewfinder. *This is it!* As President Kennedy's face came into view Beverly was awe struck. Sitting next to his pretty smiling wife, he looked pleased and happy. Beverly's admiration for the couple was at its peak and it was hard to continue filming. She wanted a better look and thought about lowering her camera as the car drove by, but then she wouldn't have something she could watch over and over. Instead, she kept both eyes open so that she could see the camera view and the real view. *Hold steady.*

Moving her movie camera in concert with the limousine as it moved toward her, Beverly heard a pop, pop sound coming from the direction she faced. It seemed to come from the corner where the limousine turned. How rude that some parents would let their kids throw those sidewalk poppers near the President, she thought. Then she heard another pop. *Hold steady.* The car was moving about twelve miles an hour as it passed directly in front of her. It then seemed to come to a stop. She continued filming wishing President Kennedy would turn around, then a loud, boom-boom sounded, and the President's head was violently thrown backward as a spray of crimson blood spouted from the back of his head. "Oh, my God . . . he's been shot." She saw Jackie pull her husband down toward the seat as if she was trying to protect him and then crawl out onto the trunk of the car to pick up something which seemed to come from the President's head. Clint Hill, who was riding in the car behind the President, ran up behind the limousine and jumped on the trunk as the car accelerated and as Mrs. Kennedy started crawling back inside, holding in her hand the fragment from her husband's head. Everything was so hopeless, somehow maybe, she thought it would make things better.

Beverly couldn't move. She stood mesmerized, her camera still in place, her finger pressed on record.

People were screaming and falling to the ground in panic. A motorcycle policeman crash-parked his cycle and raced up the grassy slope from where Beverly heard the gunfire. The limousine was powering up the ramp to Stemmons when Beverly smelled something acid in the air. It didn't smell right. A cloud of smoke drifted up from behind the fence and dissipated as it blew across the lawn.

People started running toward the fence but Beverly was too frightened to move. Someone had just shot the President in the head. There were several shots; she didn't know if someone else had been hit, nor if they were through shooting. The next thing Beverly realized, she was across the street standing on the second landing of the steps heading up to the pergola. Dazed, perplexed, she stood numb, watching a crowd of about fifty people congregating on the slope near the curb. She saw the lady in the red coat talking to some man asking her questions and wondered if anyone was going to speak with her.

Still scared, her heart pounding fast, her hands perspiring, her stomach in knots, Beverly wanted to leave. Then out of the corner of her left eye, Beverly saw Geneva's husband hurriedly walking across the steps in front of her. He was wearing part of his policeman's uniform, but not all of it. He was wearing his shirt, his badge, his trousers, but he was not wearing a hat, nor was he carrying a gun. Beverly caught his attention and realized that he recognized her even though she was wearing a dark wig; he knew what she looked like, he had seen her in wigs before. She thought he was going to go question someone. Then, she saw another policeman who she recognized from the clubs. It was Paddy (Patrick Dean). He was dressed in his uniform and was walking swiftly in the same direction as Geneva's husband.

When she saw the two policemen, Beverly thought things were going to get under control. But suddenly, her relief turned back to fear, at what–at whom, she didn't know–she just wanted to get out of there and listen to her car radio to hear what more was known about what happened.

Since Geneva's husband saw her, Beverly left thinking if they needed to speak with her they could find her. Leaving the plaza, Beverly quickened her pace, hurrying to reach her car. "What happened?" she was asking herself. *Why? The scene she witnessed kept replaying over and over in her mind. What was going on? Surely someone knows something by now.* Her thoughts shifted back to reality when she saw her car parked in the same place she left it the night before; it was the same color, it was the same make. *It wasn't a dream.*

Senator Yarborogh hurried up to the car while the hospital staff were racing to bring a gurney to carry the wounded President. Johnson was being ramroded through the crowd by a shield of Secret Service Agents calling him "Mr. President." The Senator looked inside the limousine to the most horrible tragic thing he could imagine. Mrs. Kennedy was sitting there sobbing, trying to shield her husband's bloody head in her lap. Blood was running down her leg. "They've murdered my husband. They've murdered my husband."

Beverly started her car. How could she put into words the emotions that controlled her. She was so shaken she hoped she could drive. Pulling out of the lot onto Commerce Street, she drove toward Central Expressway, her left hand steering, her right hand on the radio dial, trying to find a station reporting news on the President's condition.

"Three shots were fired at the Presidential motorcade in downtown Dallas at about 12:30 PM. The President has been rushed to Parkland Hospital. No word yet as to his condition. Governor Connally was also shot, perhaps fatally. We're here at Parkland Hospital. Everyone outside the emergency room entrance is visibly shaken. People are crying and holding onto one another."

As Beverly drove down Central, there was radio silence . . . followed . . . by someone . . . clearing his . . . throat . . . . "President John F. Kennedy died at approximately 1:00 PM, Central Standard Time, here . . . in Dallas. He died of a gunshot wound to the brain." Beverly almost lost control of the car, her heart sank so fast she felt faint. Quickly pulling to the side of the expressway, gripping the steering wheel tightly, she put her forehead on her hands and cried uncontrollably. Someone took her president away. *What right did he have–what right!* Warm tears streamed down her hands. Her heart felt the abrasive tension of sorrow fused with anger. *President Kennedy. John F. Kennedy. Poor Jacqueline.* Reason took a back-seat to emotions; there were no answers. Beverly wanted to hit someone. They had to be wrong, she tried to tell herself. They must be wrong. The insanity of what she saw was beyond her 17 year-old comprehension; there were too many things to think about, to question. *This doesn't happen in America. Who was behind the fence? Did Geneva's husband know; he was right there? Have they caught him yet?*

Flashbacks of the assassination became rapid fire–and made it hard for Beverly to concentrate on driving. She wondered what the other witnesses had seen and what she would say if anyone asked her. *I saw . . . I just couldn't have stayed longer, just couldn't.* Somehow, Beverly made it home–back to Garland. Back to the sanctity of her parent's home. Back to her room, her bed, her sheets, her sleeping pills.

The sleeping pill slowly took over, burying Beverly's grief in a groggy vacuum. Still crowding her thoughts as she battled sleep were slow motion frames of the red blood . . . the screams . . . the car slowing down, Jackie on the hood, "Oh my God . . . ."

Eugene sat in the living room–his hands wrapped around a shotgun. Beverly told him what she saw before she downed her pills. He knew the bizarre crowd she was involved with, and for some reason, felt it was necessary to stand guard. He had always protected her–even then, when he didn't know from what.

CHAPTER TWELVE

The Mourning After

Born from the darkness of the day before, Saturday morning was veiled in a sobering reality of sonic sadness and reserved restlessness. Everybody affected by Kennedy's death wanted to do something, but what? All they could do was watch . . . and care. The catastrophic mood was rooted deep into emotions which people rarely experience; a vacant, empty, physical weakness painfully experienced when a loved one is taken—forever. In a spontaneous outpouring—yet simple reverence, the world cried together and time slowed to the speed of darkness. The misery created from the senselessness of the assassination was shared universally through newspaper, radio, and televisions everywhere. Kennedy's death was a shock which reverberated in monumental grief around the world.

Taxi cab drivers in Rome parked a cab with a wreath on it in front of the U.S. Embassy. In Germany, people took to the streets of Munich, Berlin, and Bonn for torch light parades. The Schoneberg Rathaus was renamed John F. Kennedy-Platz. U.S. Charge d'Affaires William C. Truehart was greeted by thousands of Vietnamese students dressed in white cotton shirts who had marched in the rain to present their condolences. In London, Lawrence Olivier stopped his performance and requested that the orchestra play The Star Spangled Banner. And even in the Soviet Union, flags were lowered to half-mast.

Europeans, saddened with great anguish over Kennedy's murder, were faced with new questions and concern that reliance on America's protection was in jeopardy. It became evident to French Premier Charles de Gaulle and others that Kennedy's plan to curb the proliferation of nuclear weapons and keep the destructive technology in the hands of a few was superseded by the desires of a new regime, making it necessary for Europe to support independent nuclear sovereignty.

Dallas was caught in its own crossfire of despair and accountability. The bullet that took the President—wounded every citizen. Grief mingled with shame while the world watched the city try to pick up the pieces. The routine of booking the suspect for shooting officer J.D. Tippit and John F. Kennedy took place under a blind microscope.

Floating around the edge of dreams, Beverly was still wandering in the lower realms of profound slumber, relying on the intoxication of sleep to soothe her and sweep her mind of yesterday's visions, when . . . suddenly, she became involved in a vivid nightmare of the assassination. Her eyes flew open in wild panic and her heart started racing as it had the day before. The fury of the dream startled her, it was so real and she was overwhelmed with more questions than she could find answers. Beverly's sense of loss was profound. Watching the assassination from only a short distance away caused her to experience an unusual bonding with the fallen President. She felt close to him in a spiritual sense and deep down she knew thoughts of him would follow her forever. Beverly couldn't go back to sleep without reliving Friday. Seeing it over and over in her mind's eye caused her considerable anguish. For a split second, as the limousine approached her, she flashed on what was going to happen and tried to warn him by screaming . . . but he couldn't hear her. She hoped she would wake up and it would all be a dream. But it wasn't.

Lying motionless in bed, her eyes still closed, Beverly visually went through her closet of clothes. It would be so easy to stay in bed longer, but she felt it was time to get dressed and return to the living. *The white dress I wore Thursday night will work fine, or, was it Tuesday? Tuesday . . . Tuesday.* Deciding on what to wear could wait, but she needed to have her hair done, so she dragged herself out of bed and put on some clothes. *Maybe I should call Abe.*

Beverly kept her hair appointment, but her thoughts were lost in a cloud of despair. Talk at the salon was buzzing about the assassination. Everyone was shaken that it happened in Dallas, let alone anywhere, and they were grief-stricken for Mrs. Kennedy and her children. When Beverly again heard that Lee Harvey Oswald was arrested as the only assassin of President Kennedy, and that he had fired from a perch he had constructed in the east corner of the sixth floor of the Texas School Book Depository—she was confounded. Not only because she had met him, but more importantly, because no mention had been made about anyone shooting from behind the fence. It was clear to Beverly, and everyone else rushing to the fence area, where the shot which killed Kennedy had come from—why didn't they? *What am I missing here?*

There was no escaping her nightmare, not even in broad daylight. All the way home Beverly retraced the horrible event, trying to determine if there was any way she had misinterpreted what she had witnessed – but it only led to further anxiety when it always came out the same – *pop . . . pop – boom . . . boom. It came from the front . . . from the front.* Beverly was ready to slip back into bed. Big time bed. *Maybe tomorrow everything will be straightened out. Maybe tomorrow.*

Before Beverly could shed her clothes, her mother quietly approached her with a soft spoken request. "Beverly, I would like to go see all the flowers for Kennedy. Please take me down there."

Downtown was the last place Beverly wanted to be. She didn't want to face the reality of what she was trying to forget.

"Mother, I'm not up to it. I just want to sleep. As you can see, I'm not taking this very well," Beverly slurred, shaking her head, her hand reaching for the sheets. "Maybe later. Maybe tomorrow."

Beverly could tell that her mother, too, was upset by Kennedy's death, but wasn't wanting to talk about it; they never were very good at communicating with one another. Emotionally, Beverly had grown up on her own sharing her ambitions, desires, and fears with no one. Beverly and her mother were often left trying to guess what the other was thinking.

"Were you down there Beverly? Did you watch the parade?"

Beverly looked back at her mother, searching for something to say. "Yes. Yes . . . I saw the whole thing, I mean the shooting. Oh, mother it was horrible. I don't understand."

Mrs. Oliver had a thousand questions, but she could tell that they'd have to wait. "I understand. Maybe tomorrow." Beverly lifted the bed sheets and slipped back into the void.

Near 3:30 PM that day, Beverly woke up and saw her mother sitting quietly nearby gazing at her. Her mother still wanted to go downtown. It was the only thing she knew to do to pay her respect to Kennedy, the "Catholic President," who she thought was "so strong, so . . . adorable." Pleading once more to take her to see the flowers, Beverly's mother stood by the side of her bed, her shivering hand cupped over her mouth. "It won't take long. I feel like I need to go . . . I . . . I just want to do something."

The tone of her mother's voice, its slight quiver, moved Beverly. *Poor mom . . . I'm not the only one who's suffering. Maybe I'll feel better if I go and put it all . . . behind me.*

"OK, Mom. Let's go. I know it will make you feel better. Let me change my clothes."

On the way downtown they stopped at McShann Florist on Garland Avenue to buy some flowers. Beverly pulled a single long stemmed red rose from a standing vase. *Just one–there could never be enough flowers. She had it wrapped in green florist tissue.*

A few blocks from the park, Beverly started feeling ill, not just a queasiness, but a fluid bad taste that ran helter-skelter through her body. The closer she got, the angrier she got. *How could they?* She didn't say anything to her mother; how could she begin to explain what she had seen or how she felt? She wondered if the man behind the fence had been caught.

They parked in the underground city parking lot off Commerce Street underneath the old red courthouse. Walking across Houston Street to the plaza, Beverly's bitter thoughts instantaneously gave way to sorrow. She looked down at the coarse black asphalt . . . where the tires were . . . picturing the moment when the limousine turned onto Elm Street when she started filming. The effervescent energy which had electrified the plaza when the motorcade had approached had caramelized into a sticky melancholic calm. The sky was mute, cast with a clouded palette of grayish blues and bluish grays. They walked across the lawn to the area where Beverly had been filming the President. Beverly's mother couldn't hold back her questions any longer. "Who, what, where, how?" Beverly started to expound about what had happened. Her account was mechanical in detail as she explained how she found her way down there, how many people had gathered to greet President Kennedy . . . but when she . . . started describing the motorcade's entrance . . . into the . . . park, her eyes narrowed and her sense of reality evaporated. She came face to face with–yesterday. Like condemned echoes, she heard the motorcycle rumble, the cheer, the crackerball pops, the loud gunshots.

As Beverly laid her rose in the soft green grass at her feet, where she had been standing the day before, she wept.

For the first time in a very long while, Beverly's mother tenderly wrapped her arms around her in cradling comfort. "Everything's going to be OK, baby." "Mom, I really don't think so. Things will never be the same. I'm so frightened." Beverly's mother was the only person in the world who understood how delicately vulnerable Beverly was. Embraced together tightly, they rocked, Beverly's crying muffled in her mother's shoulder.

Flowers carpeted the plaza in a colorful profusion of sympathy. They were placed on the lawn, displayed on easels, arranged in pots on the pergola. They were everywhere–lilies, chrysanthemums, daisies, roses. Purple, yellow, white . . . red.

Beverly felt that somehow the country had changed on Friday. Looking around the plaza at the mourners, she experienced an unmistakable sense of foreboding. And, it wouldn't shake. Things would never be the same.

After taking a few pictures, Beverly took hold of her mother's hand and they walked away.

The East Room of the White House was eerily quiet. Candles flickered near the flag-draped casket of the late President which was positioned heroically on a catafalque trimmed in black. An honor guard stood square at absolute attention. Jacqueline Kennedy, looking worn and bereaved, paused in the doorway in woeful disarray. She was still wearing the nubby pink blood-stained suit. Her eyes were clouded and vacant. In the dancing amber glow of candlelight, she walked slowly forward, knelt, and placed her forehead to the casket. In a reverent moment reserved for the widow, she wept uncontrollably, her chest heaving in heavy sorrowful sighs. Bobby Kennedy walked up behind her, wrapped his arms around her and let her cry. It was 4:30 AM.

Sunday was sewn on the tail end of Saturday; stitched together in an endless media monotone of updates and condolences. Attention was split between reports from Washington, from around the world, and local news reports about the accused assassin, Lee Harvey Oswald. Dallas District Attorney Henry Wade waved his cigar confidently when he boasted they had their man and the case was practically closed–neat and tight: the rifle, the sales order, the bullets. Everyone did their job. Let's get on with it.

In the meantime, Beverly was buried in the soft folds of her warm sheets. Her television, still awake from the night before, was whispering in the dark, as a bedraggled and handcuffed Oswald, dressed in a black sweater, beaming that same incredible nonchalance, was marched from the police station out into a basement crowded with rabid reporters toward a car that was to take him to the county jail across town. Then, in the blink of an eye, Oswald was shot in his left gut, point blank, by someone who had muscled his way through the press. As the assailant was wrestled to the concrete floor, Beverly tossed in her sleep.

Later, sometime in the shadow of the afternoon, as evening was settling in, her eyes still closed, Beverly was awake enough to listen to the television. "The man who shot Lee Harvey Oswald this morning has been identified as Jack Ruby, a Dallas night club owner. Jack Ruby."

Beverly sprang up from her bed, trying to focus on the television screen, reaching to turn up the volume. The newsman reported that Ruby had confessed to shooting Lee Oswald in a fit of rage because he loved the President and wanted to spare Jackie and the kids the trauma and indignity of having to go to a trial.

That didn't jive. Beverly knew that while Jack was infatuated with Jacqueline, he despised all the Kennedy boys—down to the last spoiled seed. *Why is he saying that?* Beverly thought about picking up the phone and calling Shari but hesitated. She knew Jack was usually armed and that with his hair-trigger temper he possibly could have become enraged enough to blow some creep away who was charged with murdering the President, but someone who he had introduced as his friend? *Was Jack serious when he introduced us? Were they actually friends?* Beverly didn't have any answers, but was certain that the man Jack had introduced her and Jada to at the club that night was the same man that Jack shot. Beverly knew she wouldn't be able to perform that night, so she had her mother call Abe.

Editorial pages across the nation printed a sobering exposé of the temper of madness, the rudeness of hate, and the bitterness of violence. The murders of John F. Kennedy and Lee Harvey Oswald held a mirror to the nation and America didn't like what she saw. Many people tried to blame Dallas and the city's festering of volatile right and left wing fanatics. A city of virulence and lunacy which had created a climate for assassination, they wrote. The treatment of Adlai Stevenson should have served a warning, it was printed. Others however, placed the blame on America herself and that citizens across the continent should share the guilt for the political and social atmosphere which had spawned an Oswald and a Ruby. A complacency which had allowed some leaders to keep the spirit of bigotry alive through their associations with organizations founded on the principles of hate and violence. They also blamed those leaders who had failed to speak out for equality and against the degradation of democratic ideals.

Some people were shouting, "Let's pin a medal on Jack Ruby," while others felt they had been cheated and that the lid had been shut on the truth.

Some tabloids claimed that the anger which raised its ugliness in Dealey Plaza was reminiscent of slavery days when angry mobs satisfied their lust for control by getting out of control. "It's the way the south carries on its business." The violence of vigilante politics: a rope and a tree. They questioned the overt proliferation of confederate flags lining the parade route through Dallas and insisted it was a declaration that Dallas wanted no part of new civil liberties. Mark Bricklin of the Philadelphia Tribune described what he thought was the social undercurrent in Dallas, "To hell with the United States! To hell with law and order! To hell with any so-called leader of these un-united states. It means insurrection, and insurrection means violence. Murder. Assassination." It's the same old south, some papers tried to convince readers who were looking for someone or something to blame.

Monday. The television set had Beverly's attention. Black Jack, John Kennedy's favorite stallion, pranced behind the historic caisson in symbolic prose of a fallen warrior. Empty boots reversed in the stirrups, silver sword sheathed. The image of a riderless horse dug deep. Camelot was dead. The black stallion's gate was chaotic yet restrained, as if the horse was revolting, kicking up its front legs in a demonstrative buck that shouted—"No! No!" The methodical snaring cadence from a troop of military drummers provided a patriotic sobriety that kept the ceremony marching onward while the mournful sonance of bagpipes floated the wind like a good-by kiss.

Jacqueline Kennedy walked by herself, strong, upright and widowed. Heartbroken and detached; the black veil draped from her head could not mask her broken spirit—her swollen eyes spoke of lost tomorrows. Step by step, the nation tearfully walked beside her—from the Capitol Building to St. Matthew's Cathedral.

It was John John's third birthday.

Beverly learned that Jack had managed to walk undetected into the basement of the Dallas Police Station as they were transferring Oswald to the County Jail over on Houston Street. After wiring money to one of his dancers, Karen Carlin, from the Western Union office a block away from the station, Jack had pushed his way through a crowd of reporters and stuck his gun into Oswald's side and blasted him. Beverly watched the news footage over and over and still couldn't believe Jack had done it. She could believe, however, that it would be easy for Jack to enter the basement; after all, he knew practically all of the cops, and if they did see him, why would they have suspected anything? What she couldn't believe was his excuse.

Under the circumstances, Beverly managed well as she prepared to go back to work. Even with all the sleep she had gotten, Beverly didn't feel rested. And watching the funeral nearly caused her to call Abe and ask for the night off again. Beverly was determined to get the weekend behind her. But she was starting to feel frightened about the assassination. It began when she learned that Jack shot Oswald! *Jack shot that man. Right on TV! Right on TV!* As an eyewitness to the assassination, Beverly couldn't help but feel somehow involved; however, as a friend of Jack Ruby, she felt too close to the events. Not knowing what to expect when she got back to work, Beverly thought perhaps Abe, Shari, or Jada could fill her in. Beverly was wondering why no one had contacted her about what she had seen that day but still felt that someone probably would. What bothered her though, was that what she did witness that Friday was completely different than the story she was hearing in the media. When they flashed a picture of Oswald on television, she easily remembered him as the "CIA friend" Jack introduced to her and Jada, and as the antagonist Jack threw out of the club after he called Wally a Communist. But when everyone said Oswald fired from the sixth floor of the Texas School Book Depository and still hadn't mentioned anything about someone shooting from behind the fence, she was frightfully puzzled. *How could they be ignoring what was so evident? Maybe Geneva's husband didn't recognize me. That's impossible–sure he did!*

Beverly reached downtown a little early and thought about dropping in for a moment at the Carousel Club. But she decided against it, turning instead into the Colony Club. When she reached the stairs, she saw two men standing at the first landing, peering down at her. *Who are they? They don't look like customers . . . they're not here for me, are they?* Dressed in dark business suits and western hats they were quick to address her when she reached the landing. One of the men flashed a badge and introduced himself. Beverly was so engrossed with the unexpected intrusion that she didn't catch his name. "Are you Beverly Oliver?" asked the man with the badge. His partner stood quietly.

"Yes." Beverly became tense. She thought they were finally getting around to asking her a few questions about the assassination, but this was not the time nor the place; she didn't want to be late or share with those at the club what had happened.

"Miss Oliver, we understand that you were shooting film of the President when he was killed?"

Beverly's heart sank like she was guilty of something and when she realized where the film canister was, she became nervous. It had laid undisturbed since Friday inside her make-up kit, next to a tin of Prince Albert tobacco; however, the tobacco was Marijuana. Thoughts of Candy Barr's arrest raced through Beverly's mind. Candy, who had danced for Abe at one time had been set up and busted for one joint of Marijuana and, regardless of the circumstances, she was sent to prison.

"Miss Oliver. Where is the film?"

Beverly hesitated. She didn't know what to tell them. As she vacillated, the man tried to relax her, "You understand that for investigative purposes it's important that we take a look at it. We'll get it back to you in a few days."

"I have it here. I forgot about it; it's not even developed." Beverly quickly opened and shut her kit, handing him her loaded camera. As he took the camera, Beverly wondered how they knew about it, but wasn't going to ask. She wanted to hustle on up the stairs and get as far away from them as possible. *Come on, come on, ask your questions.* The man opened the camera, removing the undeveloped magazine of film, then handing the empty camera back to her saying, "Thank you, ma'am, you'll be hearing from us."

Beverly was relieved to see the two men scamper down the steps. The encounter took only five minutes but Beverly suffered for an eternity. Her heart was pumping fast. The Marijuana wasn't even hers. She had kept it for a celebrity who was in town entertaining at the King's Club. Beverly didn't understand why they didn't ask her any other questions about Kennedy's assassination, but was glad they hadn't; they seemed only interested in her film. *Maybe the answers to their questions are on my film.* As she reached the top of the stairs and stepped through the door into the club, Beverly was accosted by two reporters eager to query her about Jack Ruby. "I don't know the man!" Beverly spouted back as she huffed by.

"Beverly, you ought to cash in on some of this free publicity, it wouldn't . . . ." Chris began before she was interrupted.

"If they can kill the President of the United States, they could kill a two-bit show girl like me and it wouldn't even make the back page of the newspaper." Beverly was right and she knew it.

The FBI wanted to know if Ruby knew Oswald before he killed him. That same day they questioned Bill DeMar after he told his long time friend David Hoy that not more than a couple weeks before, he spoke to Oswald during one of his acts at the Carousel. Hoy was the News Director at Station WIKY in

Evansville, Indiana. Both DeMar and Hoy had attended President Kennedy's inauguration.

DeMar told FBI agents that he saw Oswald in the club, eight or ten days before the assassination, when he participated in DeMar's memory retention act. The agents suggested to DeMar that he go into hiding where he would be safer. Days later, when the Secret Service wanted to find him, they had to go through the Federal Bureau of Investigation.

On Wednesday of that week, Beverly and Carri Castle walked over to the Carousel Club to see if they could find anything out about Jack or where Jada was. It seemed that Jada had disappeared. Beverly had not heard from her or seen her since last Thursday night, nor did she know the plans for the club while Jack was locked up. Beverly had been told that Jada left unexpectedly for Louisiana after speaking to reporters who quoted her in Monday's paper that Ruby introduced her to Oswald in the club a couple of weeks before the assassination. Andy was tight-lipped to the girls about Jack and without an explanation he informed the girls that Jada was gone for good. He then pointed over to some hangers of clothes and asked them if they would like to buy some of Jada's wardrobe—$125.

"You're crazy, Andy. Jada will kill you for selling her wardrobe. She paid a lot of money for those costumes. That white outfit is brand spanking new. She wore it for the first time last week." Beverly said, thinking Andy was off his rocker.

"Don't worry, she won't be needing them." Andy assured the girls.

Andy seemed final and spoke with an eerie confidence that he wouldn't have to worry about a reprisal from Jada. He wouldn't say anymore about Jack or the club. Beverly was immediately suspicious that the lack of Jada's presence might have something to do with her statement about Jack and Oswald knowing each other. Under any circumstances, Jada would not have left part of her wardrobe, Beverly thought. Surely she wasn't planning on giving up dancing; she couldn't—it was her livelihood and in her blood.

Jacqueline Kennedy understood the transcending virtue of her husband's vision for America and recognized how important it was to keep the spirit of his presidency alive for future generations. His young life was taken just when his crusade for change was coming to fruition. Never before had the United States benefited or enjoyed the worldly success as with the Kennedys. They embodied a new American class to the elite in Europe; they appealed to the masses in a simple but regal way; they were unpretentious yet proud, stately yet casual. They captured the attention of America's youth and motivated them to think and to become involved. Jackie helped springboard her husband in more ways than imaginable. They were a team.

It was during their trip to France that John Kennedy realized how valuable his wife was in helping promote his message to people worldwide. Little did he know how influential she would be after his death. Jacqueline Kennedy rose above her grief and planned her husband's remembrance in a prophetic, symbolic way. Cape Canaveral was renamed Cape Kennedy, Idlewild became John F. Kennedy International Airport. The Cultural Center in Washington D.C. took the name, The John F. Kennedy Center for the Performing Arts. Then one by one, nations across the world followed suite: Kennedy Platz in Berlin, Avenue Kennedy in Paris, the John F. Kennedy Plaza in Dallas, and in England on a portion of the grassy field at Runnymede where the Magna Carta was signed, appeared a Kennedy shrine.

Jacqueline's most impressionable contribution however was—the eternal flame at her husband's gravesite. Seen flickering in the wind from its position high on a sloping hill in Arlington National Cemetery, the flame would be an everlasting reminder to her, their children, and people everywhere, that the spirit of goodwill belongs to the ages.

CHAPTER THIRTEEN

Dead End

The assassination affected Larry strangely. He was changing. He became manipulative and extremely possessive toward Beverly, demanding his way about everything. His gentle thoughtfulness had turned into a whirlpool of broken promises. Larry promised her he would file for a divorce from his wife so that they could marry. He even gave her an engagement ring. Beverly was blindly following Larry's promise, but when he started treating her disrespectfully, it wounded her feelings and crippled their relationship.

Beverly told Larry that she couldn't wait anymore on "something that was never going to happen." Beverly wouldn't compromise her values if he wasn't one-hundred percent serious about the marriage and in treating her with more respect. Besides, a southern girl and a Yankee–don't work, she joked. But Larry didn't laugh. Nor did he talk. She gave the ring back to him.

Larry didn't take splitting up with Beverly well and refused to accept it. He started following her, trying to find out who she was dating. Beverly wanted to forget about him and told him on several occasions to forget about her. However, things soon got out of control. One evening, after a late night date, as Beverly was walking back to her apartment, Larry accosted her in the parking lot–holding a loaded gun tight in his right hand, his thumb nervously rubbing the hammer.

"Beverly, I'll kill you if you don't quit running around. I'll kill you!" Larry was tense and extremely serious. His eyes were cold.

"I'm not running around, Larry. That was just a friend. Besides, I gave you the ring back and explained everything. It's over between us. I've told you before, please, leave me alone and go away. There's nothing to talk about and don't bother me again."

As Larry started to raise his hand, Beverly bravely turned her back on him, gritting down on her teeth hoping he wasn't as crazy as he sounded.

Suddenly–fortunately, a car turned the corner. A car with red emergency lights on top–the apartment security officer.

Beverly made a fast break toward her car and quickly leaped in, poking the key into the ignition as she slammed and locked the door. Larry tried to hide his gun and his intentions from the sight of the guard, then ran after her car–stretching out his hand as if he could stop her from driving away. Beverly burned what rubber she could, leaving Larry in a dangerous mood, and black tire marks as a good-riddance.

The next morning, after spending a sleepless night with a friend, Beverly couldn't find her car in the lot where she had parked it. Larry had though. He figured out where she would go, broke in and hot-wired it, then drove it to some other apartments where he assumed she wouldn't find it. What he was trying to accomplish she didn't know, but it was crazy. Just crazy. It was the last straw.

Frightened as to what Larry might do next, Beverly did the only thing she knew to protect herself–she filed a Peace Bond against him.

Beverly saw Larry in Judge Richfield's court for the bond hearing. There were no parting words. It finally was over.

Jack wasn't sitting still while he was in jail. As soon as Candy Barr had been released from prison, Jack offered her a chance to work again. This time at the Carousel Club. But there was no chance. Her release from prison was contingent upon her not returning to the bump and grind circuit. Besides, what was in it for her? The Carousel Club was crawling with suspicion.

However, after the handcuffs, after the indictment, after the jail door clanged shut on its proprietor, the Carousel Club changed without Jack Ruby. It no longer served the same people. Gone were the big shots with lots of dough looking to drop some cash on a pretty face. Gone were the parade of "people with ties;" the room became full of out-of-towners, curiosity seekers, and reporters armed with the same tired questions about Ruby and Oswald: *Who knew whom? Why do you think he shot Oswald? I hear he was friends with all the police. Do you think they let Ruby in the basement?*

Kennedy's plan for withdrawing all the troops from Vietnam by the end of the year blew away with the first wind that swept across the new President's desk.

Not three months, not two weeks, or five days, but one day after Kennedy was buried, President Lyndon Johnson, the 36th President of the United States of America, took out his pen, and on the advice of "his" braintrust, he inked the executive orders that would result in the war Kennedy feared would happen, sending American soldiers to Vietnam in a steady, seemingly unconscious current, and in a river of casualties back home.

Beverly answered the door. It was a salesman with his pots and pans: a complete set of stainless steel Revere Wear. He introduced himself, but before he started his sales pitch to gain entrance to her living room, he looked past Beverly's shoulder and pointed to a painting on the wall behind her. "Where did you get that picture?"

Beverly turned around, already knowing what painting he was talking about, "My ex-boyfriend gave it to me." she replied, thinking it was a poor icebreaker and none of his business.

"Well, I'll have you know, whoever your boyfriend was, he stole that painting from my mother. I know that painting—it was hers. I gave it to her. His name was Larry Ronco, wasn't it?"

Beverly wouldn't admit to anything, nor was she ready to wade through a pot and pan presentation. She told him he was crazy and shooed him out the door.

"Oh, by the way, I heard he committed suicide," the salesman said, as the door was about to close.

Beverly paused for a moment, then shut the door and trashed any thoughts of Larry.

CHAPTER FOURTEEN

Ace In The Hole

George Albert McGann was an immaculate and well-dressed man. Everything around and about him was clean, polished, groomed, and always well taken care of. His eyes were black, narrow, and framed by the heavy glasses he wore to correct his crippled vision; his hair was always combed back impeccably. George stood 5 feet 11 1/2 inches; he was solidly built, and trim at 180 pounds. His hands were normal and his nails were always perfectly clipped, buffed, and manicured to perfection. His handshake was strong and steady. His cool demeanor was often reinforced by the fear associated with the men he accompanied. On the outside his calm was professional, on the inside it was sinister. George was a young, clean shaven twenty-seven year old man.

When R. D. Matthews, an acquaintance of Beverly's from the club, introduced Beverly to George at an after hours poker game at the Ali Baba Club, she was immediately attracted to him. She was the guest of the club's owner Bill, when George arrived with R.D. and several others: Vernon Litton, Billy T. Dyer, and a guy called Creeper. They set up the game in the back room and immediately started dealing. George was sitting directly across the table from Beverly's date and she stood directly behind him. Surreptitiously, George kept glancing up at Beverly with a smile in his eyes. Beverly returned the favor. Eventually, George ended up with all Bill's money and her telephone number.

For the next two months George and Beverly were nearly inseparable. They dined elegantly every night. He even traveled with her to a singing engagement which she had in Bossier City, treating her like a princess every step of the way. George told Beverly he was a professional gambler, but unlike most, he knew how to win. Beverly believed him, everything about him smelled like money. George mentioned that he was born an only child in Wichita Falls and that was all he shared with her about his past. George didn't like talking about himself, so, Beverly only learned about him when he managed to bring something up.

Abe became concerned when Beverly started dating George. He called her into his office and in a fatherly fashion, cautioned her that she should not be messing around with him. "Beverly, George is trouble. That entire bunch he runs with are Trouble with a capital 'T.' You can do a lot better. Please, take my advice, steer clear of him. He's a mean man."

Beverly felt complimented that Abe was concerned about her welfare, but thought he was wrong about George. She didn't care to ask Abe why he felt that way, thinking perhaps that Abe just didn't understand or appreciate the gambling crowd. And, George was certainly not mean.

Beverly took a break from the Colony and tripped down to Houston with George to perform at the Embers Club for an engagement. When they returned, George suggested to Beverly that she move in and share housekeeping with him. Beverly couldn't bring herself to accept George's offer. It may have been splitting hairs, but actually living with someone she wasn't married to was out of the question. *Why buy the cow–when you're getting the milk free?* And even though her life was wild and loose, it still mattered to Beverly how her parents felt, and her living with someone out of wedlock seemed too disrespectful. She didn't want them to worry about her anymore than they already did. Beverly explained to George how she felt, but the words were no sooner out of her mouth, when he responded, "Beverly, I can't make a living following you all over the country from club to club, and I certainly don't want us to be apart, so, we'd better get married."

Beverly had never even seriously thought about marriage and George's suggestion caught her off guard. She knew he was serious about their relationship, and she was, too. At nineteen years old, Beverly wasn't sure what love really was. However, she knew that there had never been a man in her life who made her feel complete, the way George did, and she couldn't imagine her future without him. *It must be love–so why not? Everyone must jump in over their head sometime.* Lovingly, Beverly looked George in the eye, then jumped in. "Yes! Let's do. Yes! Yes! Yes!"

It didn't take long to set the wedding plans in motion. The day was set for July 31, 1966. They both made a few phone calls then addressed a handful of invitations. Beverly called Abe and told him about her plans and that she had decided to give up her career so she could spend more time with George. Abe paused for a moment . . . then wished her happiness, and said there would always be a place for her at his club if she ever changed her mind. The tone of Abe's voice was heartfelt, making Beverly wish she was giving him a big kind hug.

George's friends, Tony and Janie Janero, generously offered their home in Oak Cliff for the wedding and their club, The Sky Knight Club, for the reception. Beverly realized that the invitations only went out to George's friends and that somehow, her friends had faded to the background and were replaced by his. She didn't care though, George was the center of her life and their future together was all that mattered. Beverly didn't realize it at the time, but it was the start of George taking total control of her life.

The wedding day came quick. Beverly was anxious, but she had no second thoughts—she was excited to have found someone like George. The ceremony was simple and reserved. The bride and groom however, were ecstatic. Beverly's childhood pastor, Reverend C. E. Cox, had the honor of marrying them. Janie Janero was Beverly's Maid of Honor and R.D. Matthews was George's Best Man. Among the guests at the reception were George's regular gang: Creeper, Billy Dyer, Johnny Ross Patrona, and Joseph Civello. There was a lot of punch and plenty of cake. But, after Beverly's folks left with the pastor—the Champagne corks popped and the newlyweds were showered with wedding toasts.

Unknown to Beverly, R.D. Matthews and Joseph Civello were more than just gambling buddies of George's. They were known by law enforcement authorities as armed and dangerous men—weighty figures in the infrastructure of Dallas' small but growing underworld. The Cosa Nostro, or real Mafia, networked its needs in Texas and the south through a group of freelance, non-Sicilian mobsters. The chain of command ran from Carlos Marcello, Mafia Chieftain in New Orleans to his man in Dallas, Joseph Civello, who networked "requests" through R.D. Matthews in Dallas and Bill Jerden in Fort Worth. George operated under R.D. Across town there was another group of men vying for the same trade headed by Kirksey McCord Nix, Jr.

Soon after their wedding, Beverly was in the bedroom listening to the morning news, when she heard that Tony Janero had been fished out of a river earlier that morning. "George." Beverly shook her husband still asleep beside her. "George. Wake up. I just heard that Tony was found dead."

"Don't worry about it." George replied groggily, his words buried in his pillow.

Beverly was confused. George sounded as if he knew that Tony was dead, but she assumed that he was just extremely tired and didn't want to bother talking. (He had been out running with the boys until the middle of the morning.)

Beverly got out of bed and went to the kitchen to make some coffee. She couldn't believe that the man who had just hosted their wedding was dead. Life offered no guarantees. She wanted to do something, call Janie, call someone, but couldn't until George woke up. *Surely he'll want to do something.*

Beverly heard the water running in the bathroom and walked up behind him. "George, shouldn't we call Janie or maybe go over to comfort her?" George whipped around and pointed his finger at Beverly, "Stay out of it Beverly! We're not going anywhere."

Beverly was puzzled. His words where sharp, and she could tell by the tone of his voice that it was the end of their discussion about Tony. *Weren't he and Tony good friends? Did George have something to do with Tony's murder? Maybe they were friends but aren't now . . . like Ruby and Oswald. That's ridiculous!*

The next day, Beverly courageously asked George if they were going to attend Tony's funeral. George became extremely indignant, firing back at her. "Absolutely not. I told you to leave it alone–so leave it alone, Beverly!"

Later that afternoon Beverly answered the telephone. It was some guy named Joe, whose voice she didn't recognize. George took the receiver and walked into the kitchen away from Beverly.

"We had to waste him." George said. "No, we gave him every chance to pay. Are you kidding? When he threatened Stan, that's all it took. No. He signed the club over to us–then we blasted him. No. No chance. They'll never trace it to us." After a few grunts of "yes" and "no," George slammed the phone back in its cradle. Beverly walked back toward the bedroom. She didn't want George to think she overheard their conversation and she was too terrified to ask any questions. *Tony must have made Creeper horribly angry. How much money is someone's life worth? Why did George say . . . " 'we' blasted him?"*

On Monday night, the Sky Knight opened under new management; Mr. and Mrs. George McGann owned a new club. Beverly kept busy and it didn't take long to put Tony's death behind her. She rationalized that Stanley flew off the handle and shot Tony over some borrowed money, and George just happened to be there. She filed the incident in a dark corner of her mind–on with the honeymoon.

The first months of marriage to George were romantic and entertaining for Beverly. He made her feel comfortable about being married to him and honored her as being a woman. He was very sensitive and tender at all the right moments. And the income from the Sky Knight Club provided a sense of security and was more prestigious then having a "gambler" as a spouse.

The newlyweds continued dining out—parading the town like they owned it. Beverly was impressed with George's cleanliness, his preparedness, and his gentlemanly ways. However, soon after they set up house, Beverly found George's compulsion for order and control bordered on the ridiculous and it often made her laugh. If George decided to wear green he wore green everything: green suit, green shirts, matching green alligator shoes, or gray alligator shoes with gray, red with red—brown, burgundy, black, they all matched. His closet was a commercial for neatness. Shirts were systematically hung by their sleeve length and their color. Sport shirts first, then short sleeve dress shirts, then long sleeve. White first, then beige, yellow, dark blue, light blue. The same order of color was followed from the short sleeve to the long sleeve. All shirts had to be buttoned at the collar and all sleeves properly hung. Hangers were spaced evenly. All of them. As tempted as she was, Beverly knew better than to bring something back from the cleaners and put it in the wrong order. It wasn't something she thought he would find humorous.

George, positively could not stand the sight of a sink full of dirty dishes, and the first time he found some when he came home one evening, he yelled at her. Beverly reminded him that she had never done house work in her life and wasn't about to start then. "I'll spend all day outside doing yardwork, George, but dishes and laundry—forget it!"

"Fine then. You can have your choice of a maid or a yardman." George was serious. Beverly discovered right away how important it was to George for him to maintain control of their relationship. Although, for a woman she was outspoken and aggressive, he made it clear from the beginning of their living together that he wasn't going to allow her to compete for the authority. Beverly could tell from the tone of his voice when something wasn't up for discussion. She also knew that she would soon be sweating in the yard. However, it was refreshing for Beverly to let George be demanding and for her not to have to make choices, her life had almost been too full of decisions. Besides, she thought George looked good giving orders.

A woman named Eula quickly became their maid. She was an attractive black woman in her early thirties who a friend recommended. Without complaint, Eula did all those nasty cleaning jobs to George's perfection, and as an added attraction, she would cook when asked. She worked five days a week, from eight to five. She arrived and left precisely "on the dot." Beverly honored her agreement and kept the yard mowed, the hedges trimmed, and the flowers planted.

Beverly found George's eccentricity for perfection always amusing. One morning George handed Eula a weeks worth of soiled clothes and took time to carefully explain to her how he wanted his laundry starched–medium. He even spelled it for her. She took everything to the laundry . . . *medium starch . . . medium starch . . . medium starch.* The next morning, Beverly heard George scream from the bedroom, "Oh my God, she starched everything! Beverly, Eula starched my underwear." George was rabid. He waved his jockey briefs in the air like a cardboard flag trying to figure out how he was going to get into them and wondering what he was going to do to Eula when he saw her. Beverly couldn't control her laughter. "I bet it's medium starched."

George insisted that his underclothes be ironed–not starched. In fact, all of his undershirts, undershorts, and socks were all ironed and placed methodically in reserved drawer spaces which were as carefully systematized as was his closet. The top left drawer contained his handkerchiefs, the right top drawer–his socks, another had his undershirts, another, his underwear. George even went to the trouble to design and have a custom rack built to fit inside one of the drawers to the precise size of a folded pair of socks. Needless to say, there was a pair of socks to match every color of shoe and they were all arranged by the color code established for the closet. Fortunately for Beverly, she didn't have to watch him matching belts; he wore a lot of sans belt slacks. George dried his hair with a hair dryer and brush but carried a comb. A little Suave hair spray. Rarely cologne.

It wasn't long before Eula had her turn with Beverly, too. Every evening that same week, when Beverly went to bed, she would place her artificial eyelashes on the nightstand beside the phone, yet every morning after breakfast, they would be gone. Beverly thought she might be losing her mind. After four days of disappearing eyelashes, she asked Eula if she knew anything about them, but she didn't.

The next day while Beverly was getting dressed in the bathroom, she heard Eula scream from the bedroom. "Oh, Lordy! Lordy!" With fly swatter in hand, Eula was beating something on the nightstand as Beverly flew to her rescue, "My goodness Eula, What's wrong?"

"Ms. Beverly, I don't know what kind of spiders these rascals are but they sure like nesting on your table. I've been killing them every day this week. They are sneaking in from outdoors somewhere." Beverly looked closely at the spider which Eula had scooped up in tissue. The mystery of the missing eyelashes was solved at the expense of a very embarrassed half blind housekeeper.

George was serious about gambling, he had to be. Outside of the club's earnings, gambling was his livelihood and he was playing for all the marbles; so, what better way to win, than to cheat. Besides, men should know better than to gamble, he always mused. Sooner or later they're going to lose it all anyway so it might as well provide George and his wife with groceries, alligator shoes, and the mortgage payment. When George filled out his tax return and listed his occupation as an unemployed gambler, Beverly asked him if that was anything like being a "substitute prostitute."

Day or night, George was ready to play poker. He always kept several thousand dollars crisply folded in his favorite money clip—a large 14 carat gold dollar sign. The "S" was brilliantly studded in quality cut diamonds and the dollar bars with bright blue sapphires.

To maximize their opportunity, George and his associates worked in teams when they gambled. They had several lines of strategy, orchestrating a game like a Broadway play with the same happy ending: George eventually winning all the money but sharing all the earnings equally. George looked and played his part well—the part of a wealthy Texan with a talent for losing money. Like someone sent from central casting, George's grooming, attire, and debonair fit the part well, as he played the roll of the "sucker" to others. The real victim was led to believe that George had been setup to take a big fall on the table and they needed help, and of course they all would split the money taken from the sucker. Then they would introduce George as a big wheeler dealer and let the real sucker win a lot of money from him before every last dollar was eventually piled high in front of George. It worked like a charm.

When George was dealing, he used a small pinkie ring as his poker partner. The ring showcased a radiant red ruby, a deep star sapphire, and a sparkling triangular cut white diamond, with a slick smooth mirror finish on the underside. When he held the deck just right, George could read the face of the cards in the reflection on his ring as he dealt everyone their hand.

When he wasn't dealing, George complained of headaches, saying that the lights made his head pound. Donning a pair of sunshades he would implement his second strategic plan for winning. His sunglasses had special game lenses which he took great pride in having made himself. Pasted on the inside of each dark lens was a thin red film allowing him to read the backside of the playing cards which had been "invisibly" marked before the game and prior to the sucker opening what he thought was a clean, fresh, unadulterated deck.

Preparing a deck of cards took a little extra effort, but it was extremely effective and profitable. Beverly would buy George several new card decks which he would then carefully open by delicately unsealing the bottom of the cellophane wrapper just perfectly. He would then mark the cards with a special colored pen (visible only through his glasses), place them back in the box, reseal the cellophane with the hot tip of a knife, and then place the deck of cards back on the shelf of a local minute market, slipping the check-out clerk a few bucks to stay quiet. For insurance, they would place several modified decks on the shelves. Only once did it backfire, when a Fraternity of boys bought all the decks one night.

There were other rigged card decks, called strippers, which Beverly also made for George. She would take select cards out of the deck and sand the sides making them slightly smaller than all the other cards. After a good shuffling and cutting the deck, the straight flush would always end up in the right hand–George's.

A "Tommy" hand was a poor hand. A "George" hand was a great hand. By using one of these handles in casual conversation, the playing partner would be able to direct the other how to play his hand. "Remember that guy named Tommy who used to hang out at the King's Club? What a creep." Depending on how long they thought they could string someone along, George and the boys might play an easy mark for several days or as long as a week. Some chumps would be duped out of a $100,000 before they would figure it out. The fools. Doctors often got caught in their web. A plastic surgeon from Houston, a heart specialist from Fort Worth; they had the gambling bug–another day, another week, another hundred thousand dollars for the boys.

Using a ploy out of the old west, George and the boys often played cards on a "holdout" table. Octagon in shape, the table had an ingenious corduroy playing surface. As a last resort, a short-cut, or for variety, after most of the hands on the table folded, with the casual press of a hidden button, an ace or two would slip up between the tight rows of corduroy into his hands–advantage George. Holdout tables were placed at the McGann's house and at several strategic clubs around town. The holdout tables paid a lot of bills.

Since checking and savings accounts were too dangerous, the boys only did business in cash and George had to hide a lot of money all over the house. Lots of it. Money which Beverly might need was kept in the closet, stuffed in the toe of a shoe-extender horn–twenty to fifty $100 bills, that were rolled together as her household spending allowance. If Beverly needed cash she would just go and take it out of the shoe horn. It never ran out. That was the other thing Beverly liked about George.

Beverly enjoyed making the nightly rounds with George as he traveled from club to club; sometimes for business, others for pleasure. For some reason, she was usually the only wife who tagged along. But she never asked George why, nor did she care. She liked partying and singing, and did so at every chance. She cherished being with George and he with her. He always made her feel special and attractive.

George's friends also enjoyed having Beverly around; she was like having a personal jukebox with all their favorite songs–a good-looking one at that. One evening R.D. offered Beverly a $100 to sing his favorite song. Then Bill Jerden offered her $200. R.D. then countered with $300. Bill $400. Beverly collected over $4,000 that night singing *Ace in the Hole,*[1] twice an hour. George's favorite song was *I Wish You Love,*[2] by Nancy Wilson. Beverly would sing it to him in the car as they drove home, running her fingers up and down the nape of his neck; his pockets always stuffed with dough; his pants always holstering a gun.

---

1 *Ace In The Hole,* Words by James Dempsey, Music by George Mitchell
  Copyright 1909 Mitchell Music Company, 1936 assigned to Jerry Vogel

2 I *Wish You Love,*
  Copyright 1946, 1955, 1956 Editions Salabert, France
  Sole selling agent U.S.A. and Canada, Leeds Music Corp., New York

CHAPTER FIFTEEN

Shut Up!

George arranged to meet at Campisi's with R.D., Billy T., Creeper, and two other acquaintances: Charles Harreleson and Kirksey McCord Nix, Jr. As usual, Beverly was the only tagalong wife. However, there were a couple of other women whom Beverly quietly ignored. Since the men were heavy into their "shop" talk, she kept to herself and concentrated on eating dinner and people watching. Dining at Campisi's was no longer one of Beverly's favorite things to do; it always reminded her of Jack and brought a bit of sadness. For a short time she and Jack Ruby were close and shared their dreams with one another. But their friendship was taken away with the speed of a bullet. It vanished without a good-bye, a warm hug. There were no telephone calls—no letters. She wondered how different things might have been if Jack hadn't done what he did. Would he have opened his fancy club in Turtle Creek? Would she ever have sung there? Would he finally have found the class that eluded him?

After eating and returning from a trip to the restroom to freshen up, Beverly heard the men discussing Kennedy's assassination. Finally, there was a topic she felt invited to speak on. Even though it wasn't something she ever cared to talk about, she had not mentioned anything to George's friends before. Beverly sat down and at a break in the conversation, she proceeded to reveal to everyone her shocking experience at Dealey Plaza, and that she knew the fatal shot came from a gunman firing in front of the president from behind the fence. "Anyone thinking Oswald was the lone assassin is out of their ever-loving mind." Beverly commented. Everyone seemed engrossed by Beverly's commentary and startled by her statement. "Jack introduced me to Oswald at his club shortly before the . . . ."

George stood up, yanked Beverly out of her chair, and forcefully hustled her outside. His grip around her arm was painful. She was bewildered and wondered why George was hurting her. "George, what did I do wrong? Why are you hurting me?"

George became even more enraged. He grabbed her by both arms and shook her. "Don't you dare talk about the assassination again! Never! Do you understand?"

"Who appointed you my keeper?" Beverly fired back as she tried to break his hold. The look in George's eyes was cold and menacing. It was the first time he had manhandled her and she was scared. She had never seen him react so violently before. George was furious, yet in total control. He dragged her to the car and pushed her in, slamming the car door. Beverly rubbed her arm and watched as he stared at her through the windshield. His piercing eyes were hateful. She could almost hear him think as they drove silently back home. Beverly knew something was coming. George's fury was boiling. He held both hands tight around the steering wheel. No, it wasn't over.

George jerked her out of the car, pushed her through the front door of the house, screaming at her. He grabbed her by the arm, pulled it up tightly behind her. "Never, ever, ever again can you do what you did. The assassination cannot—under any circumstance—be discussed again. Ever! You don't know what kind of trouble you could bring. You don't know crap. You hear me?"

George was hurting her again and she was frightened. She struggled, trying to get free, but was helpless against his anger. "So help me, if you do, I'll kill you myself. I swear."

George threw her down on the floor and stomped out of the room returning with her box of Kennedy memorabilia; bumper stickers, buttons, campaign cards. "I swear, I'll kill you. You have no idea. No idea!" George tore up all that he could and threw it into the fireplace where the embers of an earlier fire took flame. "Never again. Understand?"

Beverly laid on the floor in fear. Why was the assassination so sensitive an issue? She didn't want to know. It was as if she had stumbled backward into a hornet's nest. What scared her the most wasn't what she knew, but what she had married. In the space of an evening, her love for George changed. She thought that she could never have anymore respect for him; their relationship seemed spiritually over. He had never spoken to her that way; he had never pushed her around before, or caused her pain. Threatening to kill her was even more serious; his tirade was delivered like a hammer driving nails. He made it sound like killing her would be strictly business.

The next day George acted as if nothing had happened between them. Beverly, however, became suspicious of everything he was up to. Beverly lost some of her respect for George and no longer felt at ease around him. Then, late one evening, George, R.D., and Beverly went to a club to meet the gang at another after hours party. Afterwards, in the early morning hours, as they were walking back to the car, Beverly's head suddenly started spinning wildly. She blacked out and fell to the pavement. George tried to snap her out of it, but she was passed out cold; not drunk—something more serious. He picked her up and rushed her to the car, laying her down in the back seat. R.D. got in, then told George that he shouldn't get mixed up in whatever was about to happen to Beverly, and if he was smart, he should just dump her off in front of the hospital and drive away. George refused R.D.'s advice. Since R.D. lived a few blocks away, he demanded George drop him off at his house before he took Beverly to Parkland. R.D. made it clear he didn't want to be around. He thought George was a fool for doing so.

Beverly was rushed into emergency and admitted as a possible drug overdose. George was asked a lot of questions but wasn't able to give them any information. He didn't know anything about any drugs.

Beverly's stomach was pumped and she was carefully monitored until she became coherent, hours later. She told the doctors she didn't remember anything except blacking out and waking up in the hospital. Dr. Blum, a psychiatrist, was called in to try and determine what had taken place; did she try to commit suicide or did she accidentally overdose on something her husband wasn't aware of? Did she suspect that someone might be trying to kill her? He told Beverly that when they wheeled her into emergency she was in hysterics and that her husband was not cooperative at all. Furthermore, they weren't able to determine what kind of drug had caused her to pass out. Beverly whispered to him that she hadn't a clue to who, what, or how, but felt that someone spiked her drink. While George waited in the hall, Dr. Blum asked her if she felt safe in driving home with her husband. He thought that George might have been responsible. Beverly was weak and confused. She didn't know what to think. Everything was cloudy and "not" going home with George was not an alternative. If he did have something to do with it, she wouldn't be safe anywhere.

Weeks later, R.D. confessed to Beverly that if he had been married to her he would have dumped her at the hospital. *Why would he say a thing like that? Did he think that I wouldn't recover?* Beverly thought R.D. liked her, so why the sudden change? R.D. had a peculiar sense of humor, but she didn't think he was joking this time. Her thoughts went back to Campisi's and the assassination discussion and George's angry threat about killing her. That was the only reason she could think that someone wanted her dead. It had failed this time—but would there be a next? But then she reasoned that if George was to blame, he would not have taken her to the hospital, and doing so, for all it was worth, showed he still cared for her.

CHAPTER SIXTEEN

Betsy

George liked guns. In fact, they were his first love. He liked the feel of their weight in his hand, the snappy jerk when he squeezed the trigger. He liked their dull metal polish and the dark hollow hole as he looked down into the barrel when he was cleaning them. His favorite was a Llama .44 caliber automatic he affectionately named Betsy.

Betsy traveled everywhere with George. She knew his darkest secrets, even those Beverly didn't. He invariably kept her close by his side, tucked tightly in his pants hidden by the custom made jackets he wore. Betsy became an extension of George's authority, the tool of his trade. It also gave him the false sense of security adopted by so many other professional killers. The Llama's short 51/2 inch barrel spit bullets with a muzzle velocity about 650 feet per second. Its trajectory and its impact didn't matter because George's targets were never more than a few feet away. Betsy frequently wore the faint fragrance of gunpowder.

Late nights had become a redundant routine: the same group of friends, the same jokes, the same rub. The excitement which first attracted Beverly to George's crowd was wearing thin and her thrills had become a product of foreign chemistry: pills, joints, a little heroin-popping. Her only joy came from singing at their club, George's Club, where they spent most of their time. The club which was once called The Willow.

It was one of those late evenings that bordered boredom. Beverly and George were sitting at the bar, engaged in the small tired talk of a Saturday night which was rapidly approaching daylight. Beverly had long finished her last set of songs and was enjoying the slow speed mind crawl of a Quaalude. She was wearing a white satin outfit and fiddling endlessly with the silver beads which adorned the top. George was drawing circles on the bar with his index finger, bobbing his head with each concentric completion. The party had been going on for hours and most everyone was knee-walking drunk. There wasn't much to celebrate, only the companionship relished by those who liked to gamble or those hell-bent on squeezing every last minute from a typical doldrum day. The ash trays were full, the whiskey bottles were half empty and the jukebox was still eating quarters.

George was getting ready for something, Beverly could tell. His concentration on what little conversation they had was waning and he had become immensely intent and momentarily withdrawn in serious thought. The circles were getting smaller and smaller, moving counter clockwise, his hand moving faster and faster, then finally, the festering urge that grated his nerves and the cold reasoning rankling in his callous mind reached its impact point.

George spun around in his chair, placed his feet square to the floor and shouted, "Does everyone remember what the penalty is for being a snitch?" Making sure he had everyone's attention, George yelled again, "I said, does everyone remember what the penalty is for being a snitch?"

George managed to get everyone's attention—he was not someone you ignored; neither was he anyone to mess with. Quickly sliding his right hand underneath his jacket, his trigger finger looking for its main squeeze, his hand palming a handle, he pulled out Betsy swinging her forward at arms full length, pointing her nose straight at his one time friend Truman Carter who was traipsing across the dance floor to the jukebox while fishing some change from his pocket. Truman turned to look at George. His face froze in disbelief as the room exploded in the loud crack of gunblast and as the first slug fatally ripped through his chest. George stood on his feet and pumped in the rest. Truman was dead. George felt vindicated. Business was business. The party was over.

Beverly was stung on the face by the sizzle of gunpowder and her ears were deafened by the piercing reports from the gunshots that killed Truman. Her heart was pounding rapidly. It happened so fast—so close. Stunned by what George had done, she couldn't take her eyes off Truman as he laid on the floor, part of his head blown away, his eyes open and staring vacantly at the crowd looking on. Blood and brain were splattered everywhere.

Apart from gambling, George was also in the business of loan sharking—loaning people money when they couldn't get any through normal channels. His interest rate was high and the penalty for foreclosure was sometimes fatal. While murder was not a stranger to George, whatever drove him to become so public with Truman's was anybody's guess. Sure, at Truman's expense he got everyone's attention and they learned what the rules were when someone didn't pay George back on time. But was it worth it? Poor, pale Truman.

George holstered Betsy in the tuck of his pants then motioned to Creeper to help him drag the corpse outside and help him stuff the loser into the trunk of his Cadillac. Trembling from the stark realization of how thin the line was between life and death in the underworld, Beverly was in a state of shock while George's friends started to wipe up Truman's blood. Using every available bar towel, they soaked, mopped, and scraped every gruesome bloodstain and splatter. The floor, the walls, the jukebox. Quaaludes have a way of desensitizing their hosts in a state of toxic bliss or paranoid confusion, and Beverly was one of them. *How can his blood be so warm and red, and Truman be so dead? He should have paid George. Didn't he know? Maybe. I don't know.* Her reaction was numb and her drugged thinking was malleable. The murder verified that George had the steel nerve and the cold-bloodedness to kill; on impulse or premeditated, it didn't matter. Killing Truman was a little of both. For the second time in her marriage Beverly was frightened of George.

Rockwall County seemed like a good place to drop the dead man. George and one of his buddies dragged Truman to a secluded culvert and dumped him like a load of dirty laundry. Truman's delinquency in paying back the money he borrowed from George had cost him his life and the disgrace of a cold concrete drainage ditch. Truman was George's testament to those in the club that rules were finite and penalties were strictly enforced.

Everything seemed in order when the boys ditched Truman. There was no one around and they assumed that it would take a week or longer before he would be found, and even longer before an identification would be made. By then, George would have time to drive Truman's van somewhere away from the club and for the mess on the dance floor to be cleaned up. They made one mistake however—Truman's wallet was laying in the middle of the road. A local farmer, on his way to church, saw the wallet and stopped to pick it up. He then noticed that the tall Johnson grass was lying flat where it shouldn't be, as if a car had driven through the field. Moseying over to investigate, the farmer followed the bent grass then stumbled upon Truman. Authorities were over at George's club with a warrant in a heartbeat. Somehow, they knew who was responsible. They didn't find George, but Truman's van was still parked out in the club lot.

Beverly watched as George threw his clothes onto a fire he had started in the fireplace. *A fire in the middle of summer—strange.* Her opinion of George had taken another dive, but at the same time, she thought she still loved him. Apart from his cruelties, she still admired a lot about him. She still wanted to love him and be loved by him, but his sudden roughness, his cold-blooded threat to kill her, and then publicly killing Truman, pitched her emotions into a tug of war. Money wise, she couldn't ask for more; he sent her flowers when he was out of town; he wrote her sweet letters; he serenaded her with whispers when they were in each other's arms. He was hurtful, yet apologetic. He was strong, yet fragile. He was gentle, but deadly. Beverly was drained trying to understand what her true feelings were. One thing she was sure of—the way things were boiling over with George, it wouldn't be long before something catastrophic would happen.

George drove down Gaston Avenue then pulled the car into the area by the side of White Rock Lake by the spillway and heaved Betsy as far as he could into the water for safe keeping. He hated to see Betsy go but he knew he'd find another one like her. She wasn't the first gun he had tossed into the lake. As he got back into the car, he chuckled to Beverly, "If the cops were smart, they could find more murder weapons than they could possibly imagine at the bottom of that lake."

George and Beverly then took off for Oklahoma. George needed the carpet in the trunk of his Cadillac replaced. It didn't wash very well.

CHAPTER SEVENTEEN

Downhill

On the way to Oklahoma City George was quiet about killing Truman. And, as the miles pushed onward, his continued silence horrified Beverly. Still flying low from the dregs of the drugs she had taken, Beverly didn't know what state of mind George was in, or what he was capable of doing after shooting someone. She even wondered if she would make it back alive, after all—*I am an eyewitness. But, there were too many people who saw what happened, how stupid.* George halted the car by a lake straddling the Arbunkle mountains, tore the sticky blood-stained carpet out of the trunk, and threw it in the water. Beverly meanwhile was replaying the events in Dallas; she was glad she was able to get the gunpowder stain out of her blouse, it was one of her favorites.

When they reached Oklahoma City, thinking it was less suspicious, George made Beverly drive the car to the Cadillac dealer to have the trunk recarpeted. He was going to call Dallas to check on things. George was told that the police had been by with a warrant to search the club and that his attorney had left word to call. When George reached his attorney, he was told that Sheriff Decker had all-points-bulletin out for him and Beverly. Unbeknown to George, his club had been "wired" and the authorities knew everything. George was advised to head back to Dallas and turn himself in. George agreed that "knowing" about a crime and "proving" complicity were often an indictment apart, so he decided to head back south. Besides, once Sheriff Decker wanted you, there was no hiding.

George wasn't a fool; he knew better then to try and outrun Decker. So he turned himself in when he got back to Dallas. When Sheriff Bill Decker placed a bulletin out on someone, a "Decker Hold" it was called, it was enforcible from coast to coast and preceded the authority of practically all other claims to a fugitive. George was arrested on the spot and locked up.

As he suspected, there wasn't any hard evidence to convict George of the crime and he beat the rap, dismissed for lack of evidence. But it wasn't long before George and his new Betsy were at it again.

George and Creeper made plans to rob a jewelry store, but were surprised to find that a hood they knew, L.B. Kelly, had broken into the store the night before and walked off with the heist which was supposed to be theirs. George and Creeper were livid and Kelly's hours became numbered. They ran Kelly down, confiscated the stolen jewels, and gave Kelly some "hot" lead in exchange. His naked, bullet-bitten body was dumped in Lake Texoma. George liked lakes.

It didn't take long before Nix got word that George had "iced" his friend Kelly, so he contracted with George Fuqua to take out McGann and Creeper. A good excuse to wipe out a few men on the other team. However, one night while smashing pool balls at the Cotton Bowling Palace, a man named Two Jumps, who was trying to get on George's good side, informed George of the contract that Fugua had on Stanley and him.

George and Creeper folded their cue sticks and left the Palace. Shortly afterwards, George and his buddy showed up at Fuqua's apartment. No chain, no noise—no problem; they made it into the bedroom where they found Fuqua in bed with his girlfriend, Doris Grooms. With a gun in their ribs, the sleepy couple followed the harsh orders and marched out to the car. George and Creeper drove them to a remote gravel road in Collin County, just north of Dallas. Watching from a few feet away, Mrs. Grooms saw George execute Fuqua then turn around and reach for her. The last sound she heard was George cocking his gun.

The war was on. Danny McCombs was next to bite a bullet. Then, George bought some plastic explosives for a buddy of his, Pete Kaye. Then Phil Hodges was blown up in a borrowed car with a witness identifying some fat man driving away, Beverly read. *Pete was fat. Did George set this up?* Beverly knew not to ask questions; she didn't know what to do. She feared George and knew she wasn't safe anywhere.

George kept busy. Gambling gave way to other activities and George became more involved in hijacking and burglary. Beverly couldn't pay attention to everything George was doing and he wasn't telling her anything. His lifestyle and livelihood had gotten out of hand and all Beverly could do was to ignore it all. Drugs helped, but when the law came knocking again, it was impossible for her to not pay attention.

George was one of eight men named in a five-count federal indictment resulting from a three-month investigation of the theft of some $70,000 worth of color television sets and stereos from a parked semi-trailer in Dallas. He was accused of a federal crime for conspiring to steal the equipment which was being shipped by Kansas City Southern Freight lines from Tennessee to Texas. Four of the men indicted were charged with the actual theft, but McGann was found in possession of some of the property and also charged in helping plan the theft.

The trial lasted four days. Prosecutors against George paraded 20 witnesses before the court, including the men arrested for stealing the merchandise. They testified that George and Harold Pruitt bought three truck loads of the televisions from them with the intent to resell them. George and Pruitt had stored the merchandise in a warehouse. Defense attorneys, James Martin, Minor Morgan, and C.A. Droby argued that the prosecution failed to prove beyond a reasonable doubt that the men knew the merchandise was stolen. They also objected that the testimony of the five convicted men be allowed. In less than an hour a federal court jury found George guilty. On November 12, George was sentenced to ten years in federal prison for receiving and concealing stolen merchandise and another ten years for expanding and conspiracy to steal the merchandise; both sentences to run consecutively. The way the legal system worked, George would have to spend the entire first sentence and three quarters of the second before he would be eligible for parole.

Beverly maintained her composure even though George wouldn't let her attend the trial. There were things he didn't want her to hear concerning the woman who had turned evidence against him. The woman not only owned the warehouse where they had stashed the sets, but she had been sleeping with him. George was very businesslike in his approach to his work and quiet about his womanizing. Jilted women were one of the hazards of his line of work. But there was always hope in avoiding the penalties of crime and it usually came in the form of "favors." George wondered where his next favor would come from.

George was not one to be left unwatched. Soon after his conviction he was arrested at Love Field Airport by city police when he and another man were sitting in George's car about to swing a deal. They confiscated several pieces of jewelry, including a woman's white gold pendant watch, gold coins and a bracelet with a gold U.S. Dollar attached. They claimed George was trying to sell the jewelry to the other man. They also confiscated $17,000 in cash. That day, while Beverly was bathing, her eyes closed and the warm water lapping quietly against the tub, Beverly heard a loud crash. Two detectives and two uniformed policemen had kicked the front door down.

Beverly was pulled from the tub stark naked and made to watch unclothed as they ransacked the house. She demanded to see a search warrant but they laughed. "We know everything that was said in here and we know what your husband did. We have the house bugged."

A lot of merchandise believed to be stolen was stacked near the door, but they continued to look around. They were always looking for the stolen gems which had never been recovered. Furthermore, Kirksey McCord Nix, Jr., who by that time had made the FBI's top ten most wanted list, left his car parked in front of the apartment. They wanted to get the McGanns for harboring a criminal.

They held Beverly naked at gunpoint for thirty minutes, then left with a few trunk loads of stuff .

Later that day George and the other man were released on bond.

Acting on a complaint, the FBI arrested George the following Tuesday and charged him with "receiving a stolen gun transported in interstate commerce by a felon." The gun, a fancy Italian pistol, was found in the trunk of George's car. Two Dallas police officers and an FBI agent testified that McGann stole the gun in Hot Springs, Arkansas and brought it back across state lines. Meanwhile, Dallas police were filing burglary charges with the Dallas County district attorney's office. They claimed that on November 27, only 15 days after his conviction, George broke into the home of Mrs. Nellie Ruth Beck of 4439 Cedar Brush and stole a wristwatch and a diamond broach valued at about $1,800. George was jailed by U.S. Marshalls after District Judge W. M. Taylor revoked his $20,000 appeal bond. *George, George, George!*

Beverly lost all her sense of security. She felt caged without a key and smothered by her future—with a man who was married to a criminal octopus that would never let go. No sooner would George be "making" money than the law would be writing more indictments and the I.R.S would be raiding what little money he kept in a bank account. George couldn't be smart forever, Beverly reasoned. The humiliating experience of standing naked in front of a gun while her house was torn apart was still with her. She wanted to leave George, but was afraid of what he might do. To top it off, Beverly was four months pregnant. Regardless of how bleak the future looked, the prospects of becoming a mother carried a sense of joy. Ever since she had given up Luwanna, she looked forward to the time she could hold one of her own babies again, one she could love and keep forever.

Beverly contemplated her limited options. She couldn't see how this time George could keep from being sent to the penitentiary, but felt that his twenty-year absence might offer the solution. Beverly began making plans to return to show business. Then, when George was locked up and she was safe, she'd file for divorce. By the time he would be released, their child would be an adult. That would offer protection for her. She knew if she brought up a divorce before he was confined, she would never be found again.

Joe Champion was a criminal lawyer, and George was one of his criminals. Joe was a very big man who was retained to help George through his mess and was doing everything he could to free George. Insistently, he prodded Beverly to help. They both camped out on Judge Taylor's doorstep for a week. Every morning, afternoon, evening, they were requesting mercy from a court not in session. Finally, Judge Taylor instructed his secretary, Della Flemming, "Write a writ and get that boy out of jail or I'm going to have to eat my Christmas turkey with that fat lawyer and George's pregnant wife."

Beverly knew that the judge's decision was influenced by her being pregnant; George was fortunate that it was the season for generosity. Although-Beverly's escape plan from George was thwarted, she thought that having his baby might change things. It had to!

As a condition for his release on bond, George was required to stay within a fifty-mile radius of his hometown, Big Spring, Texas. Dallas wanted no part of him. However, what sounded good and legal on a formal document, didn't work at all in practice. George went wherever he pleased and did whatever he wanted.

George rarely drank but found a kick in doing drugs. He started smoking a lot of pot and dropping Quaaludes. He occasionally railed some cocaine. Beverly didn't know where he got his drugs; he still didn't discuss his business or anything else with her. Joy-popping heroin was next; placing the needle into a muscle instead of a vein. It took longer to work up a buzz than mainlining and the high didn't last as long, but it was all that George needed. He didn't want to get too carried away–he still had a job to do. Beverly was popping heroin herself; just a little at first to give her a buzz. Then over the past few months of insanity, a little bit had turned into a daily routine.

CHAPTER EIGHTEEN

Big Spring—New Hope

George went right to work in Big Spring—setting up a legitimate business for his illegitimate operations. He bought Holiday Motors, a used car lot complete with a body shop and Kawasaki Motorcycle distributorship. But because his real business was so bookkeeping-intensive, George soon figured out that his car lot would not provide the means to launder the volume of money which flowed through his hands. And, since he needed to be visible in Big Spring, he decided to start a venture that was more cash-intensive. He found it in the Big Spring Raceway International, which he built at the old Sahara Drive-in on the Interstate Highway west side of town.

It wasn't long before other business followed George to Big Spring. One afternoon, a panicked Bobby Gwinn stopped by the McGanns for a visit. Listening to a frantic conversation floating down the hallway to her bedroom, Beverly overheard that the body of a friend of hers, Gary McDaniel, was stuffed in the trunk of a car parked in front of their house. She liked Gary, and a tear fell from her eye. *What in the world is this coming to? When will this insanity end? Who'll be next?*

McDaniel's body stayed parked out front overnight until George finally helped Bobby dispose of him. Twelve hours after they left, George came back. Another river—another body. It wasn't long afterwards that Bobby Gwinn's body hit the gravel on a road straddling the Texas-Oklahoma border. Beverly wondered if George was involved and if life was just as she had heard him say, "A tooth for a tooth, an eye for an eye—a life for a life."

George had an arsenal of guns at the house. Standing ready to fire by the front door was an semiautomatic rifle, and by the back door was a high powered rifle with a scope. In Beverly's purse was a small white handle Derringer and laying by each side of the bed were twin shotguns—two double barrel sawed off Remingtons. When George traveled out of town, Beverly always kept one in bed beside her as her last line of security. George convinced her that when he was away, it would be in her best interest to pay attention to strange noises, respect the dog's barking, and stay well-armed. He warned her that there were too many undesirables ready to rip him off who knew by reputation that he carried a lot of cash and stashed it in the house.

While George was out of town one weekend, their white German Shepherd guard dog, Lady, had barked fiercely outside by the backyard fence. It frightened Beverly. It was obvious someone was out there. The backyard was enclosed by a seven-foot redwood fence, fronting a large open pasture and small hill, leading into some shallow woods. Feeling scared but brave, Beverly grabbed her Remington and went to check on Lady who was desperate to get outside the fence. Beverly turned her loose. Within moments, Beverly heard a loud yell, then the sound of someone frantically running away with Lady right on top of them. Beverly tightened her grip on the shotgun and ran back to the house. Shortly thereafter, Lady returned with the shred of someone's dark blue trousers in her teeth.

The next day, Beverly was anxious to investigate where Lady had attacked the spy. She put on her boots to protect her from snakes then trudged up the hill. When she reached the top, she found a small clearing about ten feet in diameter, which was littered with soft drink bottles, snack wrappers, paper coffee cups and other stakeout signs. There was also a perfect unobstructed view into their house. Beverly could see over the fence into their backyard, through the glass sliding doors into their den and kitchen, and through the large window into their bedroom. The curtains on the windows were always open. *Someone is watching us. But, who?* Beverly knew that crooks who wanted to rob the house would not go to the trouble of a prolonged stake-out. Was it the police, the sheriff's department, or the FBI—who? And what did they want? Better yet, what did they know? Beverly felt invaded and vulnerable. George kept loaded guns around the house for specific reasons, and his precaution had finally become a reality. It made her rethink about future circumstances. If it was left to her, would she be able to pull the trigger on someone breaking into the house or creeping around the backyard? The answer seemed easy two nights before when she had a loaded shotgun sleeping beside her. But the paper cups, wrappers, and torn pants made her realize she was talking about a living breathing person who could probably react faster than she could. *What could be so dangerous about gambling? Is there something George isn't telling me?*

Beverly trotted back to the house, trying to control her anger and measure her fear. She wondered if there were any indications that whoever was spying on them had actually entered their backyard, or approached the house. She couldn't make sense of any footprints, and as far as she could tell, everything was in place. The screens on the windows didn't look tampered with. There weren't any scratches around the door latch, but hidden underneath the wooden casing of the windowsill outside their bedroom, Beverly found a small round metal device, with tiny perforated holes. It looked like a microphone, but it wasn't attached to any wires; regardless, she took it inside and promptly submerged it in water, and waited impatiently for George to return home.

George came back the next day and exploded when Beverly told him everything. She showed him Lady's trophy and the device she found outside the bedroom window. George held the thing in his hand rolling it around in his fingers. "D—D—D—. Someone's been listening to us. I wonder how long and what they heard?" With each syllable, George became angrier. Remembering what he did said, Beverly thought George was trying to get a handle on the situation and determine what kind of trouble he might be into. Whatever he was thinking, he wasn't telling. He looked up toward the hill, gritted his teeth, then dashed to his car. He popped open the trunk and pulled out the semiautomatic carbine he'd acquired on his trip. He hoofed it back to Beverly who was standing in the backyard. Then he held the weapon high over his head, shouting toward the woods, "You dirty, perverted freaks. The next time it will be me out there in the field. I'll do more than tear off your pants—I'll shoot your head off!"

George told Beverly it was probably the cops or the FBI again. That afternoon he arranged for more security for the house, their cars, and his business. He also took Beverly to the shooting range for a refresher course on firearms. George brought his entire arsenal of guns and taught her how to load and fire them all. First her brother, then Jack Ruby, then Larry Ronco, and then George Albert McGann. Beverly had a lot of training.

But when Beverly learned she was pregnant, she stopped. All her attention became wrapped in the privilege and planning of being a mother. Her life had new meaning and she wasn't going to deny herself any of the pleasures. George felt indifferent at having a child and didn't want to talk about it. There were too many other things to think about—like increasing his business.

Los Angeles was humid and sticky. Beverly and George were traveling on business under assumed names. George had a coin collection he was going to sell to an "investor," but found out that the investor wasn't backed by readily-available money. Then, they had a chance to head back to Big Spring, Beverly started going into premature labor; she was only six months pregnant. Her contractions weren't subsiding so George rushed her to the hospital; but, it was too late and they couldn't stop the delivery. Beverly gave birth to a tiny precious boy, born with no hope for survival. George Massey, who was born under an assumed name, lived two hours and forty-five minutes—then died. Beverly was in total misery. Her one hope for a wonderful change in her life and her marriage had vanished in the brief time George Massey struggled to live. Beverly didn't know if she wanted to live. Life with George, and without little George, seemed bleak. Every breath she took was painful—every thought filled with despair. *What went wrong? Why did he die? Was it the heroin? Was it a disease? Was it my fault?*

George informed the hospital they would make funeral arrangements the next day for their dead son.

George acted like nothing had happened and insisted Beverly wake-up to the fact that their baby was dead; it was over, and she had to snap out of it. Beverly couldn't understand his unemotional reaction and crawled deeper into despair. At that moment she needed his compassion. Now, more than ever, but he refused to comfort her. There were no hugs, no caring words. Nothing. Their relationship had disintegrated into something Beverly no longer wanted to be a part of. She was so tired, both physically and emotionally. George quickly checked her out of the hospital, put her in the car, and headed out to west-Texas. Beverly didn't know what he had done with her baby but was afraid to ask. She hoped that they had donated his little body for medical research. She vaguely remembered signing some papers but didn't know what they were. But she certainly wasn't going to bring up the subject.

Once home, Beverly wanted to be held more than ever. The nursery stared back at her as a testament that her entire life was screwed up and that she was going to be denied the one thing she wanted most of all—a child. She wanted George to comfort her and say that he understood her pain and then promise her that they would try again soon. But he didn't. No conversation, no communication, no baby. For two long emotionally-crippling weeks Beverly started mainlining heroin, always keeping one step away from addiction. The shadow of her smile took on the ragged lines of dejection; her once rosy cheeks became stained with yellow tears.

Beverly decided she didn't want to live with George anymore; in fact, she *refused* to live with him anymore. Needing money to relocate, Beverly felt that the $20,000 she had rifled from George's cache would do it. After all, she knew she deserved it for all the misery George made her suffer. Without a word, she slipped back to live in the serenity of her parents' home in Sachse, Texas. She had a lot to think about. What to do, where to go?

George was angry at Beverly, not only for leaving, but for taking his $20,000 with her. He was going to be the one to decide the "ifs, whens, and wheres" of Beverly's life. She had no business thinking she was in control. While Beverly's parents were at work and her sister was away at school, George commandeered two of his friends to kidnap her when she went out to get the mail. They had parked up the street, and as she turned her back, busily flipping through the mail, they grabbed her and spirited her to Via Cunja, Mexico. Once there, they aggressively tied her to a four-poster bed and started shooting her up with very rich heroin. Beverly didn't know what was going on. She thought that she was going to die and George didn't have the nerve to do it himself. The two punks who were inflicting her punishment were quiet and enjoyed what they were doing. The heroin worked its wonders, then wanted more from her. It wanted everything.

Several days later, after her conditioning, George showed up. Beverly was too confused and strung out to try and figure what he was up to. Predictability was no longer a part of their marriage. Did he want to be there for the final dose?

George sat on the side of the bed and looked at her coldly, like the cocked hammer of his gun. "Now Beverly, you will either stay with me, or you will get out in the street to support your habit. What's it going to be?"

Beverly realized that this lifestyle was going against everything she ever believed. But she was too weak to do anything but follow George back to his insanity. Surely, she thought, there will be a time she could get out of the mess she was in. It was then that Beverly started hearing thoughts not to worry, that there was something special planned for her. However, she didn't know what that would be.

Beverly found out that George had taken a mistress. Most of the boys enjoyed the pleasure of one and George felt it was time he did too. She had large pretty brown eyes. Beverly knew about her—she lived nearby. Overhearing the gossip, Beverly understood that the girl had given birth to a baby by George.

IV

CHAPTER NINETEEN

New Beginnings

Dusk hung the evening sky in shifting shades of tangerine and hot pink. Beverly drove randomly through Big Spring struggling with reluctant thoughts about going back to the house. George was unpredictable and berated her more and more for things beyond her control. It wasn't fun. Restlessness was her companion; it crawled up her spine in a pitiful craving for help. Pausing at the corner of 11th Street and Goliad, wondering what to do next, Beverly glanced up to her right where she noticed a church perched on a hill. Outside a lighted sign read, *Revival in Progress–Dr. Angel Martinez Speaking.* Beverly had never been to a Baptist church before and had no intentions of going in, but like a moth to a flame, she parked her car, walked up the steps, found her way indoors, and took a seat on the back row–the service was in progress. Beverly listened closely to a man in the pulpit telling the most beautiful story she had ever heard. Dr. Martinez was talking about a man named Jesus who loved her so much, that He gave His life for her. He died on a cross to forgive her of all her sins and save her, so that she would have eternal life in heaven.

His words flowed so effortlessly, his message blossomed and moved her profoundly. The story was simple:

"Blessed are the poor in spirit: for theirs is the kingdom of heaven. People, don't let your prejudices stand in the way of knowing God. Open your heart. Tear down your roadblocks. Ask Christ to come into your life. Accept him as your Savior. God has a place for you. He loves you so very, very much.

"Blessed are they that mourn: for they shall be comforted. Blessed are the meek: for they shall inherit the earth. Blessed are the pure in heart: for they shall see God."

Everything he talked about had relevance in Beverly's life. She knew depression. She knew grief, guilt, loneliness, worry and anger. And when Dr. Martinez said that all our past sins can be forgiven by admitting we are sinners and by accepting that Jesus had died on the Cross to wash away those sins; it was all Beverly wanted.

Although she didn't accept Christ that night, Beverly went home, thinking endlessly about what she heard. She was so hungry for His message that she found herself back in church the next morning, and night, and the next morning, and night. And on Wednesday evening something very precious, very real, very lasting happened in her life. When Dr. Martinez came to the invitation for people to let Jesus come into their lives, she didn't close her heart, mind, or mouth. She bowed her head and silently prayed a very simple prayer. She prayed for the Lord Jesus to come into her heart, to save her, to cleanse her, and to give her something worth living for.

When she left the church that night, no one had to tell Beverly she was saved—she knew it. Nobody had to tell her she was leaving the church a different person than when she came in—she knew it.

Beverly went home and shared with George her glorious feelings about her new life—but he laughed. "Beverly, it's just a passing thing like everything else with you. What do you think your new friends are going to say when they find out you have got a 'monkey' on your back? Think they'll still be your friends knowing you're strapped to a heroin needle? You'll see how much they love you then and how close these 'new' friends will stand behind you." George was getting perturbed; his fist was clenched. He didn't need Beverly witnessing to him. That was the last thing he needed. Beverly was strapped to a needle, she couldn't deny it. Heroin had become a cannibalistic friend robbing her of her dignity, her charm, her hope. She was setting the alarm clock at six hour intervals to shoot up, just so she wouldn't get sick. But then something else very real and lasting happened that night. As usual, she set the alarm when she went to bed, but when the alarm went off, she didn't feel like she needed a fix. She wasn't shaky or queasy, so she set the alarm for a few hours later, then lay back down. The alarm went off again and she got up. But she still didn't feel like she needed it. The following day was the same—and the next and the next. Beverly's standing appointment with heroin was canceled.

Beverly carried drug paraphernalia around with her for over a year, risking the chances of getting "busted" and going to the penitentiary—simply because she didn't understand that when God saved her, He divinely, miraculously, instantaneously, healed her and took away from her body and mind the craving for any kind of drugs. Beverly was aware some people who have addictions, whether to drugs or alcohol, struggle and battle endlessly with their problem after they had been saved; however, she didn't understand why God ended *her* addiction instantaneously and not other's. "But He did—and He can," she thought.

Beverly felt part of the answer might lie in the fact she was so repulsed by what she had become and that she was willing to give up anything coming between her and her Lord. Anything keeping her from becoming what He wanted her to be. She was so willing to give it up, that He was ready to take it.

George listened to Beverly tell him over and over how much her life had changed and how important it would be to her, and how critical to him that he come to love Jesus as she did, and to accept Him as Savior. George was aware that something strong and miraculous was working in Beverly's life. He couldn't explain how she had kicked her addiction overnight—heroin didn't work that way; it wasn't that easy. Cold-turkey meant death, not life. It spooked him and he didn't want to talk about it.

"George, please open your heart and accept His blessings. Jesus loves you. He will give you the strength you need to get out of this way of life. George, don't wait . . . ."

"Beverly, I will someday—but not today. I'm young. I've got too much life to live and I've got plenty of time."

Beverly could tell by the tone of his voice that he was through talking and again she was heartbroken. She knew procrastination was one of the devil's best strategies. *"Wait. Not now. You can do it later. Wait till tomorrow. Wait . . . wait."* Beverly knew God didn't promise the world a tomorrow, not George, not her, not anyone. No one is guaranteed that when they wake up each morning that they can defy all chances, beat all odds, and survive until the next day. The obituaries are daily proof of this.

George was preparing to go on a routine trip to Lubbock to collect on a debt and bookmaking operation. He carefully laid his overnight bag across the bed, pulled two medium-starched shirts, along with pants, matching socks and shoes from the closet. He pulled out his money clip and fanned the bills to see if he had enough. He also made sure he had an extra box of bullets.

Standing in the doorway to the bedroom, Beverly watched him. She felt the urge to witness to George stronger than ever. She knew what he *said* he was going to do; but what was he *really* going to do? Each time he left the house she wondered what else he had on his mind. "George, will you please ask the Lord to come into your heart before you go?" Beverly pushed one more time. She still cared about her husband, not like she used to, but now her life was full of hope about everything. As chaotic and murderous as George's lifestyle was, there was a chance he could be saved, and it was important to her that he was.

"Beverly. I will someday. But not today. I'm young. I've got too much life to live." George always replied the same way; it was his way of being as repetitious as she was. An ace with an ace.

The next day, September 29, 1970, shortly before 6:00 AM, Sheriff C. H. Blanchard got a call from a residence on the southside of town that there was shooting and two men where killed. They both were still on the premises. The caller was Ronnie Weeden who owned the property. The address sounded familiar and the sheriff remembered that only recently they had raided that same house for gambling.

George Albert McGann lay sprawled on the floor in his own blood, twenty feet from the other dead man, Jerry Michael Meshell. George was felled by slugs from both a .45 and a .38 caliber weapon. George was young, but there was no more life left to live. Meshell was shot twice with a .38.

Meshell's drivers license said he was from Lufkin, Texas. People around Lufkin said, "No he wasn't." Meshell was under indictment on federal charges of armed robbery and carrying a concealed weapon in the connection with highjacking a poker game the previous June. As it turned out, the house was full of people who were under indictment.

Three people witnessed the shooting. Ronnie Weeden, Marshall Perry of Lubbock and Frances Golden of Houston, were questioned and released with no charges being filed. Investigators found cards, dice, a little change, and a lot of liquor bottles scattered about the house. Deputies arriving on the scene, immediately after the call was placed, said that evidence pointed to the fact that the shooting must had happened much earlier.

They speculated that George was the victim of a contract placed on him by someone in Houston, because he was double-crossing the Mafia in bookmaking operations. Meshell had the contract but George shot first. A third person had to finish the job, they thought. Beverly didn't buy it, at least that was what she told the authorities. Chances were, that's just what it was, a contract; not for double-crossing, but for vengeance and control. George was felled by one shot in the abdomen and four to his back. She also noticed that the wedding band that she had made for him had been removed from his left pinkie finger and placed on his right hand. That didn't make sense. Something was suspicious, but there was no sense trying to understand what had happened.

Soon after the shooting, Attorney Blair Cherry, Jr. said that charges might be filed in connection with George's murder. He admitted they knew who did it, but they needed more evidence. Their investigation uncovered information leading them to believe they would be prepared to file charges on one or more people—which they did. Ronnie Weeden was indicted for pulling the trigger on Beverly's husband and sentenced to ten years for the murder. At the time of the murder, Weeden was out on bond on two separate charges: one from a car theft charge in Houston, and in Lubbock for receiving stolen goods.

Law-enforcement people throughout Texas who had been keeping tabs on George cheered when he was killed. They thought he was a cold, ruthless person. He was mean and extremely dangerous, and to their relief, dead.

Before his death, at the direction of Governor Preston Smith, authorities formed the Texas Organized Crime Prevention Council to advise the Texas Criminal Justice Council and the Legislature on matters of organized crime. They understood that organized crime had a foothold in Texas, but not like that of the large Eastern cities that suffered from labor racketeering and large-scale loan-sharking. Assistant Dallas Police Chief Paul McCaghren said that the Costa Nostro, that controlled the underworld in the East, was the epitome of organized crime. They were a self-perpetuating, continuing criminal conspiracy for profit and power, using fear and corruption to attain immunity from the law. Their connection to the south was through a large gang of underworld characters the police tagged as the Dixie Mafia and suspected George A. McGann as one of the reputed leaders. McGann had connections in Texas, Mississippi, Florida, Alabama and Georgia, Dallas Captain Paul McCaghren, assistant police chief claimed. He was known to also have kept company with real players in the Costa Nostro. They blamed the Dixie Mafia for 29 deaths and George with the majority of them. There would be other George McGanns, but at the time they had the pleasure of reading about his funeral in the papers.

When interviewed by the newspaper that day, Beverly denied that George had connections with any gang. "Dallas police have been playing up that thing for six months. I feel the whole thing is imagined." Beverly insisted. (They didn't refer to themselves as the Dixie Mafia, but as "Crossroaders," since they met for the specific purpose of pulling a particular job such as a burglary, gambling or hijacking.) The authorities knew they were not part of the Costa Nostro but were just as worried. The Crossroaders were organized and woke up each day with an agenda that included a long list of things which were against the law. It was hard for law-enforcement officers to corner a Crossroader because they seemed to be so insulated. The indictments that were returned against them ended up in the "case dismissed for lack of evidence file."

After George's death, two Federal agents, wanting to clear up several unsolved murders, drilled Beverly for what she knew about George's activities. She told them she didn't know what George was up to; he was always coming and going, and not sharing. They said they were aware of his involvement in at least nineteen murders. What did she know about them? Beverly knew that even if she did tell them what little she did know—she wouldn't survive a week. That was certain. She would be pocket-money in someone's fancy money clip for some other George out there. One life—a few bills.

George Albert McGann. Dead and soon to be buried. Reverend William Meagher, pastor of the Immaculate Heart of Mary Catholic Church and Reverend Jim Puckett of Baptist Temple looked out among the people gathered to pay their last respects to George and had to wonder who everybody was and what they did. There were sure a lot of them and a lot of dark sunglasses. George was buried in the Trinity Memorial Park.

Soon after the funeral Beverly was faced with the woeful task of packing George's belongings—but death was not a stranger to her. It had followed her like a curse, pouring grief on top of anger, mixing disillusionment with guilt. Self-pity with depression. However, strengthened by the promise of salvation, Beverly for once was able to control her mind over her emotions. With each folded garment, each cuff-link, each deck of cards, she constructively reminisced her life with George, reinforcing the beauty of her new life and the blessings inspired from His promise. Beverly could feel her faith growing, she wanted to share her new peace with everyone.

Secretly placed inside one of George's shoe boxes, Beverly pulled a photograph of a little smiling baby boy with big brown eyes.

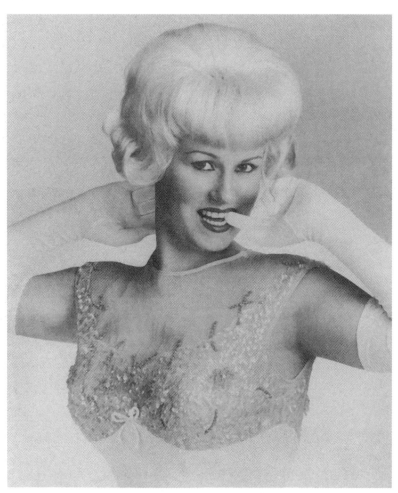

BEVERLY OLIVER IN 1963.

Beverly at 4 years-old.—1950

Beverly singing at Six Flags over Texas.— 1963

Beverly at the bus station. Photo taken by Jack Ruby.—October, 1963

George McGann and wife, Beverly at reception following their wedding. R.D. Matthews is on Beverly's left.— 1966

Larry Ronco and Beverly— 1963.
Larry gave Beverly the movie camera
she used to film the motorcade.

Scene as it appeared just seconds before the assassination. Arrow points to President Kennedy in limousine. Photo taken by Phil Willis.— 1963

Beverly Oliver, Charles Brehem, and his son in foreground witness the assassination.
Photo taken by Marie Muchmore.—1963

Beverly filming motorcade as President Kennedy is shot.
Photo taken by Marie Muchmore.—1963

Beverly watching crowd shortly after the
assassination. Note "babushka." — 1963

Scene immediately after the assassination. Beverly is still standing facing the street.
Photo taken by Wilma Bond.

The two Phil Willis photos on this page were taken shortly after the assassination. This photo shows a gathering crowd, all running toward the overpass.—1963

In this photo note that Beverly is standing at same location, not moving with the crowd. Many people are looking and moving toward the grassy knoll across the street.—1963

The Texas School Book Depository building as it appeared on November 22, 1963. An arrow points to the open 6th floor window where shot/shots were alleged to have been fired. The window is only half open. Photo by Phil Willis.—1963

Main entrance to Texas School Book Depository. Photo taken after the assassination pictures police, and numerous onlookers. The arrow points to a man who looks very much like Jack Ruby. Photo by Phil Willis.—1963

Photo of the infamous picket fence at top of the grassy knoll. Arrow and circle indicates where Beverly believes the fatal shot came from. Photo taken in 1991.

Jim Lavelle (detective who was holding Lee Harvey Oswald when Oswald was shot by Jack Ruby) and eyewitness to President Kennedy's assassination, Jean Hill (the lady in red). Photo taken in 1991.

Beverly at grave of President John F. Kennedy, Arlington National Cemetary.
Photo taken by Charles Massegee in 1993.

J.F.K. Symposium in Sudbury, Canada in 1993. Seated left to right are Larry Howard, Beverly Oliver Massegee, Charles Massegee, Ken Porter, Marina Oswald Porter, Dr. John Newman, and Jean Hill.

Judge Jim Garrison autographing the book, *On The Trail of the Assassin.* Seated left to right are Larry Harris, Jim Garrison, Beverly Oliver, and Larry Howard. Photo taken in 1991.

Beverly Oliver with Oliver Stone, Director of the movie, *JFK*. Photo taken in 1991.

Lolita Davidovich and Beverly Oliver at Dealey Plaza. Lolita played Beverly in the movie, *JFK*. Photo taken in 1991.

Oliver Stone taking aim from one of the alleged assassin's locations in the
Dal-Tex Building. Photo taken in 1991.

Gary Oldham (Lee Harvey Oswald in the movie, *JFK*) and Robert Groden,
co-author of the book, *High Treason.* Photo taken in 1991.

Recreation of Presidential limousine for the movie, *JFK*. Photo taken in 1991.

Columbia Dubose (John Connally), Randy Means (Ellie Connally), and Steve Reed (John F. Kennedy) in the movie, *JFK*. Photo taken in 1991.

Jodie Farber played Jacqueline Kennedy in the movie, *JFK*. Photo taken in 1991.

Reinactment of the slaying of Lee Harvey Oswald for the movie, *JFK*.
Photo taken in 1991.

Kevin Costner (as Judge Jim Garrison) on the overpass. Dealey Plaza is in the
background. Photo taken in 1991.

Kevin Costner with Beverly Oliver during the filming
of *JFK*. Costner played Judge Jim Garrison.
Photo taken in 1991.

Beata Pozniak, Rachel Oswald, and Gary Oldham. Pozniak and Oldham
played Rachel's parents in the movie, *JFK*. Photo taken in 1991.

Beverly Oliver Massegee, Pebbles Massegee, and Charles Massegee at President John F. Kennedy's grave, Arlington National Cemetary. Photo taken in 1993.

CHAPTER TWENTY

The Babushka Lady

A warm light breeze swept down Main Street, spilling into a vacant Dealey Plaza. Empty, quiet. Only the occasional swoosh of trucks barreling down Stemmons Freeway in the middle of the night broke the stillness. Elm Street, cast in a soft surrealistic amber light, played host to the echoes of November. The asphalt grade sloping downward from the Texas School Book Depository toward the triple overpass was saturated with thousands of questions. Those left by the many people who stood that day wondering how everything happened, where everyone was standing, and questioning why it was so difficult to piece everything together. The breeze blew along the splintered rails of the picket fence then whipped down the withered slope of the grassy knoll onto Elm Street, through the underpass, quickly traversing the countryside, silently slipping through an open window, and fanning a restless woman in a worrisome caress. Once again, Beverly fought the recurring nightmare—the gunfire, the blood, Jackie screaming.

In November 1970, at the First Baptist Church of Joshua, Pastor James Moss was readying for a revival. (Joshua is a small town about twenty miles south of Fort Worth.) Harlen Katen, the guest evangelist, and Jerry Wayne Bernard, a singer, pianist and preacher, were having lunch with Gary Shaw of Cleburne, Texas when the subject of the Kennedy assassination came up. Shaw's knowledge of the event was vast and at times it was hard not to discuss it. Shaw pointed out how vital information never made it through the Commission's investigators and into the Warren Report. How information was twisted to fit the lone gunman theory, or ignored altogether, because it didn't fit the mold. However, when all the undoctored eyewitness testimony and misplaced evidence was complied together in a coherent sequential accounting, a completely different version of the assassination was revealed. It was evident that there was more than one rifleman; that Lee Harvey Oswald was more than a kook–probably a patsy, that the Warren investigation was engineered to a pre-planned conclusion, and that the cover-up was broadly implemented. After lunch, Shaw showed his guests an actual film of the assassination, an unauthorized 8mm copy of the film taken by Abraham Zapruder. The film graphically and indisputably showed President Kennedy's head snap backward at the moment of the fatal head shot. The conclusion that he was fired upon from the front was inescapable, contrary to what had previously been reported by such luminaries as Dan Rather, who went on record after watching the film that the head went violently forward. He must have watched a different film. The discussion could have gone on for days, but the conversation ended with Shaw giving each of the men a copy of the film to take and show others. He hoped people who saw the film would become irate that they had been mislead about the presence of a conspiracy, and that public outrage might eventually lead to another investigation.

Gary Shaw and his wife went to church services early that evening and his wife reminded him that they were going to have a house guest for the week, someone in town for the revival. Walking in the back of the church Gary saw Jerry Wayne playing the piano and a young woman standing by the pulpit rehearsing a song.

"Hey Gary, come here. I want you to meet someone." Jerry Wayne shouted from the front of the church as he stopped for a moment, motioning to Gary.

"Gary, this is Beverly McGann. Gary is very interested in the assassination of President Kennedy. Beverly took a film of the assassination," Jerry Wayne commented as he introduced the blond-haired singer he was accompanying. Gary's interest was immediately piqued. He was aware of those who had taken moving pictures in Dealey Plaza. They had all been accounted for, except the one taken by a lady in a coat and scarf standing on Elm Street across the street from Zapruder; the lady (in his film) who was standing behind the limousine. Other photographs also showed the lady; still standing, still filming after the shooting–while everyone else was lying on the ground and the presidential car was speeding away. Other photographs showed her (minutes later) standing across the street with others. "Chances were," Gary thought, "Jerry was referring to her filming the motorcade–not the shooting."

"Where were you standing?" Gary asked Beverly, hoping to hear the answer he wanted.

"I was in that grassy park area standing near Elm Street."

"On the north or south side?"

"South."

"And, you filmed the assassination?"

"Yes. I had a new movie camera. It was the first time that I had ever used it."

"Did you film the entire thing?"

"Yes, everything. I started filming when the limousine turned to my right onto Elm Street, until I couldn't see it anymore." Beverly was hesitant in telling her story, but felt safe in the church, around people she could trust.

"And where is your film?"

"The FBI took it."

"Did you have it developed?"

"No. It was on the first night I went back to work after the assassination. I hadn't even thought about it; the weekend was . . . well, I was a singer at the Colony Club at the time and they were there when I arrived at work that evening. They flashed some badges and asked if I'd taken any pictures. When I said yes, they asked for it and said they'd return it after they viewed it. But I haven't seen it since."

Gary was flabbergasted. He knew this had to be the mysterious "Babushka Lady" who researchers had been wondering about. Richard Sprague, an acquaintance of his from Hartsdale, New York, had tagged the lady in an article he wrote about the application of computers to photographic evidence in the assassination. Because of the scarf she wore tightly around her head that day, Sprague referred to her as the "Babushka Lady." Sprague, like others, was interested in her film because it should have a clear shot of the picket fence at the time of the shooting. Researchers had wondered why the woman filming the assassination had never stepped forward with her film. Was she fearful after she realized the importance of what she had, or was she purposely sent to the Plaza to film it? Was she in on it?

Gary had a lot of other questions to ask but, under the circumstances, they'd have to wait. However, unknown to him during their conversation, Beverly was the house guest his wife had referred to. Beverly always arranged to stay as a guest in church member's houses when she traveled out of town; It was just a coincidence that Gary's wife had extended their hospitality.

After the service, Gary and his wife escorted Beverly to their home in Cleburne, a quick ten minute drive south. They gave Beverly a quick tour of the house, showed her to one of the girls' room where she would be sleeping, then they all joined James Moss and his wife, Harlen Katen, and Jerry Wayne at the dinner table.

After most everyone left, Gary, Beverly, and Jerry Wayne went back in the living room to continue their conversation. Beverly sat on the couch and glanced around the room; there was a lot to look at. Mementos everywhere: old pictures war medals, helmets, etc., someone in the house was a collector. Then her eyes focused at the bookshelves. Scanning the titles to see what kind of books the Shaws liked to read, Beverly was shocked when she saw the twenty-six volume Warren Commission Report on the Assassination of President Kennedy and many other books on the subject. Gary didn't have the condensed version of the report which was presented to President Johnson—he had the entire reference. Beverly became alarmed. Gary told her he was an architect, but your "average Joe" doesn't have the entire twenty-six volume of the Warren Report. Beverly assumed Gary's interest in her and the assassination had to be more than just in passing. She immediately thought about George's threat about being open about what she knew—but she had met Gary through the church.

Gary had always been interested in history. Before his fascination with the Kennedy assassination, Gary was infatuated with the Civil War and President Lincoln, then World War I and World War II. But living close to Dallas, and having met Jack Ruby on several occasions, as well as hearing all about the scuttlebutt concerning his Mafia connections, Shaw started reading everything he could get his hands on concerning the events surrounding the assassination. When he heard Ruby had shot Oswald, he became suspicious. There was more to it than what Ruby was confessing—there had to be. But after reading the Warren Report, it seemed to be a solid case against Oswald as the only assassin and against Ruby as a blowhard who became a victim of his own explosive character. Then Gary picked up a copy of Attorney Mark Lane's *Rush To Judgment* which knocked the Warren Report into a tailspin. Lane had pieced together a comprehensive case of conspiracy and cover-up that shocked a small but growing circle of doubters, and opened up a Pandora's box bigger than the government itself. This caused Gary to search for information that would verily that Oswald did indeed act alone. He wanted proof that would satisfy him. But the proof never came. Instead, he found that the tracks left by the conspirators were still warm.

It didn't take long before he realized that the conclusions that the Warren Commission came to were based on a prejudiced approach headed down a one way street. While other people played golf, Gary interviewed witnesses. The more people he talked to the more concerned he became that a travesty of justice had been perpetrated on the public. Many accounts of Kennedy's death were contradicting one another. Something was foul and he wanted to understand why anything hadn't been done about it.

Beverly kept her story casual and simple, reluctant to go into much detail. She felt compelled to talk by highlighting enough of her past to see if anything was congruent with what Gary knew. She repeated her experience about November 22, and the confiscation of her film, and also told him that a few weeks prior to the assassination Ruby had introduced her to Lee Oswald of the CIA. Beverly talked about her husband George and mentioned his private session in 1968 with Richard Nixon in Miami, which Gary found almost unbelievable.

When Beverly started reminiscing about the Colony Club Gary realized that he had seen several of her shows. Back in the late Fifties and early Sixties, there wasn't a lot to do in Cleburne so everyone went to Fort Worth or Dallas for entertainment: The Theater Lounge, The Colony Club, The Carousel. Gary and his buddies made all three clubs in a single evening because the shows were staggered right. Gary confessed to Beverly that he was a singer, as well, back in the 50s; part of a doo-wop group called the "Matadors" who backed a singer by the name of Johnny Carroll. Later, Johnny became the "head honcho" at the Cellar Club in Dallas and married Lu-Lu of Hee-Haw fame. Gary told Beverly that one night, when his group was thinking about joining AGVA, they auditioned to a committee at the Sportatorium. Jack Ruby was there. He was easy-to-spot—loud, and at times even louder. Gary recognized him from the Carousel where he was always shaking hands, patting everyone on the back, introducing himself, or sitting at a table shooting the breeze. It was whispered at the club that Jack Ruby was someone to be careful of—he was a tough guy and connected to the mob. Ruby wasn't someone you met and forgot. He was a loud character. Gary thought that Jack Ruby was a name that suited him well, it sounded tough like a mobster, like—Legs Diamond.

Gary called Beverly and asked if she would meet with him and his friend, Richard Sprague. They wanted to visit Dealey Plaza with her and see exactly where she was standing, and if she could recall any additional details. Beverly agreed, but after she hung up the phone she started having second thoughts. She hadn't been down to the grassy place since she and her mother placed flowers on the ground and tearfully embraced. Even though Dealey Plaza was a few blocks from where she worked, she avoided it at all measures, driving around it if necessary. It was another way of not having to come face-to-face with the reality of what she saw. The nightmares were enough. Beverly thought she would let the idea rest for a few days and see how she felt then; maybe going down to the Plaza would be cleansing and therapeutic, and help her shrug off the dreadful feeling haunting her and the bloody nightmares plaguing her sleep. It was worth a try, besides, for some reason it was important to Gary, and the anger she once felt over Kennedy's death was boiling again. Maybe, the real truth would eventually get out and ultimately force the public to take action to find the true killers.

The afternoon they met in Dealey Plaza, Beverly took no time in walking directly to the area where the lady in the scarf stood on November 22, 1963. Gary and Richard looked at one another as Beverly found her place; their eyes expressed confidence that she must be the Babushka Lady that Sprague had referred to. Gary had not shown her the Zapruder film, nor had it been made available to the public; but there she was, standing about ten feet from the curb looking north onto Elm Street, midway down the slope, across from where Zapruder stood. Gary couldn't believe that his and Beverly's paths had crossed so "out of the blue." Every time his focus on the assassination was directed elsewhere, something would come along and demand his attention. Beverly was one of those "things." The Babushka Lady was found. Where was her film?

Months later, Gary caught up with Beverly in Houston where she was living. Gary wanted to record her testimony which he wasn't able to do when she was staying with them; also, Beverly had pictures to show him. Gary asked Beverly to start from the beginning and retell her experiences that fateful day. What kind of camera was she using? She said it was a Yashika Super-Eight magazine load movie camera that Ronco had given her. She dug out some wedding pictures of her and George with R. D. Matthews, Tony Janero, and others. She also had a few publicity pictures taken of her during her singing career, and some Six Flags pictures, including one taken of her and Larry Ronco. Beverly told Gary about her relationship with Larry and the $50,000 offer someone made for him to kill Castro. Gary didn't believe that the offer had actually been made. Gary thought that Ronco was trying to impress her. At that time, it wasn't yet public knowledge that the CIA and the Mafia had in fact conspired and unsuccessfully tried to assassinate Castro. A plan that would be mutually beneficial to both parties. The CIA wanted to help stamp out Communism and the Mafia wanted its casinos back.

Gary also showed Beverly the Zapruder film. It was difficult for her to watch, but there it was, the whole event in all its gory infamy. How could anyone see the film and believe the fatal shot came from the rear? It was preposterous.

Everything was as Beverly remembered, including Jackie's pulling her husband forward after the final shot—as if to protect him. Beverly was breathless!

CHAPTER TWENTY-ONE

Baby Trey

Beverly received a call from a friend of George's, Jack Terry. Terry owned a bar in Houston and saw Ronnie Weedon push a few too many drinks down and become irate when he heard on the television news that Kirksey McCord Nix, Jr., the new reputed leader of the Dixie Mafia, had finally been arrested and slammed into jail. "Now what am I going to do? Nix was on my bond for the McGann murder." Weedon mumbled, not knowing that Jack Terry knew George or was fond of Beverly. Terry advised Beverly to steer clear of everybody, especially Nix. "He's not your friend!" It wasn't long afterward that Beverly learned that Stanley (Creeper) Cook was gunned down in front of the Lemmon Twist Club in Dallas. *What goes around in life–comes around.*

Beverly didn't want to hear anymore about George's old gang of friends. Emotionally, she had put it behind her. However, still tearful over the death of her baby, Beverly turned to the only thing she knew to do (the thing she did best) and that was to sing. At every opportunity she poured her soul into singing for her Lord. He led her into evangelism. The sweet voice once floating from the stage at the Colony Club was now gracing churches, tents, and meeting halls.

A year and seven-months into her new life, Beverly was singing at an evangelism conference when she heard the most Godly person she had ever listened to. She was moved by his sermon; his message was bathed in the light of the Lord. He was able to explain Biblical passages in ways that were thought provoking yet beautifully simple. His sermon spoke of love and bound the congregation in a spirit of oneness with the Savior and with one another. *By this one thing shall all men know that you are My Disciples–That you love the brethren.* Everything he said was rich with God's forgiveness and blessed with the promise of everlasting life through Jesus Christ.

Beverly and the preacher were introduced and talked a moment.

Later, when Beverly got home, the young preacher called and invited her to a New Year's Eve party at a friend's house. On New Year's Day they went to a football game together. A few weeks later he asked her to marry him and two days after that she marched him down the aisle; Beverly didn't believe in long engagements. Beverly had prayed for the Lord to send her a Godly man and He did. He sent her one that walked and talked with the Lord; a third generation preacher who lived what he preached and preached what he lived. His name was *Charles Massegee.* From wife of a Mafia hit-man to that of an evangelist, life had miraculously changed for Beverly, and she cherished it.

Charles and Beverly were married on the way to a revival, and for the next few years they lived in an Executive Motorhome, along with Rocky Shane–the first-born Massegee son. They traveled at the rate of forty-five revivals a year; twenty-two straight weeks without a rest. When they reached their destination, Charles would hook up the utilities to the churches facilities. Dinner was served at people's homes or in the church parsonage, or Beverly would cook in the motorhome. The Massegees delivered a powerful message across twenty states during that time, and led many souls into the kingdom of the Lord. As Rocky became eligible for kindergarten, it became necessary for the Massegees to build a home and to adjust their schedule.

The Massegees built a five-bedroom house on a sprawling ranch in west Texas; five miles down a dirt road and two-hundred yards from the top of a mountain. The ranch provided a serenity which transcended their expectations for a tranquil environment, away from the annoying clutter of city life. The ranch was nestled in an inspiring landscape of gentle rolling hills colored with random splashes of Indian Paintbrush, Bluebonnets, and Daffodils, and it was populated by deer, bobcats and other wildlife. The spring sun was a daily visitor and started keeping longer hours; skies were often dotted with slow-moving clouds scattered across a brilliant blue that went on forever. The air smelled clean and freshly spiced with the pungent fragrance of sagebrush. Rain could be scented from miles away. Summer days could be as still as the Sargasso Sea, the relentless chirping of katydids the only thing breaking the monotony of serene silence. But springtime brought rain and wind which often whipped through the homestead with a veracity that seemed frightfully vengeful as a roaring thunderhead barreled its way across the vast Texas countryside. The days belonged to the family, but the nights belonged to the stars. When twilight's palette left the horizon and crickets took over the chorus, the heavens were carpeted with brilliant blinking lights spreading east to west, north to south. The Milky Way was intensely awesome; so close but so far. The Big Dipper was easily defined in the lower night sky and when the moon rose it was as big as tomorrow. The Massegees were on a new frontier, their future was mapped with prayer and anchored with all the hope that could possibly be dreamed.

The tide turned one springtime when one of their prayers was answered. God blessed Beverly and Charles with a new son, *Jasper Charles Massegee, III.* Trey, they called him. He was a beautiful, healthy, and happy little boy, who came into the world weighing a wholesome ten-pounds, four ounces–his bright blue eyes beaming. The Massegees rejoiced in the joy that only the miracle of birth can bring. Trey represented the ultimate blessing from the union of their marriage and through him their love for one another grew deeper in spirit.

Life at the ranch was centered around the new baby. Beverly, Charles and Rocky relished every minute with Trey, every smile, every new expression, every "goo-goo." Beverly was finally at peace with her past. Charles was everything that George was not. His love for her was proclaimed every day in the simplest ways: the tone of his voice, the look in his eyes, the touch of his hand. Trey's presence had erased the persistent guilt concerning her failure at motherhood. Her daughter was in her heart but someone else's home; baby George was cradled in heaven, Trey was in her arms. The past was no longer burning.

With Beverly's birthday one day away, she and Charles were making plans on how they should celebrate and were also discussing plans for an upcoming crusade when she received a call from a man identifying himself as Jack Moriority with the House Select Committee investigating the assassination of President Kennedy. Beverly listened impatiently then promptly told him she didn't discuss the subject with anyone and hung up the phone. The phone immediately rang again. "Ms. Oliver! Do not hang up on me again. I am not some newsman asking for an interview. I am with an official government agency investigating President Kennedy's death. I have the authority to subpoena you and I absolutely will, if necessary, or we can sit down over a friendly cup of coffee and take your deposition."

Mr. Moriority said he was in Dallas and wanted to come see her as soon as possible. Beverly convinced him the ranch was a long boring drive away and difficult to find; directions would be as long as his arm with landmarks suspect to interpretation and that they would be better off meeting elsewhere. Beverly suggested they meet in Copeville, Texas at Charles' parent's home, (they had scheduled a revival at the First Baptist Church of DeKalb). Actually, Beverly didn't want anyone knowing where she lived. The ranch was private; her life beyond the pulpit was private; and that's the way she wanted it to stay.

March 12, 1977, was a bright day and the wind was blowing through Copeville in big strong gusts that could take your hat off or help your car change lanes. Two men, dressed in business attire, were standing on the front porch ready to knock on the door at the exact time they said they're be there. Beverly opened the door at the first knock and greeted them and insisted on seeing their identification. Her run-in with FBI Agents at the Colony Club when they took her film and their subsequent denial of doing so, had taught her to ask for and to carefully study identifications. Mr. Moriority handed Beverly his ID and when the other man, Mr. Gilbert, pulled his out of his wallet, it fell from his hand to the porch and blew away, across the highway and down the railroad tracks. The man bolted from the porch like a dog after a possum. Moriority broke out laughing as he saw him stumbling down the tracks. He knew how important that ID was and how desperate his partner was to get it. Without it he didn't belong in the depositions they needed to collect.

Card in hand, panting, he made it back to the porch and handed it to Beverly. She was satisfied that everything was in order and invited the men into the living room where she introduced them to Charles and his parents who had stepped away from the kitchen for a moment.

For over two hours Beverly answered questions about her observances on November 22, 1963, about Jack Ruby, Lee Oswald, and about the FBI confiscating of her film. Feeling satisfied that Beverly had told all she knew, the men thanked her for her time and got up to leave. Standing by the front door Beverly and Charles expressed their appreciation that Kennedy's death was getting the attention it deserved. Charles then asked if they would join in a moment of prayer. Everyone joined hands and Charles asked for God to provide a protective shield around the men as they pursued their investigation and to give the whole committee heavenly wisdom as they search for the truth behind the President's death. Amen.

Mr. Moriority was overtly touched. "That's the first time that anyone involved in this has cared enough to pray for us, thank you." He told Beverly he would be back in touch with her when they wanted to fly her to Washington to testify before the Committee and said they would be diligent and not release her name to the press. However, a few weeks later while Beverly was in Evansville, Indiana at another revival, to her dismay, she read on the front page headlines, "Ex-stripper To Testify In Washington." Beverly was irate and felt jilted. She questioned who was running the investigation and how insensitive they were to the safety of its witnesses. She felt her testimony was just a small part of the whole story but Kennedy's assassination had been riddled with unexplained deaths at every level–witnesses, reporters, government people, people who knew a lot, people who knew little, and she didn't want to be another question mark.

Beverly wondered when she would be called to Washington to testify before the Committee. She learned of another Texan who was going to tell her story as well. Audrey Bell was the supervisor of the operating room at Parkland Memorial Hospital when they brought President Kennedy and Governor Connally in. She had written an article for a publication of the National Association of Operating Room Nurses about the operating room scene the day of the assassination, recalling seeing four or five bullet fragments taken from Governor Connally being placed in a glass. If the bullet fragments could be found and shown to weigh more than the metal missing from the almost perfect bullet that allegedly fell from Connally's stretcher, "then the very cornerstone and basis of the entire Warren Commission report is no longer valid," Robert Tannenbaum, the committee's chief investigator was quoted as saying. Then on April 14, Beverly received a call from Moriority who told her that there was a ninety percent chance she would not be called to testify before the committee. He couldn't explain why. Beverly called Gary and told him about Moriority's call. She said that she questioned the sincerity of the committee in its investigation and said that her statement to the press, should they call, would be that she is "not going to be called before the committee and that's all I have to say." Beverly was disturbed that they didn't want to include her observations for the record. What were they afraid of? Was it that she could place Oswald and Ruby together two weeks before the assassination? Was it that she witnessed gunfire coming from the fence? Or was she incriminating the FBI for confiscating her film and they didn't want to deal with it?

For the next two months Trey, along with Charles' parents, traveled from town to town in a motorhome as Charles preached the gospel and Beverly sang of joy and salvation. Trey's presence made every day a spirited blessing. He was bright and playful; his little hands grasping hold of extended fingers; everyday, his eyes focusing on more and more things around him. His hair was starting to grow; his ears were so tiny, so perfect. He listened intently to every loving word coming from those around him.

Charles had no sooner closed his Bible on a successful invitation at a church in North Carolina when he started packing the equipment for the next town, Tijeras, New Mexico, over 1,500 miles away. Microphones, amplifiers, cords, plugs, everything was methodically placed into carrying cases. Beverly's Bible story-telling mannequin, Eric, was resting in his "sleep-case." After the good-byes, the thank-yous, and exchanging phone numbers, the Massegees slipped out of town and down the highway. Charles was wired from the excitement of witnessing so many lives change during the past week that New Mexico seemed just a few gas stops away. Jasper rode shotgun, Charles' mother camped in the chair behind him. Beverly and Trey were comfortably snuggled together on the couch. Happiness ran in a circular motion.

As the drive moved through the late evening hours, Beverly noticed that Trey's breathing was not quiet right and alerted Charles. His breaths were getting shorter and were irregular. Beverly became concerned but didn't think that he was in any danger. That night they stopped in Montgomery, Alabama to spend what was left of the rest of the night. Charles pulled quietly into the campsite, connected the electricity, hooked up the water hose and arranged the refuse conduit. Everyone else was asleep.

The next morning came early because New Mexico was still far down the highway. While Charles was unhooking the motorhome, Beverly checked on her baby. Trey was still sleeping but his breathing was very labored and she became worried. She called Charles and he listened closely. Beverly was right. Something was wrong; his breathing was erratic and cumbersome. He told Beverly to stay next to Trey and let him know if his condition changed. As Trey slept, Beverly sat beside him, rubbing his back and comforting him with the sound of her voice. He slept peacefully but as they got closer to Selma, his breathing became critical. Charles raced as fast as the motorhome would allow. When they reached the children's hospital, they rushed Trey into emergency with a condition the hospital listed as "respiratory distress."

Seventeen hours later, the beautiful healthy two month, 26-day-old boy, who never had a runny nose, never had a cough, never ran a fever, for no apparent reason, went home to be with the Lord while Beverly cradled him in her arms. While she held his warm little body, her life's miseries rushed before her. Everything that ever went wrong came back in a deluge of sorrow—drowning her in a rage of guilt. Beverly had never been more devastated in all her life. Trey was the child she and Charles had prayed for, and prayed for, and prayed for. Not just days of prayers, or weeks of prayer, but years of prayers. When he graced their lives they knew he was an answer to those prayers. Beverly was tangled in an emotional web of grief, despair and guilt. *There must be a reason? Why me? Oh, Lord, why me?* She struggled with her faith and questioned the reasoning behind such a cruel and untimely death but she prayed and reached deep inside, pulling her faith to the front, then like the soft touch of a comforting hand, she relaxed and was thankful she was allowed to hold Trey in his final moments when he was accepted into the kingdom of Heaven.

Shortly after Trey was laid to rest, Beverly placed a small framed picture of him on the mantel above the fireplace. Even thought she had accepted Trey's death she had many questions, most of which she knew had no answers. When Trey was born, Beverly's life was on as straight a course as it had ever been. She was keeping her body clean and drug free; she was serving the Lord in every way she could; she was on a crusade for saving lives, she was giving more than she was receiving—all the little things, too. But Trey was gone. Then the thought struck her. She remembered a phone call she received and the chilling voice warning her to keep her mouth shut and to not testify to the House Select Committee or they "would get her where it hurts." *Did they take Trey? He was perfectly healthy before he died.* The thought of such a consequence was beyond her comprehension, yet she knew how cold-blooded "those" kind of people could be, and how they took pleasure in teaching a lesson and making a statement. *Business was business. We told you the rules. But why Trey?* What could have hurt her more? Surely her testimony didn't demand taking the life of an innocent baby as a penalty. So what if Ruby knew Oswald. She wasn't the only one who knew that. So what if she said a gunman was shooting from behind the fence—who didn't? Beverly suddenly felt responsible for Trey's death, bearing the gruesome burden that perhaps she was the cause of it.

CHAPTER TWENTY-TWO
A Million To One

As time passed, Beverly still couldn't shake the loss of Trey. Little Trey—sweet baby angel Trey. His little hands, his bright blue eyes; he was gone but all around her—in every other thought. Her daily routines were engulfed in a lingering sadness; if she could only have another chance at having a baby perhaps she could be relieved of her misery. Thinking she had come to terms with death when first baby George, then husband George, passed away, she now found herself drowning in grief and self-pity. *One more chance.* Beverly wanted children more than anything in the world. When Trey was born she felt fulfilled and thought one baby and Rocky were all that she could manage. So, she (and Charles) decided she would have her tubes tied. *One more chance.* Beverly didn't feel quite right about it—it isn't the right alternative for everyone. But at the time, it was for her. In spite of the fact that her chances of conceiving were next to none, without Trey, thoughts of having another child became a daily preoccupation.

The daily battle with her anguish wore thin and Beverly finally gathered enough courage to step on her pride and ask her doctor if there was anything he could do to untie her tubes and make things work; she had heard about a procedure that could make it possible. *One more chance.* The doctor said there was a chance and explained the process of performing a tubal-reinastomosis. He explained the pros and cons and emphasized that success of such a procedure was minimal, extremely minimal. But Beverly was not to be denied any opportunity and steadfast in her decision to go to extremes to have a baby that lived, one to take home and love. Beverly asked her doctor to schedule the surgery. A million to one . . . it was her only hope.

The operation was performed the December after Trey died (in May). But Beverly still couldn't conceive. Days, months . . . years and no success. She thought, surely the Lord would bless her with another child; nevertheless, three years after Beverly's operation, hope had packed its bags and was standing by the door. But Beverly decided to keep hope waiting and see another doctor for a second opinion. She was put in the hospital for a laproscopia to take another look inside her and see if there were complications resulting from her last surgery.

"Mrs. Massegee, in your condition there is absolutely no way you'll be able to have another child. Your right tube has plenty of length, but it is completely blocked. Your left tube is only 3.8 centimeters long. You need a minimum of four centimeters to conceive. We need to go back in and unblock the right tube," the doctor stated with professional certainty.

Then there's hope, Beverly thought . . . hope. *It's not against God's will that I'm not conceiving, it's a mechanical error which needs fixing. There's still a chance.*

Dr. Michael Putnam was scheduled to perform the surgery at 9:30 AM on December 8 at Baylor Hospital, in Dallas. However, the week before Thanksgiving, Beverly believed she wasn't going to need to go through with the surgery. As a prerequisite to the operation, they required that Beverly see her doctor for a stress test. It was paramount that they measure her condition and stamina to see if her heart would be able to withstand prolonged anesthesia. When the time came for the test, Beverly informed Dr. Harvey Johnson that she wasn't going to do the stress test until after he gave her an HCG hormone level pregnancy test. He was puzzled and asked her why.

"Why?" Beverly answered, knowing he would think she was crazy. "Because . . . I'm pregnant."

"Pregnant? You're just dreaming, Beverly, bless your heart. That's just wishful thinking."

"No, I'm not going to get on that stress machine until you run a blood test." Beverly was adamant. "No way—no how!"

"Are you late with your period?"

"No."

"How far along are you?"

Beverly calculated, "Seven days, about."

The doctor laughed. "No way!"

"Right—no way, unless you stick my arm. "

A small syringe of blood was taken to the lab down the hall; Beverly retired to the waiting area. Two hours later, Dr. Johnson approached Beverly looking like the cat that ate the canary. "Beverly. What are you still doing here? You need to go home and start fixing your nursery. You're going to have a child."

Beverly knew it, she just knew it. She cried with joy as she hugged her doctor. When she told Charles he rejoiced in powerful prayer.

Later that afternoon Beverly called to cancel her surgery. "Dr. Putnam. This is Beverly Massegee. Remember when I was in your office recently and you said that the odds of me being able to conceive were a million to one?"

"Yes. I remember."

"Well, I want you to know that I serve a God who operates in those odds and wins."

"What do you mean?"

"I'm pregnant!"

"No, you're not," he said in total disbelief.

"Oh, yes. Oh, yes I am!" Mrs. Massegee, mother-to-be, emphasized.

Eight months later, Beverly gave birth to a beautiful little girl tipping the APGAR scale at a perfect "10"; weighing 8 pounds-5 3/4 ounces, measuring 19 inches. She and Charles named her *Lora Lee Andra Massegee*. Lora's older brother Rocky said that he was going to call her *Pebbles* so that the Massegees would have a "Rock" and a "Pebble."

The Massegees could not have been happier. Pebbles' presence was felt in every room of the house. Little hands, little feet . . . a million to one, and they won. Beverly and Charles often found themselves standing in the doorway of the nursery staring at their sleeping baby and praising the Lord for His blessing and basking in the delight of parenthood. Every day was the same way; little hands–little feet, big dreams.

When Pebbles was four-months old, she joined Beverly and Charles on a revival trip to California. Over the course of a few days Beverly noticed Pebbles was experiencing a decrease in her urine output. Pebbles went from five wet diapers a day–to four–to three. Something was wrong and Beverly became worried. With Trey's unexpected complications fresh on her mind, she wasn't going to take any chances and took Pebbles to the children's hospital in Oakland for a medical examination.

"She probably has a small bladder infection." the doctor remarked, undaunted by the deep concern Beverly was exhibiting and the precaution she was taking.

"Are you telling me she's not in renal failure?" Beverly asked, questioning his authority.

"Oh, no. Like I said. It's just a simple infection. I know you're concerned. I'll have her admitted and we can monitor her condition."

Beverly wasn't buying it; she knew something was wrong with Pebbles. Her intuition was screaming and no doctor or nurse had to tell her—she knew. *Mothers know!*

"Can we make it home to Dallas on an airplane? If Pebbles is going to be in the hospital I want to be near family who can help me."

"Your baby is fine, Mrs. Massegee. If you like, take her home, put her in a hospital you're comfortable with and have her own doctor check everything out. Let me know how she's doing."

Beverly called Dr. Fernando, Pebbles' pediatrician in Garland, to ask him to meet them at the airport with an ambulance. She told him that she was scared about Pebbles' health and wasn't pleased with the doctors in California and their nonchalant approach to finding out what might be wrong with her. He agreed without asking her to go into detail. Reluctantly, Charles stayed to finish the revival.

When they arrived in Dallas, Doctor Fernando made a quick examination of Pebbles and exclaimed, "Why did you get me out of bed at 6:15 AM? There's nothing wrong with this baby."

His comment made Beverly angry. "Where are his priorities?" she questioned. "Please, just take her to the hospital and have some blood work done on her. Just for me. I don't know, I'm worried."

Doctor Fernando was still upset over missing his sleep but followed through with his obligation and took Pebbles to the emergency room at Garland Memorial Hospital. Pebbles' blood samples were sent to the lab. When her results came back, Beverly was right. Something was wrong with her baby, all the tests confirmed it.

"This cannot be right! There is no possible way her blood results could be this bad and she still be alive." The doctor was astonished and terrified that the results might be right.

Pebbles was moved to Children's Hospital in Dallas where the blood tests were conducted again. It was not a mistake; Pebbles was in serious trouble, confirming Beverly's premonition. However, Beverly was told that there was no reason to have Charles rush home; Pebbles would probably be all right, her condition was stable. Charles called Beverly from California and asked what he should do. She told him how ill Pebbles was and told him to start driving home. Charles informed Beverly of the route he would be taking through Arizona, Nevada, and New Mexico, back to Dallas.

The following morning, Beverly was politely informed that if her husband wanted to see his daughter alive again, he had better get on a plane, because she was in total renal shut down. Beverly's worst fear crashed down on her. Poor tiny Trey, now sweet innocent Pebbles.

Satan seemed to sit on Beverly's shoulder and ridicule her, "You know that the God you love so much has done it to you twice already and He's going to do it to you again. Twice already. Two kids, and He's going to do it again." It was a battle. Beverly had prayed, and prayed, until she couldn't pray anymore. *It's not going to happen. Not this time.* "Two kids—one more?" *Not this time!*

Beverly's sorrow turned to alarm; she hadn't heard from Charles and didn't know where he was. She had her personal secretary, Betty McDonald, call the California Highway Patrol to see if they could help. Her call was passed around the station from person to person until finally Betty reached a young Christian highway patrolman who told her not to worry, "I won't stop until I find him and put him on a plane."

Charles was tracked down just outside of Phoenix and put on a plane to Dallas.

Beverly sat in the bathtub in Pebbles' room. Pebbles laid close by on her bed hooked to three monitors and several I.V.'s. It looked so unfair that a young baby should suffer so. "God, I just don't know how to pray anymore. I don't understand it but I trust in you." In the quietness of solitude and in the middle of prayer, He sent her the words of a song with which she was familiar but had never learned:

He didn't bring us this far—to leave us. He didn't teach us to swim—to let us drown. He didn't build his home in us—to move away. He didn't lift us up—to let us down.[1] "Beverly, I didn't bring you this far to just let you down and kick you. Trust me. Go through the doors that I've opened for you."

Hours went by and there was still no word from the doctors about Pebbles' diagnosis. Beverly stood at Pebbles' bedside, watching her, contemplating what God meant—saying He had opened doors for her. She was torn between hope and fear. Finally, a group of doctors walked into Pebbles' room and asked to see Beverly in private. "Mrs. Massegee there is nothing more we can do. We've done all that is possible. The only thing left is for you to take your four month old organism home and let it die."

Beverly was shocked that they had the audacity to refer to Pebbles as an "organism" and an "it." She fired back at them, "That's not good enough. As long as my daughter is breathing there is hope." She informed them that she wanted to take Pebbles to see Drs. Lee and Jay Hammer, who she knew in Atlanta, to see if they could help. They were brothers who were both practicing chiropractors, who worked with the science of kinesiology.

It seemed like an eternity after her conversation with the doctors. She felt isolated. Pebbles' prognosis was far from Beverly's thinking that doors were soon to open. She was struggling with her emotions when Charles, Beverly's best friend, Vicki Vaughn, and Dr. Arant arrived. Shortly afterwards, Dr. Arant was given the task of informing them again just how serious Pebbles' condition was. "Pebbles is going to die. There is no hope for her. There is nothing medically we can do for her. There is no place I'm aware of that can help her. I'm afraid to say, but you need to know, Pebbles' death will be very painful and not pleasant."

Beverly and Charles held steadfast and told him that they wanted to take her to see some doctors in Atlanta whom they thought could help.

"Beverly, you two don't need to go chasing rainbows. You just need to accept the fact that she will die. When she does, you need to have a thorough autopsy done and have her soft tissue sent back to us so we can do a definitive diagnosis and study the disease." Dr. Arant then clasped Beverly and Charles' hands. "I've told you what I'm supposed to as a doctor, now, I want to share with you my thoughts as a man and a daddy. You go anywhere you need to go, do anything you need to do, and chase any rainbow God puts in your path to try to save your daughter." Dr. Arant then bowed his head and prayed with them.

Beverly and Charles made up their mind that Pebbles' only hope was away from that hospital and they didn't waste any time in getting away. Charles pulled out all the I.Vs strapped to his daughter then carefully wrapped her warmly in a small blanket. The hospital staff went crazy. They screamed at Charles, "You can't take that baby out of here! What do you think you're doing?"

"I'm taking my child where she can be loved and cared for. She isn't an organism. She is a living, breathing, immortal soul who is going to have life as long as God has breath! She is God's gift to our family."

Pebbles made it to the airport hanging to life by a prayer, and flew to Atlanta and the home of Dr. Jay Hammer.

Dr. Jay Hammer invited the Massegees to stay in his home. He made Pebbles his priority. Trying to diagnose her problem was difficult and treatment even harder. For five days, Beverly and Charles fought a life and death battle to keep Pebbles alive. Betty noticed that Pebbles had stopped breathing and without thinking grabbed a heavy duty body massager and administered it to Pebbles chest in a desperate effort to revive her.

Through the grapevine a doctor by the name of Julius Sherwinter heard about Pebbles and called the Massegees. "I hear that you're in town with a baby who's in distress. I want to help you. Here's my home phone number, my hospital number and my office number. Call me anytime day or night."

Beverly and Charles were elated that there was someone who cared enough, who had the confidence to try, to take the initiative to call on them and offer help with Pebbles. Then, when Pebbles started bleeding at the slightest touch, they called Dr. Sherwinter immediately. Pebbles lay comatose, bleeding from her ears, and from her naval. From all appearances, she didn't seem alive, but part of another world.

"Bring her out right away. I'll dialyze her once to clean her out and see if the enzyme treatment the Hammers are performing on her is working."

Dr. Sherwinter didn't expect Pebbles to respond to the dialysis; she was very young to be going through the procedure. When they met with Dr. Sherwinter in Atlanta at the Shriner's Hospital for Crippled Children, he immediately ordered blood work. They determined that Pebbles' platelet count was 19,000, necessitating a transfusion to increase her blood count before they could even place the catheter into her for the dialysis. Pebbles received fifty units of pack cells building her count up to 80,000; they were only hoping for 50,000. Once the Jackson Pratt catheter was in place they began her dialysis and were amazed at how well she responded. She was given another fifty-pack of platelet cells building her count up to 150,000. At that point, her blood miraculously started manufacturing its own cells again. They weren't expecting that; there were a lot of things going right with Pebbles that the doctors didn't expect.

It was suspected that Pebbles' condition was probably an extremely rare genetic disorder called "Primary Hyperoxaluria." But they weren't positive.

The next day Pebbles was still being dialyzed even though she was doing so well. Beverly then told the doctor. "Dr. Sherwinter, I'm extremely pleased with the progress you've made with Pebbles. But I understand that the University of Minnesota is the only place in the world that is conducting a study of this disease."

"Beverly. I'm ahead of you. I've already called them. I went to school with Dr. John Scheinman, who's the head of pediatric nephrology there. He has a bed waiting for Pebbles. All we need to do is get Pebbles stabilized to make the flight—making sure there is no brain involvement." Seven days later the Massegee family were on their way to the University of Minnesota. In a small twist of fate, Pebbles's life had miraculously crossed with the only person in the world who could save her.

But before they left, at the doctor's request, they arranged to have Trey exhumed and the large bone from his leg sent directly to the University so that it might provide clues and confirmation about Pebbles diagnosis; the disease was so rare. (If indeed Trey had the same disease, then Beverly's guilt from giving her testimony to the House Select Committee could be forever put to rest.)

The medical staff told Beverly and Charles of a procedure that was just then being introduced to the medical profession—pediatric transplant. Dr. Scheinman and Dr. Michael Mauer asked Beverly who the donor would be should they proceed with a transplant?

"I will." Beverly said without blinking.

"Mrs. Massegee we can't take your kidney because you have Lupus." Beverly had been suffering for several years with Lupus, a systemic blood disease, and was surprised that they knew about it. However, they already had all the family medical background they needed.

Beverly knew that Charles's bloodtype, "A" positive, wasn't compatible, and that both she and the baby were "O" positive and a match.

"I'm going to do it." Beverly insisted.

"No, you're not."

At this time there had never been a kidney transplant for a baby that small. The next week, they transplanted a little boy, P. J. Strunse, the same age of Pebbles, with his father. It was very successful. The further miracle of the operation is that the adult kidney shrinks to the size needed to perform its functions in the body of a baby. (Sadly however, P. J. died a little more than a year later.)

While Dr. Najarian, who was to perform the transplant, was out of town, Beverly urged the medical staff to put her in the hospital to do a tissue match and a donor work-up, pushing her candidacy to be the donor. When the results came back they found that she and Pebbles were a great match and that if Dr. Najarian would agree, they would allow Beverly to be the donor. After he returned, he looked at the lab results and agreed. He then looked at Pebbles' picture, bowed his head momentarily and then exclaimed with great confidence, "I can do it. I can do it!"

For the second time in medical history and the first time for a baby with Pebbles' disease, a kidney was transplanted from an adult into a baby. The God who the Massegees served was still working miracles.

1 *He Didn't Lift Us Up To Let Us Down,* words by Phil Johnson
Copyright 1976 Dimension Music.

CHAPTER TWENTY-THREE

Who Were Those Guys?

Gary Shaw and Beverly became friends and kept in touch with each other over the years as he thought of more questions to ask her. Still curious about who Beverly might have crossed paths with while she visited Jack at the Carousel Club and in her marriage to George, Gary asked if she would mind scouting through a binder of photographs he had compiled containing hundreds of photographs of people somehow associated with the Kennedy case. Randomly placed in the binder were pictures of policemen, FBI and Secret Service Agents, mobsters, etc.

Grabbing his book of photographs, Gary drove to Omaha, Texas where the Massegees were conducting a revival at the First Baptist Church (Richard Longino, Pastor). After the service, Gary met with Beverly and Charles, and two friends of theirs, Bob Bynum and his wife.

As a control measure, none of the pictures in Gary's book were labeled, nor were there any clues as to their identities. Beverly flipped through the book scanning each page carefully; some photos she studied long, others she glossed over quickly. One of the first men she recognized was a strange looking man with black hair and screwy eyebrows. "I knew him. He was at Jack's club a lot. I think he was Jack's assistant-manager for awhile. He was a strange, but intelligent man." Beverly had identified David Ferrie. She then pointed out two men who were also at the Carousel Club prior to the assassination: Guy Banister and Emilio Santana.

She then identified New Orleans attorney Dean Andrews, with whom Oswald had consulted during the summer of 1963. He was also the attorney someone called to represent Oswald after he had been arrested.

Within 24 hours after the assassination, David Ferrie was wanted for questioning by the FBI. Oswald had on his person—Ferrie's library card. In late 1966 David Ferrie was implicated by New Orleans District Attorney Jim

Garrison in a conspiracy to assassinate President Kennedy. He died under questionable circumstances soon afterwards on February 22, 1967. According to the autopsy report, however, Ferrie died of natural causes, a cerebral hemorrhage resulting from an aneurysm. But the two notes he left, including his signature, were typewritten, leading to speculation that he was murdered. (The New Orleans Crime Commissioner also suspected that Ferrie was murdered.) Some people believed Ferrie spent most of his pre-assassination time at the Town and Country Motel conferring with Carlos Marcelos on his upcoming trial (which was brought about by Robert Kennedy's war against him) and planning Kennedy's "hit." The FBI said they suspected Ferrie was a money- runner for New Orleans Mafia chieftain Carlos Marcello. What we do know is that Ferrie was a pilot, a hypnotist, and a rabid anti-Castro and anti-Kennedy fanatic. Also that an audit of his bank account indicated that he had made a deposit of $7,000 in the weeks following the assassination.

Banister was an ex-FBI agent who worked out of the Chicago office. He was involved in the John Dillinger ambush and during World War II was reported to have worked for Naval Intelligence. After the war, he returned to the FBI, was forced to resign after brandishing a weapon in public, then moved to New Orleans where he set up a detective agency bearing his name at 544 Camp Street. Several people had connected Banister with setting Oswald up with the Fair Play for Cuba Committee. It was ironic that the address listed on the pamphlets Oswald was handing out for the committee when he was arrested was also the resident address for the anti-Castro insurgents headed by Banister, who died in 1964. His official death was ruled a heart attack, but researcher Robert Groden said that a bullet was found in his body. Banister had never been questioned by the Warren Commission about his connections to the case. Santana, whom Beverly identified, was a Cuban hood.

Beverly then identified a photograph of Jack Lawrence as a man she danced with once at the Cabana and someone she had seen on several occasions at the Carousel Club. She then asked Gary if he'd found anything out about Larry Ronco and his whereabouts. Gary said he had been working with Henry Hurt, who authored the book, *Reasonable Doubt,* and that a private investigator he kept on retainer had checked with Kodak for both Larry Ronco Jr. and Sr. in Rochester, New York, and the surrounding area, but couldn't find a trace of Larry. Six Flags was a dead-end as well. They refused to provide any information.

Jack Lawrence was the subject of serious accusations that he, too, was somehow involved. At the time of the assassination, he was working for a car dealership close to downtown. Soon after news of the assassination reached the dealership, Lawrence was seen slipping through the showroom to the bathroom where he threw-up. His clothes were muddy and he looked pale. The company car Lawrence was driving was found parked behind the picket fence. When questioned later, he denied everything. He said he abandoned the car because he couldn't manage to maneuver through all the traffic.

There was no photograph of Larry Meyers, so even though that was how he was introduced, Beverly could not confirm that it was Larry who accompanied her and Jack to Campisi's on the eveninng of November 21, 1963.

Towards the middle of the mugbook, Beverly looked up at Gary and then back at a picture. "That's him. He's the one who took my film. I'm positive. That's him!" Beverly placed her finger on a picture of FBI Special Agent Regis Kennedy. Earlier, Beverly had told Gary that a man, whom she later identified as someone who was not only an agent, but was suspiciously involved in the case, had identified himself as an FBI agent and had confiscated her film. This intrigued Gary. If there was someone who could have known about the film and was in a position to take it, it would have been Regis Kennedy.

Regis Kennedy was the New Orleans Federal Agent assigned to Mafia boss Carlos Marcello when Robert Kennedy was on his campaign to clean up organized crime. Robert Kennedy had made Marcello one of his top four priorities and was angry that the FBI, who was successful in wiretapping the other suspected bosses, couldn't penetrate the Marcello organization. Regis Kennedy's questionable surveillance of Marcello led him to consistently report that Marcello was nothing but a real-estate investor and salesman for the Pelican Tomato Company. Agent Kennedy also provided David Ferrie an alibi on November 22, 1963, by saying that Ferrie was in the courtroom during Marcello's deportation case hearing. Several researchers speculated that Agent Kennedy was on the Marcello payroll because he wasn't able to get the scoop on Marcello's activities in New Orleans and failed to turn up the heat when the U.S. Attorney General demanded it. In fact, the two areas that information concerning Mafia activities was suspiciously void was New Orleans and Dallas. Later, when push came to shove, and interest in Marcello became a priority again and his surveillance was reassigned, it didn't take long for Federal authorities to sneak into his office, wire the place, and acquire the information they needed to arrest Marcello.

Beverly then easily picked out George's buddies: R.D. Matthews, Joseph Civello and Johnny Ross Patrona. Why they were in Gary's book? Beverly didn't ask. She also identified Charles Harrelson, who was dining with her and George at Campisi's the evening when she tried to discuss the assassination and George threatened to kill her if she brought it up again.

One evening, Gary picked up Bernard "Bud" Fensterwald at the airport and drove over to Mary Ferrell's house where they were going to meet Beverly. Both Fensterwald and Ferrell were anxious to meet her; one of the missing puzzle pieces. Fensterwald was a Washington D.C. attorney, a researcher, a one-time friend of Jack Kennedy, and founder of the JFK Assassination Archives Center in D.C. and co-founder of the JFK Assassination Information Center in Dallas. Mary Ferrell was a Dallas resident and one of the most renowned and respected Kennedy researchers. She once worked as a legal secretary for New Orleans District Attorney Jim Garrison and was credited with bringing to the House Select Committee's attention that there was a Dictabelt recording from an open police microphone of the gunfire in Dealey Plaza. It was from an audio analysis of the recording that the committee concluded that Kennedy was probably killed as a result of a conspiracy–they determined that there had been four shots fired.

Beverly called Gary from a service station close to Mary's home and got the final directions. Everyone stood by the window waiting for Beverly. When she pulled up out front, Mary said excitedly , "That's her. That's her."

Gary had met Mary through news reporter and pioneer assassination researcher Penn Jones, who was also editor of the Midlothian Mirror newspaper. In the mid sixties, when Gary's interest in the case started growing, he read an article in the Fort Worth Star Telegram about Penn Jones' second volume of his book questioning the authenticity of the Warren Report called *Forgive My Grief*. Since Gary often went to Dallas, he stopped by to meet Jones on a regular basis. It was through their mutual interest that Penn later introduced Gary to Mary and a few others who were "on the trail of the assassins."

Beverly was introduced to the others interested in the assassination. She then told her story of meeting Lee Oswald, her walking to the Plaza, filming the assassination, and her encounter at the club with the FBI. She then answered as many questions as she could comfortably answer. To their satisfaction, she knew a lot about the Dallas Club scene and people peripherally associated to the assassination and the underworld. However, there were areas and people she refused to acknowledge for fear of her life. There were people still alive who would kill her for breaking the code of silence about their activities. While some questions seemed pertinent to the assassination, others didn't. But when Mary showed Beverly her file on George McGann, she was caught off guard. Mary obviously had some inside connections, because the information she had on George was exhaustive. Someone had been keeping a tight eye on George and knew much more than Beverly thought possible. What was an ex-secretary doing with a room full of file cabinets and office equipment? Beverly was awe-stricken, just as she was when she met Gary and saw his Warren Commission library. "Who is this woman?" she thought. Is she more than just a researcher?

Beverly left the "interrogation" two hours later, still not sure about who everyone was or why they felt her story was so important. She wished she had never gone down to the Plaza.

Beverly and her secretary had taken Pebbles to the Children's Hospital in Dallas for tests. The hotel across the street from the hospital, where they usually stayed, was full, so they stayed at the Cabana because it was the closest.

Checking into the Cabana Hotel was eerie. The hotel held a lot of memories for Beverly. They enveloped her the moment she parked her van in the exact place she had everyday for the several months she had lived there in 1963 when she was dating Larry Ronco. The irony of it all was that when she checked in she was given the same room.

Walking through the front door, Beverly flashed back to the night before the assassination when she stood waiting for her ride. That night was the last time she saw Jack. He seemed happy and pleased with the way she looked. She again thought about the club he wanted to open in Turtle Creek and about how much he loved those steaks at Campisi's. Then, her heart sank when she thought about the fact she would never hear Jack's voice again. *I never got to thank him for being kind to me. That dress was so thoughtful.*

Beverly's queer feelings followed her down the hall and into the room. The room had changed in a few ways that slipped her notice; she saw it through a veil of yesteryear. In the hot steam of a shower, her mind continued to wander back in time, and around town. She visited her time spent with Larry and wondered how it all fell apart and if what she heard was true about his death. Visually, she had taken herself back to a time she was in the room getting ready to go out with Larry when . . . she remembered.

Beverly jumped out of the shower, pulled on some clothes, and told Betty to get up and follow her. They jumped in the van, took a right away from the hotel, whipped over to Commerce Street East, took a right on Houston Street, and drove across the viaduct. Just across the bridge, tucked to the right, down a small hill near the St. Andrew's Miniature Golf Course, were the apartments where Larry lived. Finding the apartment was like finding a puzzle piece that had fallen from the table and hid under the sofa. After she had spoken with Gary, trying to piece together the events surrounding the assassination, it bothered her that she couldn't remember where he lived. Not that it had any significance, but finding it would just be something she could check off her list.

Looking up the walk at his apartment, Beverly shuddered, experiencing a morbid anxiety she wasn't prepared for. Not knowing why she felt that way, Beverly continued to stand there. Then she remembered the last time she came to see Larry. She remembered she was going to surprise Larry for some reason— he wasn't expecting her. But as she walked closer to his apartment she heard or saw something that caused her to run away before knocking on the door. She stood there trying to think what it might be, but her mind was completely blank. Whatever it was frightened her intensely and caused her to fear Larry. It then dawned on her that it was at that time her feelings toward Larry started crashing.

Driving back to the Cabana, Beverly replayed her visit to Larry over and over, but still . . . no answers.

CHAPTER TWENTY-FOUR

Going Public

Secretary, Betty McDonald, kept up with the profusion of books and articles published about the assassination. But Beverly purposefully avoided them, refusing to read any. She wanted to keep her memory of the event undisturbed and unclouded by public opinion. Actually, after her confrontation with George about the assassination, she had conditioned herself to avoid and ignore it. She was still fearful and trusted her intuition that silence was her best ally. Betty, however, started to read aloud specific passages referencing Beverly and her experience both during and after the assassination. Beverly became angered that people she had never met before could talk about her and distort her story as if they were there or knew better. Other than Gary Shaw, Beverly had never met any researchers or spoken to any reporters. How did these people know who she was? Surely they didn't get all their information from the short summary Gary had written in his book *Cover-up,* or did they?

Betty answered Beverly's phone on the third ring. It was a lady named Sheila Kogan asking to speak with Beverly Oliver. Betty asked the nature of her business and Ms. Kogan replied that she worked with Nigel Turner of British Independent Television. Mr. Turner was filming a documentary on the assassination of John F. Kennedy and he wanted to film an interview with Beverly. As usual when people called the "Babushka Lady," Betty quickly responded that Beverly wouldn't be interested, "Beverly isn't granting interviews to anyone at this time. I'm sorry. Thank you for calling. I'll let her know."

When Betty told Beverly that the Nigel Turner from British Independent Television had called, she simply shook her head. *Will it ever be over?*

A few days later Ms. Kogan called again and the same conversation took place between her and Betty, "Beverly isn't granting interviews, thank you." A third time, Ms. Kogan called and Betty politely advised her that if Mr. Turner wished to speak with Beverly he would have a better chance if he called personally. The next day he did call. Betty asked Mr. Turner to leave a telephone number because she and Beverly were headed to the hospital in Dallas with Pebbles, who was running a high fever. Mr. Turner mentioned he was aware of Pebbles' kidney transplant and that he understood. After conferring with Beverly, Betty promised that when they got settled, Beverly would call him back.

"How did he know about Pebbles?" Beverly asked Betty. "How do these people know these things? What's going on out there?" Betty and Beverly were unaware that newspaper articles about Pebbles' operations had been reprinted in a popular assassination newsletter at the time called *The Continuing Inquiry,* published by Penn Jones. Why Pebbles was of interest to assassination followers had them baffled.

After Pebbles was comfortably placed in the hospital's care at Children's Medical Center, Beverly called Mr. Turner back. After listening to his sincerity about the project, Beverly agreed to meet with him and to hear about the documentary. She was beginning to think that going public might be the best solution. Then everyone would have the answers they wanted and perhaps the phone calls would stop.

The next evening, Pebbles' condition had stabilized and she was feeling better when Nigel came to see them. Wanting to get away from the clinical smell and stainless-steel surroundings of the hospital ward, Beverly and Nigel went to the coffee shop and talked at length. Nigel's accent was fascinating to Beverly. His approach to conversation was very cordial and his understanding about Beverly's reluctance was very sincere. He told her that his production would be nothing short of first-class. Beverly became convinced it would be. Kennedy's death was also a tragic blow to Britain and the rest of Europe; he was very well loved for his progressive leadership and attitude toward world peace and they were infatuated with his boyishness, gaiety, and spontaneity. And while most of America kept its head buried in the sand about assassination conspiracies, Europe was trying to understand what actually happened and solve the crime. After all, they lost a great leader as well.

"Nigel, I'm concerned about being hounded by people calling me all the time, threatening me and all the other garbage."

"Beverly, chances are, this production will not be shown in the United States. Your government is still very guarded about this subject and the networks are accommodating them. For some reason, they want the public to stay in the dark about your President's death."

Beverly reacted favorably to Nigel's request but wanted Charles to meet Nigel and give his consent as well. After all, even if the documentary wasn't shown in the States, with publicity of this magnitude, Charles's life could be affected, too. There were always going to be crazies out there and the Massegees didn't want anymore threatening phone calls or harassment of any kind. Furthermore, how would it affect their ministry? Appearing on the documentary required serious thought and she didn't want to make the decision alone. During the drive home, Beverly decided that it was important that her testimony was publicly-recorded and more importantly—correct. Both Betty and Gary Shaw were in favor of her doing the interview. But Charles would have to meet Nigel.

Later in the week, Beverly and Charles met Nigel for dinner at Bay Street Restaurant. It wasn't long before Charles, too, was won over by Nigel's warmth and cordiality. Charles was convinced that the production was well-planned and would be professionally implemented. Nigel mentioned again that much of the information in his documentary was controversial and the film would probably not be shown in the United States. Beverly and Charles agreed that she should do the interview. However, to minimize contact with the public, Beverly asked if she could sign an exclusive agreement with British Independent Television so that should anyone call, she would have a legitimate reason for not speaking with them. Nigel agreed.

Morning came early the day Beverly was to film her interview and she laid in bed—sick to her stomach, wishing she had decided not to do it. Her mind was cluttered with all the "what if's" about proceeding, but the decision to go public had been made, and there was no turning back. She'd just *have to get over herself;* something she once said about Jack when he was upset about her dress.

Nigel must have known Beverly better than she thought and she was grateful for it. To help calm her down and ease her into the interview, he insisted she record his favorite gospel song for him to use in the documentary. Beverly was flattered; a recording studio was one place she felt comfortable, Dealey Plaza was not.

"Amazing Grace how sweet the sound, that saved a wretch like me . . . ."[1]

Beverly concentrated hard during her singing but was bothered by visions of the assassination. To sustain the intensity of her singing, she tried to picture Kennedy with his wife and children during the times she saw him on television, the times he was happy. It worked.

"I once was lost but now I'm found. Was blind but now I see . . . ."

Beverly finished recording the song, and in doing so she felt she knew Nigel better as well. But the ease that enveloped her while singing began to dissipate; she knew it was time for the "Babushka Lady" to go back to the grassy place. Not since Gary Shaw and Richard Sprague had taken her to Dealey Plaza had she been back. Beverly wondered if any of the film crew, other than Nigel, could possibly understand how difficult it was for her to revisit the plaza on Elm Street. She wondered if other witnesses to the assassination experienced the same crisis and suffered the same nightmares.

It was important to Nigel that Beverly's interview take place where she stood as the motorcade passed her, holding her camera, filming the smiling, hand-waving president—where she stood as the sound of gunfire split the air and the President's . . . .

As the film crew arrived and Beverly followed them to the "grassy spot" down by the triple overpass, she felt that they were trespassing on the past. That small triangular open space was haunted and always would be for Beverly, and thousands of others. Melancholy would always permeate the air. For Beverly, it was a comprehensive feeling layered with fear, anger, sadness, retribution, hopelessness. She didn't understand how she could feel so many different ways at the same time. But that feeling was there on November 22; it was there when she went back with Gary, and it was still there—as if it waited for her to come back.

While the camera crew was busy setting things up, Beverly began questioning her decision. *Why in the world did I sign that contract? Will I ever be ready for this? What will become of this investigation? Does any of it matter—will anyone actually be brought to justice?* Beverly sighed, her eyes darting over at the fence, then back up at the window, over where Mr. Zapruder stood, where the lady in the red coat stood, the man with the little boy, the limousine, the blue sky, the crack-crack, boom-boom, the President's head . . . .

Beverly's mind always tried to avoid the "scene." But it was impossible; it had awakened her too many times. She'd seen enough of it. She thought about Jackie, wondering what on God's earth raced through her mind the moment her husband was shot. How did she tell their children? How did she reply to their questions about—"Why?" Did she say, *"Children, the world is crazy and life can be cruel. Your father was a gentle person—a caring father and a great man . . . ."* Did Jackie really believe that Lee Harvey Oswald pulled the trigger? How is she going to react about a gunman behind the fence, or, has she closed that chapter *completely?* Beverly didn't have any answers to her questions. *This can't happen again. America votes its leaders out of office, it can't murder them! That's the way democracy works–at least that's the way it should.* A spark of patriotism was lit and Beverly's seething anger manifested itself as a personal demand for justice. *What can I do? I can tell my story and hopefully, it will help wake-up the public to what really happened.*

"Beverly. Can I have your attention, please. We're ready to roll." Beverly snapped back to the situation at hand and what they had come down to the plaza to accomplish. Once again, Nigel explained to Beverly how he was going to film the sequence and reinforced that there was nothing for her to be nervous about. This was 1988, not 1963. She was safe. Beverly pulled all her inner strength together, said a prayer; the action went live and she told her story.

With the filming complete, everyone went out for dinner together where conversation about the assassination continued. Beverly remained calm but was still angered by the travesty of justice. It was amazing to her that emotions which she had suppressed for so long were now boiling over. *Where is Kennedy's justice? Did the people who planned his assassination ever stop to look back? Did they laugh, have a party to celebrate? Someone got away with murder. The fact that they never caught the man behind the fence is proof enough. Surely, the conspiracy was bigger than one man behind a fence and another in a window. There had to be someone giving orders.* Beverly knew how "hit" contracts worked. The men with the guns could only be hired killers and could not have been the masterminds behind the order to kill Kennedy. It simply didn't work that way.

The exclusive contract Beverly and Charles negotiated with Nigel came in handy. Occasionally, a reporter from some random journal called wanting to speak to the "Babushka Lady" but were turned away, "Beverly's under an exclusive agreement with British Independent Television not to discuss anything prior to release of a documentary she participated in. You will have to go through them." One afternoon Betty answered a call from the offices of veteran journalist Jack Anderson who was preparing his own special report on the assassination and wanted to interview Beverly. "Sorry," Betty replied.

Betty drew a blank stare from Beverly when she said that Jack Anderson's office called wanting to arrange an interview with her. Betty knew right away that Beverly hadn't a clue as to who Mr. Anderson was. Betty chuckled, "Wouldn't Jack Anderson be surprised if he knew there was someone out there who hadn't heard of him."

"What?" Beverly said as Betty was walking out of the room.

"Nothing." Betty replied. "I was just talking to myself."

Anderson's office called again. The routine was the same. Betty again informed the woman calling for Mr. Anderson that Beverly wasn't granting interviews and that Mr. Anderson would of had a better chance speaking to Beverly if he had called himself. That afternoon the phone rang and it was Jack Anderson.

Betty was surprised. She excitedly told Beverly that Jack Anderson was holding and then had to coerce her to speak with him. "Beverly, just talk to him. You don't have to agree to do an interview, just be courteous. After all, he did call, himself."

"Beverly. This is Jack Anderson."

"Yes ..." Beverly paused, waiting for him to speak again, but he was waiting for her to continue.

"Do you know who I am?" Anderson asked.

"Mr. Anderson, I honestly can't say that I do." Beverly was wondering just who "he" was. Betty was impressed, so he must be somebody, Beverly thought.

"Really. I'm a Pulitzer-prize winner."

"Well, that's OK. I don't know anything about boxing, either," Beverly was quick to point out. Listening close by, Betty couldn't imagine why they were talking about boxing. Mr. Anderson quietly remained on the line, probably thinking he was speaking with a proverbial dumb blond, a Texan at that, but Beverly was just playing her cards tight to her chest.

Finally, Mr. Anderson broke the silence by informing Beverly that he was filming a television special on the assassination of President Kennedy in tribute to the 25th anniversary of his death, then asked if she would be interested in being interviewed for the special. Beverly told him that until *The Men Who Killed Kennedy* was released, she couldn't participate because of her contract arrangement with British Television. It worked, she thought, as their conversation came to an abrupt end. She was thankful the contract was in place, and wondered if the "boxer" had other people to call.

The trees were still clothed with leaves and a cool November wind was whipping sporadically from every direction. Cornish hens roasting in the oven and a steaming palette of wild rice cooking on the stovetop saturated the house with a mouthwatering aroma. The dinner table was set for an early evening meal and the Massegees were waiting for their Thanksgiving guest.

Rarely did Beverly invite people to her home, but she was grateful to Nigel for everything he had done. After all was said and done, she felt comfortable about going public, and was relieved of the pressure of having to keep the knowledge concealed. Telling Gary Shaw her experience happened so unintentionally that it hadn't effectively lifted her tension. Besides, she had grown fond of Nigel's British ways and his continental manners, and it was time for an American "thanks."

When Nigel arrived, he brought a video copy of *The Men Who Killed Kennedy*. After God's blessing (prayer) was asked and everyone stuffed themselves with the bounty of Thanksgiving dinner, they made themselves comfortable in the living room to watch the production.

Watching the film in its entirety provided Beverly with a thoroughly new insight into how broad the assassination conspiracy actually was. For the first time, Beverly realized that other people in the plaza that day witnessed and experienced some of the things that she did. Most of the people in Dealey Plaza thought gunfire came from the fence. She remembered everyone rushing toward the fence but was confused when the investigation didn't head in that direction. She also became aware that there were other people who had their film confiscated. Gordon Arnold was a young soldier who was standing in front of the picket fence and reported that he was confronted by a uniformed policeman who kicked him and demanded his film. Mary Moorman was taking Polaroid still photographs and handed all of them over to the "authorities." Nevertheless, one of them slipped through the net and made headlines all over the world.

Beverly felt an odd sense of security knowing that other people shared her feelings that shots were fired from behind the fence, and that others had their film taken. She then became angry that her film was never returned and wondered what options she had in trying to get it back. There was no doubt in her mind that her film would show the picket fence at the time of the fatal shot. What a difference that would make from an accountability standpoint. The government would be force into reopening the case, and where would that end? Who was behind the fence and is he still on the loose? And if Oswald wasn't shooting from the window, then there's another assassin walking among us. The French connection presented in *The Men Who Killed Kennedy* was intriguing and sounded plausible. Were those the real assassins? She shuddered to think.

The documentary held Beverly spellbound. It was very well researched. The thought that it took an English production group to reveal the conspiracy to the public, coupled with the suspicious way the FBI confiscated her film and refused to admit testimonials supporting the fact that Ruby and Oswald knew each other, made her question just who was in charge of the investigation, and if they really cared that the truth be known. Something wasn't right.

Beverly was pleased with the way her testimony was presented in the documentary. It showed her walking across the grassy place to the spot she was standing on November 22, 1963, then mixed through to the Stars and Stripes flying above Dealey Plaza. In the background, Beverly was singing, *"Amazing Grace, how sweet the sound that saved a wretch like me. I once was lost but now I'm found, was blind but now I see."* Beverly was touched. Her love for John F. Kennedy was still very real.

1. *Amazing Grace,* words and music by John Newton.

V

JFK: The Movie

Action!

The Wake-Up Call

Roscoe White

The Carousel Club: Rewind

It's A Wrap!

CHAPTER TWENTY-FIVE

JFK: The Movie

While Oliver Stone was filming his classics about the Vietnam War, *Platoon* and *Born on the Fourth of July,* he discovered several political inconsistencies leading him to question the assassination of Kennedy and its ties to the war. The closer he looked at the events in Dallas the angrier he got. He saw strings tied everywhere. The assassination unfolded as a conspiracy involving a cross section of elite power moguls directly benefitting from the heat of battle—the "military industrial complex" to which Eisenhower frightenly alluded. Stone was on a crash course to film the JFK assassination story.

Even before Stone's movie about Kennedy had been given a name, the script finished, or contracts signed, there was a major effort to stop the film from being made—let alone shown. Spearheaded by the New York Times and sheepishly followed by its major allies Newsweek and Time Magazine, a media campaign sprang forth trying to discredit and destroy both the film and its director. Suddenly, the attention of mainstream media was maddeningly directed toward the making of a movie. At one point, the "other guys" stooped to stealing Stone's script and releasing it to the print sharks as a matter of "national security." Reading of the script resulted in an article by George Lardner in The Washington Post. Never before had a Hollywood production attracted the attention of so many poisonous, viscous attacks.

Some articles written about the movie were by the old guard such as Gerald Ford, Richard Mosk, and David Belin, who still had their integrity to protect because of their direct involvement in preparing the Warren Commission Report. Others were written by those who were armed with half truths and little knowledge of how far the research community had taken the conspiracy investigation. Stone was upset that history had somehow been delegated to newsmen who were upset that a movie maker was ready, willing, and prepared to correct their reports. "History is gossip," or so Stone quoted Herodotus and

Homer. *Stories heard around a campfire, passed down from generation to generation.* How was history going to interpret the Kennedy assassination? What would go unsaid?

The barrage of ridicule and heady editorials lasted well after the movie opened to record crowds everywhere. But then, articles surfaced praising the merits of *JFK*, not only as a cinematic adventure, but as an important lesson in historic and creative representation.

"Do you know who Oliver Stone is?" asked Gary Shaw when he telephoned her.

"No." Beverly said, without a second thought.

"Have you seen *Platoon, Born on the Fourth of July, Talk Radio* or *Wall Street?*" Surely, he thought, she has heard of his movies.

"No. I don't go to movies." Beverly was only being honest. Going to the movies was not a luxury, it just didn't happen unless it was something special for Pebbles. Any movies showing on television took a back seat to the news and weather or the Cowboys. The TV was usually tuned to CNN for background noise and weather flashes. During tornado season she always kept an ear out for those ominous little beeps alerting people to severe conditions.

For a moment, Gary thought he would be swimming upstream in trying to convince Beverly to be agreeable about meeting with Stone. The ghost of George always haunted Beverly when the subject to the assassination came up. She was very guarded about speaking with people. With the exception of Nigel's film, she had always shunned publicity. She was afraid of it. Her silence and anonymity the past twenty seven years kept her alive, she insisted. Gary understood her reluctance and was hesitant in proceeding further.

"He's filming a movie about John F. Kennedy and I just thought you might be interested in meeting with him, he's going to be in Dallas this week."

"Well Gary, let me think about it," Beverly replied, not knowing what to do. She had recently learned that Nigel Turner was trying to swing a deal to air *The Men Who Killed Kennedy* in the States. This was contrary to what he had told her, but it was something that was probably inevitable. She did not like the idea of losing her privacy, but was beginning to feel that the truth was bigger than she was. As her friend advised, it was important to become visible, but–*Oliver Stone* visible?

Beverly let the idea float around for a few days, mulling over how public she wanted to be. She was happy and secure living reclusively in Ranger and did not want to be hampered by obscene or threatening phone calls. Beverly had become a serious and popular evangelist with her husband Charles. She was knee-deep in rabbits, and was struggling with her Lupus. *What were the risks? Whatever happened to Jada?*

Finally, Beverly decided to commit to meeting with Stone and take it from there. *Who knows?* Perhaps the opportunity would be refreshing, but more importantly, she felt that if someone of Oliver Stone's stature had committed his talents to publicly expose the truth, she would do what she could. She wondered how the American version would be different from the British one. Beverly called Gary to arrange everything, and then started to plan what she should wear.

Charles and Beverly drove to Dallas and met Gary and his wife Karen for dinner at the West End. Afterwards, they walked over to the JFK Assassination Information Center in the Marketplace. Beverly was dressed in a black skirt, black satin shell, fuchsia blazer, and four-inch spike high heels adorned with a big pink bow. Black looked good on Beverly with her light-golden blond hair.

Walking toward the Center they passed a man dressed in a sleek black leather jacket, black pants, and sporting a bright red shirt. Beverly did a double-take as she passed him, only to find him looking back at her.

Gary introduced the Massegees to his partner and co-director at the Center, Larry Howard, his wife, Daryl, and Larry Ray Harris, the Center's Director of Research. For some reason, Larry looked familiar to Beverly.

Both Beverly and Charles were glad to learn that the assassination had become so public. Books were one thing, but an exhibit and bookstore dedicated to November 22, was something else. They were glad people like Gary and the two Larrys were dedicated to pursuing the truth behind the President's murder, but wondered why they had selected a mall like the West End Marketplace of all places. It was later explained to them about the difficulties they had trying to find anyone who would rent to them. Someone was still pulling strings.

The center was filled with photographs: Jack Ruby, Lee Oswald, Kennedy, Kennedy, Kennedy. It was difficult, but Beverly was able to block it all out. She still didn't want to face her memories of the event—not yet anyway. Larry Harris was thrilled to meet Beverly, her historical status had preceded her. He had a "million" questions, but understood they should wait until the proper time.

Beverly took a rain check on his invitation for a tour through the JFK exhibit. So they left to go meet the director.

The Stoneleigh Hotel's charm lies in part to its location in the breezeway of Turtle Creek, close to Downtown, but far from its hustle and bustle. Many new old timers who frequented Dallas thought the Stoneleigh was a well-kept secret. And thanks to the Mansion on Turtle Creek and The Crescent Court Hotel, who filtered off many of the Stoneleigh's original guests, there was usually always room.

It was late January, but still standing inside the hotel, trimmed in dusty mauve and custard-cream ornaments, twinkling all the way from the elegantly-carpeted floor to the high ceiling, was a towering Christmas tree. Just the right touch, Beverly thought, for meeting new friends.

Everyone ventured into the bar. At a table tucked in the far right corner of the room was Oliver Stone, Alex Ho, Jeff Flach, Joe Reidy and a few others.

Beverly noticed that Stone was wearing a bright red shirt, a sleek black leather jacket, and the same boyish grin she saw when he passed by her at the Marketplace earlier. Gary introduced Beverly to everyone, but it was Stone who spoke up. Raising his eyebrows in curious salutation he asked, "Have you seen any of my movies?"

"No, have you seen any of mine?" Beverly quipped in her odd sense of humor. Only Beverly knew she was serious.

Stone "broke up." He didn't quite get it.

Beverly couldn't put her finger on it, but she instantly admired Stone and they enjoyed immediate rapport. During the course of conversation, she felt like they had been friends forever. Influenced by Stone's kindred spirit and his sensitivity to everything she said, Beverly trusted him immediately and would have done anything to help with his movie.

The next day Beverly made up her mind that she was going full speed ahead with Stone's offer. The night before had been inspiring and refreshing. She wanted to become a part of it all. Everyone was so kind and enthused about the project that lay ahead of them. A magical spontaneity flowed through Beverly. It was more than being a part of Hollywood. It was being a part in the remaking of history. However, there was an unusual apprehensiveness that they were treading into an area of history that was still dangerous.

Who is more prepared to portray the "Babushka Lady" than me, Beverly thought. Why not? After all, once an entertainer, always an entertainer. Beverly convinced herself that she should audition for her own part under one of her old aliases, June Massey. It wouldn't hurt. Besides, Beverly could use the money. There was never enough money to keep up with the family's hospital bills.

Chris Nicolou stood about five-feet tall in heels. She was an explosive, spunky, *what you see is what you get* petite gal, and responsible for directing the casting in Dallas. She received June Massy's request and arranged for her to audition at her studio along with four other girls. When June Massy walked in however, Chris immediately recognized Beverly as the luminary she was, and quickly introduced herself. Beverly was a little disappointed that she couldn't do the reading anonymously.

Looking around the studio, the reality of what Beverly was attempting slapped her in the face, but did not shake her unbending confidence. Under the circumstances, everything went smoothly, considering that Beverly was recovering from pneumonia and wasn't able to perform at her best. Chris did not want Beverly to leave with high expectations, so she mentioned that Mr. Stone might have already hired a "star" to play her in the movie. Beverly felt complemented that her role was important enough to merit that type of status, but curious as to why, and who? If he had already made up his mind to use someone else, then why go to the trouble to have others audition?

Regardless of their intentions, Beverly left a portfolio of her career for Chris to give to Stone. It presented an overview of her talents and accomplishments, and contained a tape recording of her singing. The thought of someone beating Beverly out of playing herself was bizarre. How can someone be more you than yourself? *How can someone absorb your life by reading a script and do a better job?* When Beverly left she felt that her chances were nil. However, she was going to pursue the part.

Chris called Beverly back to the Stoneleigh to read for Stone and a couple of other people. The hallway on the forth floor where the readings were taking place was a mad house, crowded with wanna-be's and sure-to-be's. Hopefuls were busy glossing over scripts, mumbling to themselves, fretting, smiling, fuming, crying. People were pacing, walking up and down, up and down, standing up, sitting down, standing up.

"Next!"

Once again the irony of auditioning for a role built about herself was awkward, yet, while Beverly gave it her best, she did not feel the part was hers and knew Stone wasn't going to lead her on. After her reading, Stone was noncommittal about her part, but eager to have Beverly on the set. "Would you like to work for me as a Technical Consultant?" he asked. Beverly agreed immediately and assumed that his request meant a "no" to her chance to play Beverly Oliver. Stone walked Beverly down to meet his production manager, Clayton Townsen, and explained to him his desire to hire her as a technical advisor. Mr. Townsen was agreeable and Camelot Productions had the "Babushka Lady" on the payroll.

Soon after the cattle call was over and the initial hysteria left town, Beverly wrote Stone a letter explaining how nervous she was at her audition but how prepared she was to play herself. Stone wrote her back in a short sincere letter explaining that her role had been given to a "star." He convinced her that for realism and authenticity, it would be better if a younger person played her part. He also reminded Beverly that he was just as nervous as she was.

CHAPTER TWENTY-SIX

Action!

Stone introduced Beverly to Lolita Davidovich who was given the part of playing the Babushka Lady and Beverly couldn't have been more pleased. He asked Beverly to spend a few days filling Lolita in on her life, and how to act like herself. *How does one teach someone to be you?* "How are you going to make this petite Canadian red head look and sound like a big blond Texan?" Beverly asked with raised eyebrows.

Stone cocked his head, looked Beverly squarely in the eye, and grinned. "That's your job."

Beverly liked Lolita a lot; she was bubbly, easy going, and like two silly teenagers, they sat cross legged on the bed swapping stories about growing up: little girl stories, big girl stories. Stories with laughter, heartache, pain, joy and horror.

Before filming started, Lolita made a quick trip back to California, and when she returned, she brought Pebbles an entire gift bag full of creative art presents and a copy of her latest movie *Blaze*. Beverly felt honored that someone spent quality time thinking about what a child with special needs might want. She remembered how excited Jack Ruby became when he bought presents for children he didn't know.

During rehearsal week, two weeks before filming, Stone was standing behind the pergola on the north side of Dealey Plaza and motioned Beverly to join him. Standing next to Stone was an ordinary-looking man who was paying no particular attention to anything, but absorbing everything. He was clean, unshaven, decked in old faded blue jeans, a polo shirt, sunshades, and a gimmie cap. Pasted across his face was a cunning, half smile—half grin.

"Beverly, this is Kevin." Stone said, smiling.

Beverly did a double take. "As in Costner?"

"Yep, that's me." Kevin said, just like any old redneck from Ranger. Beverly once again felt at home. Costner exhibited a casualness that put her at ease. Beverly wasn't used to meeting so many people outside of revivals, and it was comforting that both Stone and Costner were people she could relate to.

Kevin Costner was playing the lead role in *JFK* as New Orleans District Attorney Jim Garrison. His success in many recent movies should have made his face familiar. But under the circumstances, Beverly thought he looked just like any old redneck from Ranger, albeit a good-looking red neck. Introducing people to Kevin must have been a "kick" for Stone. Watching and judging people's reactions, especially women. Beverly must have been a "hoot."

"Beverly, come join us, we're going up to the sixth floor," Stone said, thinking she would be happy to tag along, as everyone took flight up the stairs of what once was the Texas School Book Depository. But she wasn't.

"No, I just can't. I feel uncomfortable." Beverly folded her arms in refusal. She had no specific logic for not going–she simply was not emotionally prepared. Bob Hayes, the Director of the sixth floor Museum, overheard their conversation and walked over. He was introduced to Beverly and invited her personally as his guest, but the look in Beverly's eyes was steadfast. She wasn't going anywhere.

"Listen, I'm sorry Mr. Hayes. I don't feel like going. I haven't even been through the JFK Center exhibit, and they are my friends," she said pointing over to Larry Howard. Beverly took a seat on the porch as everyone scuttled off. It wasn't long, however, before Larry came back and told Beverly that Kevin wanted her to come up. That did it. Beverly really wanted to be included and it was this last invitation that turned the tide.

Beverly followed Larry, taking the elevator to the sixth floor where she was greeted by Kevin who gave her a hug for coming up. Everyone was deeply engrossed in the exhibit as they wound their way through the labyrinth of photo and film presentations, following President Kennedy and his wife and their fateful trip to Dallas that November.

Beverly avoided looking at any of the exhibits, but over her left shoulder, she saw it–the boxes, arranged in neat stacks as to block the view of anyone accidentally intruding in the middle of an assassination. She saw the window behind it. The cold corner. The hard solid brick. The perch.

Beverly walked over to the window, her eyes fixed on Stone, who was standing by a window looking out over the Plaza . . . the kill zone.

Strangely, Beverly didn't sense any morbid or unusual vibrations near the window. No squeamish thoughts. But then again, Beverly never thought the President was shot from there. She had seen it differently. Someone might have been firing from there, but she was convinced that the shooter . . . never mind.

Everyone was still engrossed with the exhibits, trying to get a better sense of the history behind the movie. Why was the President coming to Texas? What was the weather like that day? What was the scene like at Love Field? What route did the motorcade take? What were the initial reactions to the gunfire? How did local law enforcement respond–Parkland Hospital, The Texas Theater, Dallas Police Station, Lee Harvey Oswald, one rifle, three bullets? No matter how long everyone stared at the photographs, it was unbelievable that the truth about the assassination was so completely different from how it was portrayed that dark afternoon in Dallas. Beverly had had enough. She turned away from the window and waited reverently by the elevator.

A lot of people wanted to visit the JFK Center to see the other side of the story, the conspiracy and the cover-up, so Beverly's van was commissioned to shuttle them on the three-block excursion. Larry grabbed the keys from Beverly and scooted behind the wheel; Kevin jumped in the front seat. Beverly, Lolita, Kevin's bodyguard, and Roy Hargraves slipped in the back seat along with Ellen McElduff, who played Jean Hill. Hargraves was another technical consultant, hired for his insight into the Cuba crisis.

As they pulled up to the Marketplace, Beverly handed Kevin a Sharpie felt-tip and girlishly asked him to autograph her sunvisor. "Larry, take a picture of this because no one is going to believe that Kevin Costner actually signed my visor."

"Everyone get out, cuz I'm going to write something mushy." Kevin demanded humorously.

When Beverly saw that Kevin had written a "letter" on her visor she said, "Kevin, I wanted Oliver Stone to sign that visor, too."

Kevin snickered, "There's a little space there in the corner. It doesn't take much space to write Oliver Stone."

Once upstairs at the Assassination Center, Kevin dragged Beverly reluctantly to the back to see the exhibit, in case he might have any questions she could answer. Beverly had visited Dealey Plaza just three times since 1963. Seeing it again in large blown-up photographs taken that day was sobering. Kevin wanted to know all about it, how she got there, how the crowd reacted, what did she hear, see? And what she was thinking at the exact moment the . . . .

Beverly paced her breathing. It was difficult masking her emotions, but she had become good at it. She was excited at being part of something so interesting–but those pictures.

Kevin walked her away from the assassination photographs and pointed to a picture of gangster Frank Nitty and FBI legend Elliot Ness. "I got to kill that gangster, Nitty," Kevin remarked proudly, referring to his role as Ness in the remaking of *The Untouchables*. Beverly felt that Kevin was sincerely disgusted with what had happened to America. How organized crime had muscled its way into everything; taking what it wanted, when it wanted it. Was the Kennedy murder the same thing? Kevin was a patriot she thought. God, country and apple pie. *Apple pie . . . that's Kevin.*

Standing in front of a huge police photo of Jack Ruby in handcuffs and jail whites, Kevin asked what kind of person Ruby was. What was he like? How did he act around her? Around others? What about the time he introduced her to Oswald? Why did he shoot him? What about this Ferrie character? Was she ever scared? What does she think happened to her film?

Beverly gave Kevin a short tutorial about Jack and answered his questions. Beverly thought differently than many people about the "Why" part. She believed that Ruby's mission was to rescue Oswald and whisk him away to Redbird Airport where David Ferrie was waiting. Ruby wasn't expecting the army of reporters he saw in the basement and instead of taking him out of there, he just "took him out."

"Jack had the tip of his right index finger bitten off in a fight, or so he told me." Beverly added. "Someone was trying to convince me that the reason Jack held the gun the way he did, using his middle finger as the trigger finger, was because his entire index finger had been bitten off-from the knuckle down. Ha! I know why Jack held the gun that way. It was an assassins grip. His index finger was pointed straight along side the barrel, like the old gunslingers. It was a fast way to point the bullet at whoever you were shooting. I should know, Jack taught me how to fire a gun."

Out of professional courtesy, Beverly kept calling Kevin, "Mr. Costner." which began to drive him nuts.

"Beverly, please. Don't call me Mr. Costner."

"What should I call you–Kevin?"

"No, I'd rather you call me–Darling."

Beverly lightened up. Kevin's little strategy worked.

Beverly missed the first day of filming as the cameras broke the silence of history and set the JFK grassfire which is still burning. The first scene filmed was the episode of Lee Bowers in the railroad watchtower back in the parking lot behind the fence. Bowers observed three unauthorized cars cruising the secured parking lot; he saw two men suspiciously pacing back and forth behind the fence right before the motorcade arrived. He saw them step up to the fence; some commotion, a puff of smoke, pandemonium, policemen; he saw three "hobos" get into a train car. Stone, armed with his walkie-talkie, made sure everything and everybody was in place: Bowers, the strange cars, the hobos, the policemen, the witnesses, the shooters. There was an undefinable feeling of anticipation as Stone mentally moved toward the moment that the celluloid would slip through the 70 mm spindles to record the first scene of an epic movie. More than a year's worth of study, planning, writing, rewriting, backfires, roadblocks, progress, was now coming to fruition.

Stone called Larry Howard up to the director's perch in the tower. "Larry, I wanted you to be here and look through the camera as we start to roll this film. We're making history."

"Action!"

Technical Consultant, was a big word for Beverly's responsibility, she thought. She was to make herself available at all times in case Stone or someone needed a quick answer or verification on the accuracy of something. There were no guidelines for her to follow; no persons to report to; no expectations other then to stay close and away from the camera's line of fire.

Dealey Plaza was alive with action, and full of yesterday. The City of Dallas granted Camelot Productions the exclusive use of Dealey Plaza and the Sixth Floor of the School Book Depository, so everything was vintage 1963. The Texas School Book Depository even bore a 1963 facelift, all except the Hertz sign. The trees lining Elm Street were trimmed to their original height; vintage lamp posts were placed in position; the Stemmons Freeway sign seen in Zapruder's film was reconstructed, everything was all too hauntingly familiar. At the close of her first day watching the production, Beverly became keenly aware that there was no way on earth she could have relived the assassination, playing herself in front of a camera. No way.

Beverly lingered behind the short brick wall in front of the Depository waiting for the motorcade to crank up. She had been readying herself for weeks to be able to watch the scene, repeating to herself that it was only Hollywood.

For twenty some odd years Beverly avoided the Plaza, taking every way she could around it. But there she was in a realistic remake of her worst nightmare, November 22, 1963.

Suddenly, the sound of the motorcycles roared awake, trumpeting the start of what was going to become the most realistic, comprehensive recreation of the motorcade to ever be staged. Beverly could hear the powerful engines revving-up over on Main Street, waiting for the signal to begin the procession. The loud noise filled the Plaza and everyone within earshot with surreal anticipation. Chris looked over at Beverly. She sensed something was wrong. "Beverly, are you sure you're going to be all right?" Chris asked, affected by the swelling of Beverly's sorrow and again realizing that the pain would always be there for her.

"Sure." Beverly answered bravely, thinking she would be.

"Action."

When the motorcycles made the 90 degree turn onto Houston Street, Beverly felt queezy. As the caravan moved closer she could see the waving hands, hear the crowd cheering. She looked up at the sixth floor window of the School Book Depository and saw a rifle barrel; she glanced over toward the picket fence, knowing what was . . . waiting. When the procession made the wide fateful turn onto Elm Street, things worsened—Beverly bolted for her van. All the heartache, anger, and sadness, knotted in her stomach and churned in a sickening feeling. When the gunshots popped, she lost it. Nothing could have desensitized Beverly, or the other witnesses, for the remaking of the Dealey Plaza scene. Nothing. Henceforth, someone always made sure Beverly was notified before the filming of the head-shot sequence began. She could not bring herself to stand there and watch it. The exploding mechanism employed in the scene was too real, Larry told her. Too real!

After a few days of filming in Dealey Plaza, Beverly finally mustered enough fortitude to leave her secure area behind the short wall and walk back behind the picket fence. She was drawn to the area, not knowing why or what to expect when she walked right smack into the middle of one of her other nightmares. There, dressed in the dark blue uniform of a Dallas Policeman, was Richard Rutowski, playing the assassin behind the fence. He had a rifle. She had the memories.

Oliver Stone was honored by the Film Director's Guild as "Director of the Year" at a special affair in Dallas where they presented a screening of his movie,

Born on the Fourth of July. After seeing the movie, a touching story about personal tragedy resulting from the Vietnam war, Beverly knew she made the right decision to accept Stone's request. To Beverly, the movie proclaimed that, not only was Stone successful in maximizing the impact of his subject matter, more importantly, he was sensitive to the anguish suffered through historical tragedy. A lot of questions crossed her mind about the war in Vietnam. History wasn't stagnant; it was perpetual, something to study and learn from. Beverly wasn't trying to be philosophical about her reasoning, she was releasing her pent-up patriotism. Larry Howard had told her Kennedy wanted to pull out of the war and had already initiated a plan of withdrawal. That was one of the reasons he met his fate in Dealey Plaza. When they pulled the trigger on the President, it took the lives of 58,000 men. What a horrible thought.

Afterwards, at a cocktail party at the Adolphus Hotel, Beverly was speaking with Jane Sumner of the *Dallas Morning News,* bringing her up-to-date on Beverly's flight from the Dallas night club scene. Nearby, Stone was approached by a snide young woman who questioned his dedication to realism. "If you're such a realist," she accused Stone, "Why are you filming the motorcade scene while the trees and grass are still green?"

Stone raised his eyebrows. He knew there was a reason; after all, no one told him to spray the grass brown or remove the leaves. "Beverly." Stone motioned her over. "Why are we filming the Dealey Plaza scene with green trees and green grass?"

"Well, first of all, the trees in Dealey Plaza are live oaks and green all year long. Secondly, that particular November, Dallas had not yet had a frost and the grass was still a bit green. Sometimes we don't get a frost until late December."

Beverly commented further that even though people were wearing all-weather coats that morning, it was not cold, it was windy and it had been raining throughout the morning. Stone was satisfied and glad there was a reason.

CHAPTER TWENTY-SEVEN

The Wake-up Call

During the doldrums of filming a series in Dealey Plaza, Beverly visited with Lolita between takes. Lolita was standing directly where Beverly stood November 22. Beverly felt awkward, and her mind began shuffling between what she was actually doing to the reality of "that" day. The lady in the red coat, the man and the little boy, the man across the street standing on the wall taking pictures. These were people she repeatedly saw in her dreams and now . . . they were flesh and blood again. Looking at Lolita standing next to her, dressed in a tan overcoat, her hair bound in a babushka scarf, camera in hand—was "spooky." Beverly showed Lolita how she moved her camera to follow the President, and how she watched as the . . . then she was standing across the street on the the the concrete stairs leading up to the pergola. Strange, she thought. She couldn't remember crossing the street. Everything else was so vivid. *I don't remember walking over there.*

During filming, when they weren't busy on the set, Larry, Larry Ray, and Beverly usually stayed close together near the School Book Depository so that everyone could easily find them should there be any last-minute questions. During the fifth day of filming the two Larry's felt neglected and unofficial because they were the only ones without walkie-talkies. So, they shelled out some big bucks for two at Radio Shack only to discover they could not access the same frequency that Stone was using. They were only able to speak with one another. Stone was smart enough to have his walkie-talkies calibrated in California to keep the media spies at bay—confused and wondering who shot the President. At least they were able to keep in touch with each other and Beverly.

Beverly didn't know everyone on the set and was careful only to give information to those to whom she'd been introduced. One transient researcher annoyingly asked Beverly the same question over and over about her where-abouts late on November 21, 1963, simply rephrasing his question each time in hopes he could catch her off guard. *Wrong.* Finally, Beverly convinced the man she would not answer his question no matter how many ways he reworded it. Beverly was introduced to three researchers she felt comfortable with and learned to admire: Robert Groden, author of *High Treason,* Mark Lane, author of *Rush To Judgement,* and Jim Marrs, author of *Crossfire,* a book Larry Howard assisted with research. They, too, acted as consultants to help direct historical and theoretical authenticity. *How do you direct theoretical authenticity?*

As the movie began to take shape and its multilayered script began to develop into a complicated labyrinth of political sabotage, it was hard for Beverly not to hear more about the assassination and the many theories about who killed Kennedy. For the second time, she was confronted with information confirming everything she had thought about a second gunman being present, and that Oswald, Ruby, Ferrie, and others were all somehow connected. Outwardly, she was naive, yet interested in why Kennedy was killed; inwardly she couldn't shake the sadness. The magnitude of the conspiracy and its cover-up confounded Beverly. Listening to Groden, Howard, Harris, Marrs and others reawakened her anger. She could no longer try and push aside what she knew, or try and keep from learning more.

To avoid being directly in the line of filming, the "advisor" troops moved their base of operations from in front of the Depository to the south side of Elm Street, underneath the trees by the fountains. Just as they settled down, Beverly met a friend that she hadn't seen in years, Madeleine Brown. Beverly was thrilled to visit with her. They didn't know where to begin, there were so many things to talk about. Later, Beverly met another eyewitness, Jean Hill, who had come to the set to consult with the woman playing her role in the movie.

Wearing a bright red coat, Jean was standing at the curb a few feet away from Beverly at the time of the Kennedy's assassination. Appearing in many photographs taken at the time, Ms. Hill was referred to as, the "Lady in Red." Standing next to Ms. Hill was her friend Mary Moorman, who was snapping pictures with her Polaroid camera. Jean was in the Plaza to see her boyfriend who was riding in the police motorcycle escort.

The Warren Commission hadn't liked what the "Lady in Red" had to say, so they changed her testimony, altering it to coincide with what they wanted to hear. She was livid then, and still was when Beverly met her. "They" also tried to discredit the "Lady in Red" because she said she saw some commotion in the back seat of the Presidential car as it drove by. She thought she saw a dog sitting in Mrs. Kennedy's lap. David Belin, chief "go-for" researcher for the Warren Commission berated her and challanged everything she said. Beverly understood. Her experience with the House Select Committiee taught her that the investigation of witnessess is questionably selective.

It had been twenty-seven years since they both had witnessed the same horrific scene as they stood only a few feet from each other. Later they survived the anguish and fear of being dissenting witnesses. Now the "Babushka Lady" and the "Lady in Red" finally meet. Now, more than ever, Beverly wanted the nation to wake up to what really happened on November 22, 1963.

CHAPTER TWENTY-EIGHT

Roscoe White

Rain was falling lightly in Dealey Plaza while Kevin was filming a scene on the triple railroad overpass that spanned the three streets funneling through Dealey Plaza. In the movie, Jim Garrison was trying to get a feel for the area where Kennedy was shot. He wanted to talk to witnesses and see for himself the proximity of the witnesses to the *kill zone*. What could they have seen? What was impossible to see? Garrison wanted to see the series of turns the motorcade had to make; how close the limousine was to the School Book Depository and the picket fence area. From the vantage point on the overpass he had an excellent panorama of Dealey Plaza. A visual which he would use over and over as he listened intently to people share their story.

In this scene, Garrison was standing on the overpass with witness Sam Holland, portrayed by James Harrell, and his assistant, Lou Ivon, played by Jay Saunders. Holland remarks in his slow-but-deliberate Texas manner, "I made it very clear to the Warren people that one of those (shots) came from behind the picket fence. I heard the report and saw the smoke come from about six or eight feet above the ground, right out from under those trees. There is no doubt whatsoever in my mind . . . ."

While Kevin was busy filming, Beverly, Larry, and Cindy were playing with Lily Costner on the railway tracks behind the shoot. Larry and Beverly got into a discussion about who was behind the fence. Larry told Beverly about how a young man from Midland, Texas who had approached Larry Harris with information that his father had acted on orders from Naval Intelligence to "end a threat to National Security." He asked if the center would help prove that his father "didn't" kill President Kennedy. His father's name was Roscoe White.

Larry pointed to the area where Lee Bowers saw the two men he described and where Ed Hoffman saw someone fire a rifle and afterwards toss it to an accomplice. When police investigated the area, they found evidence that someone had been pacing for quite some time, leaving a pile of cigerette butts. They also found mud on the bumper of a car parked close to the fence as if someone had stepped on it to look over the fence.

Beverly was enthrawled with everything Larry was telling her. She had heard bits and pieces about the man from Midland while she was on the set, but still hadn't tried to string it all together.

"Well, what did you find out about the boy's father?" Beverly inquired.

"A lot and not enough." Larry hesitated. It would take the rest of the evening to explain in detail everything about the case he was still working on. "To make a long story short, we know from his father's diary, which his son had read before it was secretly taken by the FBI: that he was in the same U.S. Marine outfit as Oswald; he was classified as an expert marksman; and was supposedly working on orders from Navel Intelligence. There were two other assassins; one named Saul, another named Lebanon—his code name was Mandarin—he was employed by the Dallas Police Department, and for a short time his wife worked for Jack Ruby . . . ."

It then dawned on Beverly who Larry was talking about. He was talking about Geneva White's husband, Roscoe. Beverly had been approached on a couple of occasions about Roscoe: once by Larry Howard and Gary Shaw when she was in the hospital recovering from surgery. She was under medication and vaguely remembered meeting Larry or what she might have said. But the fact of the matter is, she knew Roscoe White only as "Geneva's husband." She did not know Roscoe. Larry's mention of the name Mandarin got Beverly's attention. She told Larry it was a name she had heard used in Jack's club the week all those strange men were in town. She distinctly remembered the word because she thought they were talking about Mandarin Duck, something she almost ordered while dining out with a friend several days before. Beverly wondered why all of a sudden everyone was interested in Mandarin Duck.

Standing near the train tracks with an overview of the area behind the fence, Beverly cringed. She had seen Roscoe near the fence soon after the shots were fired. And, he saw her. Maybe that's why she never heard from the police.

Larry also told her that a young military man standing in front of the fence heard a bullet wizz past his ear. He claimed that a policeman had grabbed a roll of film the young man had taken of the assassination and walked off with it. Beverly rememberd the young man from *The Men Who Killed Kennedy.* She wondered if he was the man she had seen up by the fence before the shooting and if that's how the FBI might had learned of her film. If Roscoe was in on it, and he knew she had taken a movie film, he could have directed them to her. But then, that implicated the FBI. But that was fair game, because the agent who took the film was known to have a questionable relationship with Carlos Marcello. Beverly did what she didn't want to do. She became involved in trying to figure out the entire mess.

Larry told her that they found among Roscoe's possessions a film cannister matching the right description, and written on a piece of tape stuck to it was the word military man. It was the correct vintage, but when they had it developed, it was spoiled.

Larry wanted to learn what Beverly knew about Roscoe and was sorry that his visit with Beverly in the hospital turned out to be a dead-end. Now, it was beginning to make sense. Beverly's identification of Roscoe by the fence tied up one huge loose end–he was in the area. Not a block away, not fifty-feet away, but right there.

Lily became bored, so Larry invited Beverly and Cindy to walk over to visit the JFK Center at the West End. Beverly baited the hook by telling Lily about all the arcade games and how much fun she could have.

Lily's eyes lit up, "OK, OK, Lets go."

Larry and Cindy took the elevator up to the Center while Beverly and Lily walked down the stairs to "tilt" for some arcade action. A "zillion" quarters later, Beverly was afraid that Cindy might be getting concerned about Lily's being gone so long. After all, Beverly was sure they weren't in the habit of letting her race off with people they hardly knew; so she and Lily started up the stairs.

On the way out of the arcade, Beverly bought Lily a white puppy puppet which Lily named, Lolly-pup. Being an accomplished ventriloquist, Beverly was able to make Lolly-pup come alive for Lily. Lolly-pup "gabbed" all the way up to the third floor. Lily listened intently as Lolly-pup told her all about armadillos. Beverly had a soft spot for little girls, and Lily stole her heart.

The rain had stopped and it was time to go back to the Plaza and check on "Dad." Leaving the Center, Lily was holding tight to Beverly with one hand and to Lolly-pup with the other.

"You are the prettiest movie star I've ever seen." Lily shared with Beverly as she looked upwards to her new friend.

"Oh, Lily. I'm not a movie star." Beverly said, feeling a rush of joy.

"Well, what are you?"

"I'm just a Mommy."

"Well, you are the prettiest Mommy I've ever seen!"

Beverly looked over at Cindy and felt that without a doubt, she must be the exception.

Kevin wanted to meet Jack Shaw, Roscoe White's pastor, to whom Roscoe gave a deathbed confession that he had killed people on both foreign and domestic soil for his country, thus lending credence to the diary that he was a military assassin. Jack Shaw was teaching Sunday School at the First Baptist Church in Dallas, and interestingly, Pebbles' physician, Dr. Billy Arant, was in Jack's class.

Beverly called Dr. Arant to get Shaw's number. She then called Reverend Shaw, asking if he'd meet her and Larry Howard at the JFK Center to drive over to the hotel for dinner with Kevin Costner. He agreed. Costner's wife Cindy and daughter Lily were there when they arrived but they didn't join in for dinner.

Kevin asked Reverend Shaw more questions about Roscoe than he cared to answer. How did Roscoe die? What about his covert activities? Shaw seemed quite nervous, but Beverly couldn't tell if it was due to meeting Kevin or because of the subjects being discussed. Larry listened intently for new information about Roscoe.

Throughout the attempted discussion, it was hard for Beverly to keep her attention at the dinner table. She did not like discussing Roscoe White. There was something sinister about the man that frightened her. Instead, she focused on watching Cindy playing with her child. Beverly was developing a growing admiration for Cindy Costner that grew beyond the fact she was Kevin's wife. She admired Cindy for her simplicity. Cindy glowed on the outside from a rich spirit radiating inside. Beverly wondered how hard it would be married to a mega-star like Kevin. How does Cindy maintain her own identity and self-worth and carry the responsibility of rearing three gorgeous children in a normal environment? Beverly was impressed with Cindy's success. Cindy was truly—a mega-mom. Soon, the conversation took a turn and Kevin started talking about his family.

"How did you meet Cindy?" Beverly asked Kevin.

"She was *Snow White* at Disneyland." Kevin gleamed.

"How did you get up enough nerve to ask Snow White out for a date?"

"Easy," Kevin smiled, "I was her *Prince Charming.*"

Beverly thought of the irony of Kevin and Cindy's relationship. Every woman would think that Cindy is the luckiest woman in the world to be married to Kevin. Beverly felt just the opposite. Isn't Kevin blessed to have found and married a person so spiritually rich and beautiful as Cindy?

To make her commute to the set a little easier Beverly stayed downtown at the Plaza of the Americas Hotel. The morning after her dinner at the Costners, and before she had a chance to wake, Beverly's telephone rang.

"You've already been told once to keep your mouth shut. Why won't you listen?" The caller demanded in a deep whispery voice. "You might want to know that Larry Howard, the man you're placing your confidence in, is with the CIA . . . ."

"Who is this?" Beverly asked, thinking perhaps it was a joke. "Who is this?"

She hung up when they wouldn't answer her. She thought they would call back and explain the rouse, but when they didn't, she called down to the hotel operator. She told Beverly she hadn't placed any outside calls to her room. The call came from inside the hotel. Beverly still thought one of the boys was pranking with her and decided not to let it bother her, until the next day when she heard that Oliver Stone also had received a threat, which included the same comment about Larry Howard and threatened to throw Oliver out of the fourth floor of the hotel. (Someone didn't want the movie to be produced.)

"The idea of Larry being a CIA agent is preposterous," Beverly thought. "Or is it?" Beverly was too new at this game, where things seemed to be different than what they really were. Who were the good guys? The bad guys?

Never being one to sit around, Beverly approached Larry with the accusation.

"Beverly," Larry said. "If I was with the CIA or FBI or anybody who feared what you might have to say, I'd have gotten rid of you long ago. Be serious."

Beverly buried her thoughts and hoped she wouldn't get anymore calls.

CHAPTER TWENTY-NINE

Carousel Club: Rewind

The day was over and so was Beverly's job with Camelot Productions. Clayton had told her earlier that since her part was finished she wasn't needed on the set any longer. Everyone was standing outside the bar area in the hallway saying their "good-nights," Beverly was saying her "good-byes." Beverly stuffed her melancholy inside and left to go back up to her room when she passed Stone and Alex coming out of the elevator. Beverly sadly said good-bye and thanks, holding back some of her emotions. It wasn't easy.

"What do you mean good-bye? Where are you going?" Stone asked, quite perplexed.

"Clayton told me you didn't need me anymore."

"Wait here for a minute, I want to check on something." Stone said. Beverly didn't know what he was up to, but wasn't going to argue. Stone darted off.

Ten minutes later, Chris came down and approached Beverly, "Mr. Townsen asked if there is a possibility for you to stay on a few more days?" Of course she could. (She was hoping they'd ask.)

Beverly was offered the small part of a cocktail waitress in the Carousel Club scene and excitedly accepted the offer. *If Jack only knew that, finally, I would be working at the Carousel.* Stone asked her to work with the three strippers, teaching them how dancers worked the stage back in 1963. She agreed, as long as she wasn't given any screen credit. She could see a Baptist preacher's wife getting credit for choreographing the "strippers." Stone laughingly agreed.

The week before filming the club scenes, Beverly worked strenuously with the girls, developing their skills in the art of strip-tease. Most of the girls didn't know the old art of stripping. After doing a little research for her new job as a choreographer at a local gentleman's club, the *Cabaret Royal*, Beverly learned that 1990's girls do two routines very well: with clothes on-with clothes off. The bump and grind had become passé. They became more proficient in dancing and acrobatics instead of mastering the tease in shedding their clothes. Little by little. A peek here, a peek there. They'd learn.

As a personal tribute to her missing friend Jada, Beverly wanted desperately to help a young dancer named Carolina McCullough capture Jada's essence. Beverly became sentimental as she told Caroline about Jada and how she controlled an audience. The only film of Jada was a poor quality, low budget film titled, *Mondo Exotico,* about a young girl deciding to travel to the big city, and eventually becoming an exotic dancer. But for Beverly, that wasn't enough. Beverly wanted Caroline's performance to be her own tribute to Jada. She wanted Caroline to become Jada incarnate: the sizzle, the animalism, the magnetism, growling, panting.

Somehow, Jada's disappearance was harder for Beverly to understand than the President's death. *Did she just get in the way? Was she dead or somewhere hiding? Why doesn't anyone know where she is?*

The night before the actual filming of the Carousel Club scene, Beverly and Caroline were working hard on old fashion bump and grind routines to of all things a song called *Tequila.* It was tough. They worked long into the early morning then decided to give the dance a tryout on the runways. The new Jada took stage, the music cranked up, the crew woke up. They loved it. For that short little moment, caught in the twilight of make-believe, in all her radiant glory, a little known legend came back to life.

Morning came early, especially for Beverly. She hated mornings to begin with but after only three hours sleep, you can imagine. However, once awake she was ready to get on with the big day.

The club set was buzzing. Movie extras, dressed for a 1960's cocktail party, were making small talk to clutter the background with laughter, whispers, secrets and invitations. Beverly thought if Jack Ruby were looking down, he'd be proud of the way Camelot had chosen to portray his club, the Carousel. It was finally a joint with class. Just what Jack always wanted. Maybe it was easier to make a place look "classy." It would have been impossible to recreate the Carousel that Jack had personalized.

Beverly was on the run trying to get her girls ready, not to mention that waitress they hired. Here . . . there, that way, this way, up–down. Stone was exercising his walkie-talkie privileges by calling for Beverly again and again. Then he had the audacity to ask why she wasn't in wardrobe. Men! She thought.

No sooner was Beverly in wardrobe than she was paged again. *This must be important, pulling me out of wardrobe. Something must be wrong.* They were filming the scene where Beverly is confronted by the two FBI agents who take her film. She still needed to get dressed but she wasn't about to keep the director waiting.

Rushing frantically to the set where they were filming, Beverly started thinking about the FBI and how she really believed that they were going to return her film to her. *How did they know I had it? What did they do with it?*

Stone was standing in the hallway pointing to Lolita. "Beverly, is this the color of the makeup kit you had that night?"

"Oliver," Beverly began, controlling her temper. "There are only three people who know what color my makeup kit was: Regis Kennedy, his sidekick and me. Yes, white. That's the color it was. And please don't ask me why I'm not in costume!"

Beverly was never one to be late. Years of working on the stage, whether at the Colony Club, the Chateaubriand, or one of countless churches, Beverly was always ready to go. But that day, she had too many distractions. *It'll take me five minutes to finish my hair, five minutes to get on my . . .* whoa! Beverly was suddenly airborne. Her right shoe hit something slick pummeling her down the stairs, landing on her knees. She was in pain. There was no one in wardrobe to help her so she managed to get up and struggle back to her van to get the dress and shoes she selected for her waitress scene. There was no way for her to hobble back to wardrobe to have her dress "approved." What's the sense anyway? Beverly was part of the 60's, she knew what kind of clothes waitresses wore. Besides, there wasn't anyone there she reminded herself.

Luckily, Stone was standing in front of the Honey Wagons. Still wanting to follow protocol Beverly asked, "Oliver, you're the boss, can't you approve this wardrobe?" They were short of time and Beverly knew her outfit was a good choice. There shouldn't be anything for him to worry about. But that's what a perfectionist like Stone does.

"OK," he quipped. "But hurry up!"

Beverly hurried, aching knee and all, got dressed and was back on the set, taking a seat on a bar stool just in time for Joe Ready to yell, "Action!" It was Beverly's turn. She picked up a tray of drinks and headed over to serve them to Ruby and his friends who were sitting at a table directly in front of the stage ramp. Ruby was engaged in light conversation with David Ferrie and Lee

Harvey Oswald, when Beverly Oliver walked up and was introduced to the two men. "Beverly I'd like you to meet my friend Lee Oswald. He's with the CIA" (Beverly already knew David Ferrie), Ruby said as he pulled out a chair for Beverly. Smiling as bright as a neon light, Beverly joined in the smoky talk of a typical evening. Beverly, the waitress, set the drinks around the table and when she gave Beverly Oliver a shot of Tequila, she flashed back to herself twenty-eight years earlier. Actress Lolita was a mirror image. Beverly serving Beverly. She couldn't look at Lolita anymore. 1991–1963. Joe Pesci and Gary Oldham broke character. They blew their lines.

"Stone. That's nothing but a mind blower!" Pesci chortled. They did another take. Another and another.

Between takes, Darla, Camelot's set nurse, kept Beverly's swelling knee packed with ice. Otherwise, Beverly would have missed something she had worked so hard to be a part of. She was extremely grateful to Darla. More than she could express.

The hard work paid off. Caroline was Jada . . . beautiful, gone Jada. For one day, the Carousel Club was back. Anthony was behind the bar, Jack was Jack, talking that talk. The club was alive with mischief and the sound of clinking glasses, racy conversations and half-naked girls.

(Months later, all but ten seconds of Jada and all of the waitresses would end up as celluloid clips curled in forgotten frames in the editing room. That's Hollywood!)

CHAPTER THIRTY

It's A Wrap!

The next day was the last day of filming in Dallas for Camelot. It was May 17, 1991. The original filming of the graveside scene was scheduled for Washington, D.C. but was moved up to be filmed in Dallas. With a simple addition, Lee Park was transformed into Arlington National Cemetery. Lee Park is a tribute to the gallant men who gave their lives for the Confederate Army during the civil storm that raged across America. High on the hill was a replica of General Robert E. Lee's old home which stands close by the Kennedy grave.

A solemn and forlorn Jim Garrison stood at the graveside looking down at the flickering flame, the eternal symbol for the man John F. Kennedy. A man strong in his conviction for world peace. A man who recognized that his country must think anew and set new world standards for racial harmony.

Ironically, a man, looking like Martin Luther King, approached the gravesite with a young boy, taking a place in front of the gravesite beside Kevin. Then, softly floating on the spring breeze wafting through the park, a special song took everyone's breath away, sending tears streaming down their cheeks. *Has anybody here seen my old friend John, can you tell me where he's gone? There's been lot of freedom, now it seems the good die young, Abraham, Martin and John* . . . .[1]

In a tearful moment, Beverly came to terms with her own loss and was finally able to bury the slain President, whose memory cried so often in her heart. It was a healing process which had taken many years to fulfill.

The hotel had put on its evening dress for a wrap-party. Like everything Oliver Stone commandeered, the affair was elegantly detailed, great food, great music.

Beverly walked out onto the balcony overlooking a hot Dallas neon skyline and her old Skynight Club next door. The memories came flooding back; memories of George that she had buried long ago. My, how things have changed she thought. George holding a gun to her head, pulling back the trigger; George pumping her little veins full of dope; George running off on another "hit." And now, radiant with love and hope, Beverly was standing on a balcony with Oliver, Kevin and others. People she had grown to care for.

Beverly was experiencing a sequel to her emotions, needing to say good-bye once more. The crew was heading to New Orleans and taking their stardust with them. Good-bye to Oliver Stone, good-bye to Kevin Costner, to Alex Ho, to Joe, Chris and Darla, and all the Camelot production staff and crew –especially Jeff Flach, whom Beverly had grown to admire and respect. He was an honest, down-to-earth human being. She didn't know if their lives would ever cross again. She hoped they would. When Camelot came into town they brought movie magic and Beverly realized that when they left the next day they would take it with them. *Parting is not sweet sorrow. Nine weeks of bonding does not make saying good-bye easy.* (Maybe it was for Hollywood, but not for Beverly.) Beverly left the party early; the pain in her knee was increasing as was the sorrow in her heart.

Awaking the next morning, Beverly could not stand on her leg. It wasn't working. *Thank goodness I packed the day before.* She mumbled to herself. Again she tried to stand thinking it was just morning stiffness, but it was more than that. Beverly finally realized that her knee might be seriously injured. Calling down to the production office, she told Lee Ann that she was immobilized and needed to see a doctor about her knee as soon as possible. Lee Ann sympathized with Beverly and said she would call the set doctor, Dr. Chris Renna, immediately.

Shortly thereafter, Dr. Renna came to the hotel and checked Beverly's knee. It was red, swollen and very painful. Shaking his head he left and went down to the drug store for some pain medication and anti-inflammatories. Beverly you need to get home, pack your knee in ice and stay off it."

Beverly had only one problem facing her–going *home* required a short drive of only 125 miles, with a clutch, and she knew her knee wasn't going to cooperate. But, leave it to Doc. First he drove by his house to get Beverly a leg brace; then with his wife Belinda following he drove Beverly to the highway, aimed the car in the right direction, minimizing the need for her to shift gears. "Beverly, I recommend that you see an orthopedic specialist. You'll probably need surgery."

Beverly looked at her knee. *What a problem you've been. Why won't you get better?* The thought of surgery didn't appeal to Beverly, but it had to be done. Other than the infection which settled in her knee, the operation went well. Beverly looked at her knee again. Another week in the hospital, all because of a stupid little fall while rushing around. Stupid little fall, crude little infection. Big bills.

Pebbles was concerned that their planned trip to Florida would be in jeopardy due to her mother's knee problem. But Beverly wasn't going to let that happen. Not only were they going to Florida, Beverly made arrangements for them to drive through New Orleans to visit the Camelot people while they were filming there. Christina Hare was very accommodating and arranged for Beverly and her family to stay at the same hotel with the same Camelot discounted room rate. Christine also asked if Beverly would stay for them to film her testimony for a documentary that was being made about the filming of *JFK*–the real events and people behind the assassination. Beverly was thrilled to oblige. The thought of getting to see everyone again helped her recovery.

NEW ORLEANS

Camelot was busy, busy, busy in New Orleans. Most people in America, including Beverly, didn't know that much of the drama of the Dallas tragedy was staged in New Orleans and that it hosted the only trial bringing someone before the courts for conspiracy in the assassination. The names of David Ferrie, Clay Shaw, and Guy Banister were going to be discussed across the dinner tables all around the world.

Oliver Stone received most of the "heat" from the media about his story because of the Jim Garrison connection. Utilizing artist's privileges, Stone took information uncovered by a variety of researchers throughout the twenty-plus years of investigation and rolled them under the mat for Jim "Costner" Garrison to find. True, there were peculiarities about Garrison, and his investigation into the assassination raised questions. But, Stone said that he was presenting his story from the Garrison perspective, not because of the quality of his findings, but from the human interest standpoint of one routinely investigating the assassination from a unique perspective–someone who finds links to a conspiracy network with global implications.

Stone said that he wanted John Kennedy to be the focus of the film and not Garrison, so he didn't create a controversy around Garrison. Stone just wanted to use Garrison's investigation as the "narrative framework" of the film. Unfortunately, the media sharks went after Stone through Garrison with a technique used for a long time in the research community. If you have trouble with someone who is too close to the truth, find a weak spot to discredit him so that when the truth comes out, it too will be tainted.

Filming

In the original courtroom where Jim Garrison prosecuted Clay Shaw twenty-some odd years ago for conspiracy to murder John F. Kennedy, Kevin Costner was in the middle of his most intense, climactic scene. Garrison had finally brought his investigation to a hurried close and it was time for America to learn that it had been hoodwinked. Fingers were crossed that the evidence didn't fall apart or that key witnesses would still be around to testify. After all, Ferrie wasn't. And oh, boy, what he could have offered, if he told the truth. The opening remarks, presentation of the facts, the evidence, the closing arguements. Garrison's case was weak but his sincerity was unshakable. While he was on the right track in trying to bring Kennedy's killers to courtroom justice, he stepped out of bounds, many people thought, by ignoring what seemed to be an obvious connection to the New Orleans Mafia. A saint, a sinner. The D.A. had too much going against him—the perpetrators, the government, the media.

The courtroom was small and well-secured for the filming of the final courtroom scene. Beverly asked Kevin if her husband and children could go on the set to watch. "Come on in. I want you to watch me film this scene. Stay out of camera range."

Kevin absorbed everything around him as he launched into Jim Garrison's summation. The inflection in his voice was fractured with sorrow but forceful and driving.

Between takes they met and visited with Tommy Lee Jones who played the accused conspirator Clay Shaw. His performance "blew Beverly away." He played it with such gritty class. *And he's a Texan.* Beverly also met Sparky, Jim Garrison's son, and gave him two pictures she had taken of his father on the set in Dallas. His father, tongue in cheek, played Commissioner Earl Warren in the movie. Sparky told Beverly that his father was in the hospital intensive care unit but was stable. "Why don't you go see my dad?" Beverly knew that only family members would be permitted and declined his suggestion. She regretted that she would not get to see the big man again and silently said a prayer for his recovery.

Kevin made sure to have his picture made with the girls and to visit with Beverly. (Pebbles didn't quite know how important Kevin was until she saw *Robin Hood* later.)

Once back in the van Beverly looked up at the sunvisor and remembered something she had left undone. Stone had another autograph to sign. The novelty of having Kevin and Oliver sign them was silly and she knew it, but who was keeping score? She spent a lot of time in her van. Hopefully, it would make those long treks into Dallas shorter.

The documentary interview was filmed without any complications. Beverly answered the standard questions about where she was standing, what she saw, and who took her film. No one ever asked her how she felt about losing Kennedy as a President or who she thought was responsible. Once again, she was faced with good-byes. Once was hard enough. Twice . . . thrice.

Stone had the last good-bye. As Beverly went to check-out, Camelot had "comped" the bill. Furthermore, their company had taken care of all her medical expenses. Beverly was impressed that there was a group from Hollywood that were givers–not grabbers. Oliver, Kevin and Alex.

December 20, 1991 was a stormy, rainy night. Texas was dumping buckets of the wet stuff on North Park Cinema and the Texas premier of *JFK*. "Huge" buckets. Slicing through the wet deluge, large white beacons shot upwards to the low clouds. Beverly was excited. She was dressed in a black velvet bolero suit trimmed in gold braiding and multi-colored gemstones accented by a stroller-length silver fox coat. She and Charles were with their friends Dr. Harvey Johnson and his wife Fredi. Dr. Johnson was interested in seeing how the film portrayed the Garrison investigation. He was from New Orleans and had personally known Jim Garrison.

The premier was packed. Oliver Stone, Michael Rooker, and others were there. The film received a standing ovation and left its audience with a million questions.

After the premier of the movie in the lobby of the theater, Beverly was approached by a young lady. "Are you Beverly Oliver?" she asked. "I'm . . . ."

"I know who you are. You're Rachel Oswald." Beverly said knowingly.

"How do you know that?"

"Because, I've got pictures of you and Oliver Stone together taken at the Pacific Pearl Restaurant."

Rachel Oswald placed her hand on Beverly's shoulder looking her straight in the eye, "Did you really know my daddy?"

"Yes, darling. I met your daddy and never believed that he fired the shots that killed the President. If this movie does only one thing—ease your pain and suffering, then it will be worth it." Beverly could see the longing in her eyes for her dad's vindication. Rachel looked very much like her father—Lee Harvey Oswald.

1. *Abraham, Martin and John*
   Copyright 1976, Motown Record Company.

VI

CHAPTER THIRTY-ONE

The Geraldo Show

The Kennedy assassination was a hot topic and Dan Weaver's *Geraldo* team knew it. While Oliver Stone was directing his entourage around Dallas filming *JFK,* there was another crew working the same streets, sometimes following directly on the heels of the Camelot production. Director Stephen Davis however, had a considerably smaller budget and was focusing intensely on the enigma of a Dallas night club owner in a movie simply called, *Ruby.* Who was this man who killed accused assassin Lee Harvey Oswald; and, what do we really know about him and his obscure motives? This fascination with November 1963 prompted the Geraldo Rivera Show to host a segment called *The Trial of Jack Ruby.*

In March of 1992, Beverly was at the JFK Center visiting Larry when she received a call from Dan Weaver, Senior Producer for the Geraldo Show. He asked if she would be willing to come to New York as a guest for a special segment on Ruby. He mentioned the names of the other guests, but other than Tony Zoppi, she wasn't familiar with any of them. Beverly listened intently as he explained what they were trying to accomplish on the special, but Beverly wasn't interested in further publicity and quickly declined; besides, her knee was bothering her terribly and she couldn't imagine herself limping around Manhattan. She thanked him and they hung up.

Not wanting to accept "No," for an answer, Weaver called Madeleine Brown right away in hopes that she could convince Beverly to accept the offer before she left the JFK Center. She did. "Beverly, they really want you to go up there. They're very interested in what you have to say. They'll treat you like a queen. Go on, do it. You'll have a good time."

Beverly was still hesitant. "Beverly, not many people knew Jack like you did." Besides, Madeleine pointed out, it was important that the public, who hadn't yet awakened to conspiracy theories, know that people had seen Ruby and Oswald together before Ruby shot Oswald on national TV. Maybe this single fact might wake a few people up, she thought.

Madeleine was right. It was important that people know that the relationship between Ruby and Oswald was not what they were led to believe by the Warren Commission. Oliver Stone's determination and sincerity in the making of his movie came to her mind, acting as a further catalyst. It really is time for people to tell the public what they know, no matter how small our part was, Beverly thought. Perhaps after all the little stories are woven together, everyone will get a clearer picture of what happened—not the portrait that the Warren Report falsely painted. Additionally, Geraldo reached a daytime market that probably has people who haven't seen Oliver's movie.

"If they fly you up too, I'll go," Beverly decided, knowing that if Madeleine went they would make a fun time of it.

Madeleine gave Beverly Dan Weaver's telephone number and Beverly called him back. Not intending to sound pugnacious, but wanting to make sure that they were on track with each other's expectations, she explained that she would accept their invitation with certain conditions. First, she did not want to be in a position to have to defend her story; or, "I will walk off the show." Beverly said that she would answer questions truthfully and describe Jack as she knew him and events that she saw with her own eyes. Secondly, she would not discuss the night before the assassination—it was irrelevant and wouldn't change anything. Thirdly, Madeleine Brown must accompany her on the show for personal support. After all, she knew Ruby, too.

Weaver was agreeable and was more than pleased that Madeleine would be accompanying her. The "Trial" was set.

On the flight to New York three days later, Beverly ran into Zoppi whom she hadn't seen since they went out to dinner with Joe Pesci during the filming of *JFK*. Tony wanted to meet Pesci once he found out they were from the same neighborhood in New York, so, Beverly asked Larry to set it up with Pesci and he did. And, of course, Campisi's was the place.

Zoppi no sooner settled into his first class abode, reading a book, when he jumped up and went back to see the ladies in coach, holding a copy of David Shiem's book, *Contract on America*. He was raving mad. "Can you believe that they've got Jack Ruby tied to the mob?"

Beverly and Madeleine shook their heads. They weren't ready for Zoppi and thought he was coming from left field. This was not the time or place to be discussing the assassination and he took the hint, changed the subject and avoided any further discussion.

The Texas trio were received at the airport in a limousine and whisked away to their hotel. That evening Weaver brought the soon-to-be released movie *Ruby* over for everyone to watch prior to the show. The movie was just days from theaters and he felt that it was important they use it as a point of reference.

Halfway through the movie, Zoppi shows up and "pops off" again, "Can you believe that they've got Jack Ruby tied to the mob?"

"I don't have any problem with that at all, Tony." Madeleine started in on Zoppi. "Tony, you know that Jack knew all those people."

"No, that talk was a lot of crock."

Beverly guffawed. What's going on here? she thought, staring at Tony. Did we know two different Jack Ruby's? Did Jack present himself differently to Tony than he did us? Was it possible? Perhaps. Beverly didn't know if Zoppi and Jack were close or not. She never actually saw the two of them together and Jack did seem to have the ability to modify his character. For instance, Beverly knew many people remarked that Jack could get pretty rough with women, but with Beverly, he was nothing but a gentleman. Beverly was willing to give Tony the benefit of the doubt. Maybe Jack really did mask his mob life to Tony, after all it would be to Jack's advantage. Tony was the entertainment correspondent for the Morning News and it was probably better that he wasn't enlightened about Jack's ties. Who knows what Jack was thinking? But what was confusing to Beverly was what Betty had told her about Tony's alibi for Jack, the day of the assassination. Zoppi said that during that morning, just before the assassination, Jack had come to see him at his office to place an ad in the paper. Later, when Jack was being interrogated, he said nothing about seeing Zoppi that morning. Was this another example of misinformation? Did Zoppi just infer that they saw each other by saying Ruby stopped by to place an ad. Who knows?

Rabbi Hillel Silverman, Ruby's rabbi, visited Jack many times while he was incarcerated and made the statement that he believed Jack didn't have anything to do with the assassination, or he would have confided with him. Why would Jack share that information with him, she thought? Beverly always felt Jack believed he was going to walk out of that jail a free man. He never gave up hope of being exonerated and becoming the hero he thought he should become. Another confusing thing Betty had told her was that Jack visited the Rabbi the night of the assassination. Why did he do this? It was out of character from what she knew. Jack didn't frequent his worship services. Why did he go see the Rabbi then? Was he trying to get right with God before doing what he was told to do; or, was he fearful that he didn't have long to live? Beverly struggled with these thoughts. She wasn't sure if she wanted to know the answers. Still, it was puzzling that Zoppi gave Ruby an alibi and he didn't go along with it. Where does the story of Jack Ruby end, she contemplated?

Beverly was eager to see the movie and determine for herself how much of what she heard through the grapevine was true. She was moved by Danny Aiello's performance. He did a superb job of bringing out Jack's volatile personality, including his dark side. Aiello's portrayal on screen brought Jack back to life and the way he barreled his way through that short chapter in her life, taking time to be sweet and sensitive; his anger, his intensity, the softness, the occasional smile. Yeah, that was Jack. But as the storyline developed, Beverly shook her head at some of the inconsistencies and became quite irritated with the character Candy Cane in the movie, portrayed by Cheryl Fenn. Ms. Fenn was beautifully vivacious and curiously familiar. Had someone been reading Beverly's diary? Candy Cane was this chance character that arrived downtown via bus, accidentally meeting Jack Ruby; they dined and chatted together; she got a job as a singer; she and Jack became close friends and traveled together when he had business in Las Vegas and New Orleans. And strangest of all, she sang Beverly's songs, almost in the same order. How did someone know all of this? She had never told her story to anyone. And, there were never any films made of her performance that she was aware of. As dark as the club was, it would have required too many lights and she would have known they were filming. Candy Cane wore her hair in a bobbed flip the same way as Beverly. She walked the same route from the club parking lot; and stood in the exact same spot in Dealey Plaza filming the assassination.

Dan became sensitive to Beverly's escalating anger and was surprised when she informed him that she had already contacted an attorney about her rights to her own story. Weaver was quick to arrange a meeting between Beverly and the Ruby scriptwriter, Steven Davis, for lunch at The Plaza Hotel the next day. He didn't want anything to go wrong during the show.

"Beverly, I wasn't writing that part about you. When I originally wrote the manuscript, it was for a play of mine called *Love Field*. I didn't know that the

'Babushka Lady' had been identified,." Steven Davis said, trying to explain where his character Candy Cane came from.

"Then how come her hair was the same color as mine? How come she wore it the same way as I did? She even looked like me! How did you know I was one of Jack's good friends—who started out as a dancer in an amateur hour—ending up as a singer. How did you know what songs I sang? Ninety percent of that character is me!"

David tried to convince her that he just made her up. Candy Cane was a composite of several people: Candy Barr, Judith Exner, Marilyn Monroe, the "Babushka Lady" and others.

"Then either you are the biggest liar in the world or the best clairvoyant in the business. And if the latter is true, then you're in the wrong business." Beverly quipped. She wasn't prepared to go into a full blown tirade but she was "steamed." Beverly didn't deal in half-truths. They were worse than telling a lie. Both were deceitful. You cannot pick and choose which parts of the Bible are true. It's either all true or it's all false. You can't pick and choose which of the Ten Commandments God wanted you personally to follow.

Candy Barr wasn't in circulation at the time the story portrayed and she wasn't a singer. Judith Campbell Exner wasn't a singer, nor did she frequent the club or travel with Jack Ruby. As for Marilyn, well . . . Beverly left well enough alone.

Beverly was waiting with Stephen for their escort to the show; however, once Tony learned that David Sheim, author of *Contract on America*, was going to be in the same car with him and Madeleine, he took a cab instead. Beverly reminisced quietly about the time at the club Tony had introduced her to Addie Addison of United Artists. They went to dinner a few times and months later, she received a call from Addie asking if she could pick up actor Robert Mitchum at Love Field. The next day when Robert failed to show up for an interview in Denver, United Artists became worried and called Addie, who called Tony. Addie told him what alias Robert used when staying out of town and Zoppi remembered that Beverly used the alias "June Mead" so, he started canvassing the town. After who knows how many phone calls, Tony found June Mead staying at the Ramada Inn at Love Field. Mitchum made it to Denver, Beverly made it back to the club.

As a courtesy limousine pulled to the curb, Beverly was again impressed. *Geraldo has "class." There's that word again.* Beverly lightened up, she was beginning to enjoy herself. Watching the people stream by, often moving faster than the car, Beverly cleared her mind and relaxed.

Dan Weaver was waiting curbside to greet everyone and usher them past the waiting throngs to the *green room* for make-up and to wait until time for their appearance. Jack Ruby's Rabbi was there; so was Stephen Davis and Zoppi. Then as David Sheim walked into the room it became the stage for a preliminary bout between him and Zoppi. The men came close to rolling up their sleeves and taking a swing at each other.

In his book, Sheim claims that Zoppi was part of the Mafia manipulation media and an integral part of the cover-up. He says that Zoppi stuck his neck out for Ruby with alibis on several occasions that backfired. Once about Ruby's trip to Cuba and then again concerning his where abouts at the time of the assassination.

As the fireworks started, Dan came and rescued Beverly. He didn't want her to get scared and walk out. He took her back to Geraldo's dressing room.

Things calmed down and the show went before a live audience.

Every time Tony had a chance to answer, he attempted a long filibuster, defending his character and chastising Sheim for his book. Zoppi was at war. Sheim managed to remain dignified and hold to his position and his diligent research. Geraldo called them down several times to move the show along.

When the show was over, Beverly put her flats (shoes) back on. Geraldo shook everybody's hand, thanking them for coming. Zoppi complimented Beverly, saying she stole the show, then again remarked, "Beverly, I just don't believe that you saw Oswald and Ruby together at the Carousel Club."

"That's OK Tony. I know I don't believe what you have to say either, but does it have to affect our friendship?"

Beverly couldn't understand why Tony insisted on taking this stance. It was almost not worth the bother trying to understand his motive—certainly not worth an argument. By this time, through the efforts of researchers and authors like David Sheim, John Davis and Seth Kantor, the general public was fairly convinced that Ruby was connected to organized crime. She flashed back to the many times that she was in the middle of casual associations between herself, Ruby and the Mob. *Whatever*, she and Tony hugged and departed as friends.

Two weeks later Beverly received a call from Dan. He called to thank her again for joining the program and mentioned that they received more compliments from peers about the *The Trial of Jack Ruby* show than any they had done in a long time. The grassfire started by the *JFK* movie was still spreading. Beverly was glad that Geraldo was a man of his word and did not try to discuss things she wasn't prepared to talk about. He was courteous, professional, and better looking in person, she smiled.

CHAPTER THIRTY-TWO

"Were We Controlled?"

In a sad, simple but dramatic moment, the *JFK* movie brought to Beverly's attention that Robert Kennedy's murder was possibly executed by the same political octopus that killed his brother. That made what happened in Dealey Plaza all the more horrible. She knew there was a conspiracy behind John Kennedy's assassination for the simple fact that Ruby and Oswald knew each other, and, there was no question in her mind that there was a gunman firing at the President from behind the fence. Beverly thought that whoever wanted control of the country had to be just as threatened by Robert Kennedy as his brother and when the Senator seemed destined for the White House, the only course of action was one which had worked so well in Dallas.

During the thousand days of President Kennedy's tenure in office, the brothers shared a spiritual bond and political savvy. They shared the same goals, relished in the same victories, and demanded full attention from their political constituents. The missile crisis and the civil rights turmoil proved that Robert Kennedy had guts and fortitude to stand his ground and administer his power. Camelot could never be resurrected, but a single knight could carry the torch; and, in the hands of Robert Kennedy, it would only be a matter of time before the country was burning with the same desire to pursue peace among the nations and races of man, usurping the power from those who controlled it.

The chain of command from the assassins to their superiors was too interwoven and obscure for Beverly to even begin to speculate about. The many angles she learned about after watching *The Men Who Killed Kennedy* and during the filming of *JFK* were overwhelming. Even though she had her suspicions, she didn't want to be caught in the table-talk of, "Who Shot J.F.K?" However, Betty told her something she read about Robert Kennedy's assassination which frightened Beverly—the controversy concerning the mysterious lady in the black and white polka-dot dress. She was perhaps the last person to talk to Sirhan Sirhan before he pulled out his gun and killed the Senator. A diary which Sirhan recorded had led to the speculation that he had been hypnotically programmed to carry out his diabolical plan. During his interrogation, Sirhan admitted that his last recollection before his apprehension was meeting a girl in a coffee shop and handing her a cup of coffee. Then, shortly before he pulled the trigger, he was observed standing next to this same girl–who seemed to be whispering in his ear. She was wearing a black and white polka-dot dress. In the margins of Sirhan's diary he had scribbled over and over, "RFK must die . . . RFK must die." Also scrawled was a curious passage, "practice practice practice; Mind Control–Mind Control–Mind Control."

When Betty told Beverly what she had read, Beverly felt as if she had been hit by a sledge hammer. The episode with Jack about the green and white polka-dot dress had always bothered her; why, she didn't know. He bought it specifically for the party they were going to on November 21, 1963 and, uncharacteristically, went out of his way to have it gift wrapped; yet, even though he objected to her wearing it to see President Kennedy, Beverly felt at the time, that he might have been confirming that she "was" going to wear it to the parade. Betty further pointed out that the Warren Commission said David Ferrie was a practicing hypnotist, and brought to her attention that Bill DeMar who was entertaining at the Carousel Club the week prior to the assassination, was also a hypnotist.

The thought that she might have been used in the assassination plot nauseated Beverly. Could it be true? When she first heard the theory that she might have been involved because she never made herself or her film public soon after the assassination, she laughed; however, she began to question if she actually was an unwilling participant. Beverly thought about her conversations with David Ferrie and Bill DeMar. Bill DeMar–she remembered him but didn't recollect ever speaking with him, other than perhaps a hello. Neither could she think of a time she was with Ferrie that lent itself to hypnotism; but then again–was she programmed to forget? Betty informed her about the speculation that Oswald might have been programmed while he was in Russia and that even his mother, Marguerite Oswald, had concerns about his changed behavior when he came back. A book entitled, *Were We Controlled?* by Lincoln Lawrence (a pseudonym) published in 1967, stated that the author knew personally that Oswald was the subject of an advanced technique of mind control. Supposedly, while Oswald was in the military hospital under anesthesia, two control devices were covertly implanted in him making it possible for him to respond to radio transmission and ultra sonic signals. In effect, they could control programmed activities and erase the memory of the event from his conscience. This information corresponded to a CIA memo from CIA director McCone to Secret Service chief James Rowly saying that Oswald might have been "chemically or electronically controlled" during his surgery in the Minsk hospital for an adenoid operation. Oswald was in the hospital for eleven days for what should have been a three day procedure. His mother wondered how that little scar on her son's neck got there.

The Rockefeller Commission Report on CIA Activities Within the United States, released in 1975, revealed that the CIA was probing the possibilities of controlling human behavior and actively searching for a method to design a "programmed" assassin. In the book *Appointment in Dallas,* the author Hugh McDonald claimed to have a conversation with a former high ranking CIA official, Herman Kimsey, who said, ". . . Oswald was programmed to kill–like a medium at a seance. Then the mechanism went on the blink, and Oswald became a dangerous toy without direction . . . ." Kinsey further told McDonald before he died three weeks later, that "the assassin was code-named Saul" and "was hired by a private group with strong government connections."

Lawrence went on to say that Jack Ruby was also controlled; probably hypnotized by Bill DeMar while he was performing at the club. He quoted that in his psychiatric report on Ruby, Dr. Walter Bromerg noted, "Definitely there is a block to his thinking which is no part of his original mental endowment." Furthermore, McDonald referenced Ruby's comment to the Warren Commission, "Very rarely do I use the name Oswald. I don't know why. I don't know how to explain it." Was this because Ruby had been hypnotized to disassociate himself with Oswald? An interesting footnote to the Lincoln Lawrence saga, pointed out by Dick Russell in his investigation and book entitled, *The Man Who Knew Too Much,* is that Lawrence's attorney Martin Schieman was found dead right after the book was published with a bullet to the brain and a gun in his hand. And, Damon Runyon, Jr. who provided a condensation of the book for *National Inquirer* was killed by a suspicious fall off a bridge.

Further research at the JFK Center revealed that the government was interested in hypnotic techniques that would allow a subject to be secretly programmed for a specific function, then go about his daily routine until he received a phone call triggering the implementation of his instructions. Was this the case with what went wrong at the School Book Depository? Did Oswald not receive his phone call? Or, did he, or did he not see the green and white polka-dot dress when he was up there moving boxes because Beverly had worn a coat over it? If one would look directly down from the sniper's perch to where Beverly was standing, it would be directly in line with the crossfire.

The details of the government's interest and pursuit in mind control techniques were overwhelming. Beverly didn't want to listen to Betty anymore. It all seemed too preposterous; yet the thought of being hypnotized to film the assassination couldn't be ignored and struck a nerve which caused Beverly to retreat into a depression she hadn't experienced in years. The more she thought about it, the more ridiculous the thought seemed, and the more disturbed she became. If murdering the President was simply a power play for those involved, perhaps having a home movie of their victory was just part of the game.

Beverly tried to deny it, but it was obvious to Betty that she was struggling with the theory and all its implications; wondering if her writing a book was such a good idea after all. Beverly struggled with whether or not she actually wanted to know the truth behind the speculation and vetoed the suggestion to visit a hypnotist to uncover details she couldn't recall.

Beverly remembered what Larry Howard told her about his theory concerning Oswald. He thought Oswald was indeed designed to be the patsy, but several things went wrong in the Book Depository which complicated their open and shut case. The first thing which happened was that whoever was firing from the sixth floor window had his rifle jam, causing a misfire. Losing precious time, he then missed his target which necessitated that the man behind the fence finish the job. After it was said and done, there were too many bullets to account for the three shell casings laying on the floor under the window where the "single assassin" knelt. Another thing that went wrong; Oswald wasn't killed or apprehended before he left the building. Oswald was seen in the lunchroom drinking a Coke within minutes after the assassination. He seemed calm, full of breath, and appearing unlike someone who had just murdered the President, hidden a rifle, and raced down eight flights of stairs.

As the chill of winter was replaced by the tranquillity of an early spring, Beverly crawled slowly out of her depression; thinking positively again about the book and the importance of helping perpetuate the truth about the assassination. While so many things about 1963 were crystal clear, her memory of other moments was distinctly blocked. Not vague, but altogether— invisible. She thought that locked up somewhere in her mind were the answers to her questions, that for some reason, were inaccessible. For instance, there was the time that she went to see Larry Ronco, and for some reason ran from his place before she even knocked on his apartment door—scared and threatened. What did she hear that shocked her into running away, and why didn't she remember anything so frightening? Then, there was the moment in Dealey Plaza, after she stopped filming the motorcade, when several minutes later she realized she was standing across the street—not remembering having crossed it. Beverly accepted the advice that details were important to the readers who want to know everything she experienced. So she decided it was important to come to terms with everything about the assassination, including the green and white polka-dot dress. She agreed that under certain conditions she would be hypnotized to try to uncover some of her hidden memories: the hypnotist must be reputable; there must be someone else in the room to monitor the session; and the late night party in Fort Worth, the night before the assassination, was off limits—it was private and had nothing to do with the importance of the case as some researchers were beginning to speculate. That she knew, and it was nobody's business.

After making a few inquires, Beverly was referred to Dr. Michael Stower, president and founder of the Hypnosis Institute in Dallas. She scheduled an interview with him at Lombardi's Restaurant in the West End to learn about hypnosis before she made a decision. There was still part of her that wanted to know the truth, and the other didn't. Regardless of what information was gathered; if Beverly didn't know the truth she would be haunted forever by something that most likely wasn't true to begin with. (She admitted that she had felt depressed ever since Betty told her about the lady in the black and white polka-dot dress.)

Beverly and writer Coke Buchanan met Dr. Stower at the JFK Center; then they walked over to Lombardi's and sat at a table outdoors. Coke had explained very little to Dr. Stower—other than the fact that he was writing a book with a lady who witnessed the assassination of President Kennedy. Also, that they were interested in the value of hypnosis to see what information could be retrieved after thirty years of hibernation. Coke mentioned to Dr. Stower that Beverly knew Jack Ruby. The rest would be discussed at lunch. Dr. Stower said that he had never worked before with anyone on the assassination. His specialty was helping people deal with pain, both emotional and physical. There was also a fair share of people he saw who wanted to lose weight, quit smoking, study harder or find something they misplaced. Coke told him Beverly was bothered by recurring nightmares about the killing and if that was something he could relieve her of it would be valuable. The thought of going back to November 22, 1963, fascinated Dr. Stower.

When Coke introduced Beverly to Dr. Stower back at the center, he noticed a smile come across Dr. Stower's face. When they sat down with their menus, Coke found out why.

"Beverly, it's a small world." Dr. Stower said. "Coke didn't tell me your name until we were introduced at the center. I was surprised when he said the name—Bevery Oliver. It was a name I hadn't heard in years. Back in the sixties I used to cut Chris Colt and Toi Rebel's hair, as well as several of the other girls. I've heard you sing many times. In fact I knew Jack Ruby as well."

Beverly became suspicious, thinking: *If Dr. Stower knew Jack and Jack knew George and R.D. and all that gang, maybe we shouldn't be talking to him.* She asked Stower how well he knew Ruby and if he also knew George McGann; then she went down the list of names. Dr. Stower didn't think much of Jack; thought he was rudely loud—Stower didn't know the others. However, the more he talked, the more at ease Beverly became. Perhaps Dr. Stower was genuinely interested in her; not so much at uncovering lost conversations and providing detail, but in helping her come to an appreciation and understanding of how powerful her mind was, and the control it had in relieving her of the dreadful anxiety of the assassination, that followed her like an unwanted shadow.

"Beverly, what do you think hypnosis is like and what do you expect to gain from being hypnotized?" Dr. Stower began.

Beverly looked at Coke for the answer. After all, he suggested she be hypnotized. "Well, as I mentioned Dr. Stower," Coke started to explain.

"Call me 'Mike.' I'd like to know what Beverly wants out of this. This is her life and it's important that she knows where she's going and what she wants to accomplish. If I don't know what is important to her and focus on satisfying you, Coke, then I won't be doing my job."

Beverly perked up, "Dr. Stower. There are several things I'd like to accomplish. I have decided to write a book about my experiences so that people who are interested will have a testimony with as much detail as possible, even if it's significance seems trite. I want to record my story, get it behind me; then get on with my life. Oliver Stone's movie has stirred up a hornet's nest and I keep reading about the Babushka Lady, from people who have never talked to me to confirm what I may or may not have said, and I want to set the story straight. I understand hypnosis can help me recall things more clearly and that's what I want to do. I am also interested in knowing if I could have been hypnotized to have filmed the assassination for someone else and if the dress I was wearing that day could have been a visual signal, triggering a program for the assassin or assassins to fire."

"I understand. Coke also tells me that you suffer from recurring night-mares or replays about the assassination and that they keep you awake at night. Wouldn't you like to put those behind you as well?"

The thought of ridding herself of the dreams was something Beverly hadn't thought about and the purpose of Beverly's hypnosis took on an added value. If that was the only thing she accomplished, it was worth the effort. Mike handed Beverly a salt shaker and told her to grab hold of it and squeeze as tight as she could.

"Imagine you've been holding onto that for thirty years. Keep holding it. Your muscles are already getting weak I can tell. Now let go." Beverly let the shaker fall into his hand. "Now tell me what felt better: holding on or letting go?"

"Letting go." Beverly replied.

"What does hypnosis feel like? Is it like sleep? Are you afraid of someone else controlling you?"

"No, its not really like sleep. It's more like falling asleep. Hypnosis is a scary word to some people. Perhaps you might feel better if I used the words *meditation* or *alpha awareness*. Words are words; whatever you feel comfortable with. Hypnotism is not magic. It's not voodoo; and it is not dangerous. It's physical relaxation and mental concentration. You will never be unconscious. Just the opposite. You will be aware of everything that goes on. All you have to do is cooperate and concentrate on the things you want to have happen. It's simply a matter of the hypnotist and the subject working together so that a pleasant state of awareness can be brought about to help you. Hypnosis is deep mediation and is very natural. I would like to show you how it works. You should enjoy the feeling very much."

Dr. Stower was saying all the right things and Coke could tell that they were moving forward, even though Beverly said she would have to think about it some more.

It felt refreshing to be dining outdoors. There was a steady breeze and the smell of hot garlic bread made their mouths water. Everyone who walked by was smiling. Two blocks to the southwest, Elm Street passes through a small park where the camera shutters never stop.

It took only a few days before Beverly agreed to have Coke call Dr. Stower to set up an appointment, provided Coke could sit in on the session. The more she thought about the therapy application of hypnosis, the more willing she was to participate.

"Let me tell you a little about hypnosis, what it is and what it isn't." Dr. Stower began. "Hypnosis is not a truth serum. You can tell whatever you feel is necessary at the moment. If there is something you don't want to talk about, you won't, your conscious mind won't allow you. What is beautiful about the subconscious mind is that once the conscious mind is relaxed enough to say, 'OK, I feel safe now, I'll let the feelings come forward, that for whatever reasons, were kept in the recesses of the subconscious.' Some people relive an experience instantaneously, others take a few sessions to retrieve the whole picture. I don't know what will happen when we get started. Or as a recognition factor you will need a composite artist to draw a picture as you detail it or have a group of photographs from which to point out who resembles who you saw in your trance.

"Every event you have ever experienced is recorded permanently in the subconscious mind from the time you were born throughout your life. We are a compilation of all these past moments up until the present. The subconscious doesn't keep things in chronological order. It doesn't have a time space continuum; time doesn't exist in the subconscious so there is a lot of time distortion. Memories are stored according to the hierarchy of the emotion tied to the event, therefore, those events associated with much pain or fear usually are the easiest to reconstruct under hypnosis. It is easier for one to recall the first time they suffered a traumatic experience rather than a happy one; feeling bad has much more emotion tied to it than feeling good. Once we begin and start stirring up those old feelings of yours, even after the session is over, the process will continue until there is some resolve; it could happen over a few days, a few weeks, a year—we don't know. Of course the more emotion that you put into acquiring resolution the quicker it happens. For instance, if a man keeps a messy desk and is chasing some lady, they are going to put a lot more energy into catching that lady than cleaning the desk because of the emotion tied to it."

With respect to Beverly's concern about her being "programmed" to film the assassination, Mike told Beverly that logically, and in practice, it is easier to motivate someone to do something which is normal, rather than persuade them to do that which goes against their beliefs or they would resist. The same is true with hypnosis he told her. Getting someone to sing a silly song or flap the arms like a bird in public does not go against their primary instincts. On the other hand, suggesting to a normal person that she rob a store or kill someone would not work at all without the mind-altering conditioning of drugs and deprivation techniques, etc. Getting someone to watch the President when he came to town and film him with a camera that they already had would not be difficult; having them shoot at the President would be next to impossible. "Wearing a particular dress at a particular time could have been easily arranged; but logically, why would someone go to the trouble of setting up an elaborate political assassination which rested on something as weak and uncontrollable as making sure that a complicated set of sequential events happened before the shooting could take place—such as getting Beverly from Fort Worth to Dallas and then to a particular spot in Dealey Plaza while wearing a dress she wore the night before. There were too many things which could have stopped Beverly from getting to where she was supposed to be. The plan would be too weak and unreliable."

Beverly was relieved that Dr. Stower's thinking was in concert with hers. The scheme was too ludicrous and she was almost sorry she brought it up.

There were several "memory" sessions Beverly participated in to help recall specific information: her activities on November 21 and 22, the evening when she was threatened by her husband to never bring up the assassination again, her meeting with David Ferrie and Jack Ruby, and the session which follows.

Dr. Stower begins, "Relax as you've been doing and as each moment passes give your body permission to relax more completely, realizing that with each sound of my voice, as we have worked together in the past, each sound of my voice allows you to drift to a nice peaceful place, a place where you can feel safe and secure—a special place.

"I'm going to count backward from ten to one. As I say each number, allow yourself to relax twice as deeply as the previous number. In order to communicate with me, I want you to choose a finger on either hand and each time you have achieved a level of relaxation twice as much as the one before; then let that finger pop up. And to do that, subconsciously, is not even a conscience move. If that's agreeable with you, let me know now. Good. Perfect.

"I'm going to count backwards. With each number, I want you to relax yourself twice as much. Don't let your finger come up until you feel that you are twice as relaxed. And you'll find that the lower I go in the numbers, the harder it will get to lift that finger. Even just a little movement of that finger will be sufficient to communicate to me that you have been successful in doubling your level of relaxation.

"I'll begin to count now. 'Ten.' Now double your level before I go to the next number. I'll wait."

Stower then proceeded counting backward toward one, each number taking Beverly deeper into a state of complete relaxation.

"Two. Doing so very well. Go even deeper now. Now the next number will bring a very profound state of relaxation. Number 'One.' Way down . . . with each moment that passes let it take you deeper into relaxation. With each breath that you take becoming deeper relaxed. Each moment that passes will take you deeper. This is your time. It's a healing time. It's a time when you can take for yourself to reach your higher-consciousness. Begin to give yourself feelings of good health, peace of mind, peaceful, comfortable feelings. This is a time to heal yourself inside and out. Realize that from this moment on your mind is now learning much more about you; that's its function—to learn about you; learning how easy it is to relax when it's in your best interest; learning to sleep a complete night through is so beneficial for you; sleeping a whole night through is so beneficial—the mind responds, the body responds; contentment and peacefulness overtakes you. And with each moment that passes . . . you go further and further into a beautiful state of peaceful relaxation, allowing your mind to wander here . . . and there, realizing that there are some areas of your life that are very important to you; some areas are more important at particular times than others, and that others are more important at their particular time and place in your life. And for this moment, as I talk to your subconscious mind, I want you to let yourself drift back as an observer to another time—another place in your past. Allow the pages of a calendar to fall off like those in a movie. And as the pages fall off, notice that time is taking you back as an observer, simply as an observer. You are more observant—more aware about things that are important to you. And as you go further back in time, you feel even more relaxed and calm—you even feel more youthful . . . younger, as you travel back to another time, realizing something that you've been wondering about is about to reveal itself to you; that makes you a stronger and more powerful person. You are learning the power of your mind and how to utilize it to your best interest. Realizing that once you get answers to these questions, an inner peace and calm will come over you at the moment of your awareness. Whatever it is that you are about to become aware of, will bring you a feeling of peacefulness and calmness—more than any other time in your life. Going back, you visit different episodes of your life. And as you travel back, I'll remain silent for a moment. As soon as you are ready to begin uncovering information and reviewing it aloud . . . becoming aware of episode number one in your life which we talked about . . . just take your time. As soon as you get back to that day and that place of importance—just let me know and I'll wait . . . .

"OK, wonderful. Now Beverly, you have a choice. You can either get into the scene and see what happened, hear what happened, and feel what happened, or you can look at it from a slightly different perspective of your choice and observe it more clearly from a distance. If you want to participate and get inside what happened—as it happened, let me know now. If you don't, move your finger, meaning you want to view it as an observer. If that's what you want let me know now. If you want the first one lift your finger once; if you want the second one lift your finger twice. Take your time and decide which one gives you the better information. Good. Take a moment now and see what you can see, hear what you can hear, and feel what you can feel. Get inside the scene and notice if it is day or night, if you are inside or outside, if you are alone or with someone. As soon as you are ready to review out loud the events that are now taking place in your minds eye, you may do so.

"Is it day or night?"
"It's night."
"Are you inside or outside?"
"I'm outside."
"Are you alone or with someone."
"I'm by myself."
"What's going on?"
"I'm standing out in front of Larry's apartment."
"Look down at your feet. What's on them?"
"A pair of . . . black leather high heels."
"Where are you standing?"
"In front of the picture window."
"What do you see?"
"I hear voices—he's supposed to be by himself tonight."
"Listen in a little sharper."
"I can't tell who it is, but there is a crack in the window. I can see someone."
"Is it male or female?"
"It's a man."
"Sitting or standing?"
"They're standing. I can't see the one on the other side of Larry, but the one facing him is the guy that was up at the club at the party night before last. Saturday night."

"Did you meet him?"

"Yeah."

"Were you introduced?"

"Yeah."

"Listen to his name . . . watch the lips move . . . its not important, go on . . . what are you hearing . . . listen real close now . . . take your time . . . just turn up the volume . . ."

"They have a gun."

"Take your time . . ."

"I don't want to."

"Turn up the volume . . . report what's going on . . . who has the gun . . . where is it?"

"(Sigh) Roberto has the gun. It's got an ejection . . . whatever it's called . . . on the side and he's moving it back and forth and looking through the scope."

"Is it a handgun?"

"No it's a big rifle of some kind."

"Does it surprise you?"

"[Sigh] It surprises me that he's in Larry's apartment."

"What else do you hear . . . turn up the volume . . . see his lips moving . . . who's he speaking to . . . listen closely . . . who's saying what . . . who's speaking . . . who's lips are moving?"

"Roberto's."

"Listen carefully to what he's saying. Is he talking in a loud tone or a soft tone?"

"I can't really understand him."

"Can you see his lips moving?"

"Part of them . . . shooting something."

"Is anyone else responding?"

"I don't know. I can't see."

"How do you feel right at that moment?"

"Really scared. I want to leave."

"What do you do next?"

"I'm running back to my car."

"Does anyone see you or hear you?"

"I don't know."

"Is anybody behind you or near you?"

"No!"

"So no one saw you or heard you? Do you feel safer now, a little bit?"

(Sigh) *"Yes."*

"Do you remember where you were? What apartments you were at? Look at the entrance. See yourself ready to drive out. What do you notice?"

"It's out the back."

"What street are you on?"

"Off of Sylvan . . . I don't know what street I'm on . . . I just know how to get here . . . ."

"You've been there many times?"

"Just about every night . . . I don't understand . . . ."

"You don't understand? What are you thinking about as you drive away?"

"I don't know why Larry has them in his apartment."

"Did you recognize someone else there?"

"I couldn't really see him."

"Was he white or dark?"

"He's . . . he looked like the other . . . I'm not sure . . . he looked like the other guy that was there (at the club) that night . . . he has little mustache . . . I don't know . . . he's dark . . . sleezy looking . . . ."

"OK, you are driving away, thinking about who was there . . . ? "

(Sigh) *"I'm going to stop and call Larry."*

"Where are you calling from?"

"The Holiday Inn at North Central."

"What do you do next?"

"It's safe . . . I told him that I was going to come over to the apartment . . . and he tells me not to . . . he doesn't feel well and he's going to bed . . . ."

"How do you feel when he says that?"

"I know he's lying to me. I don't know why he's lying to me."

"What happens next?"

"I'm telling him to have a good night's sleep and I'm hanging up the phone."

"What do you do next?"

"I go to the bathroom . . . just off the lobby . . . and I'm getting in my car and I'm going home . . . to Garland . . . ."

"Are you still thinking what he said?"

"Umm . . . it's confusing."

"You saw him with that rifle. What's he doing?

"Pretty big rifle, wasn't it? Or was it a small rifle?"

"It was a big one . . . I don't know what kind."

"Were they looking through it?"

"Um . . . ."

"Have you ever seen that rifle before?"

"No. I've never seen a rifle like that before."

"Did you ever see it again? Take your time."

"I don't know . . . ."

"So you go home . . . ."

"Larry's a good shot though . . . he's probably just trying to buy a gun." (sigh) *"I'm home."*

"How was it you were aware that Larry was a good shot?"

"Because, he takes me shooting."

"Where do you go?"

"At a gun range off of Talley Road in Garland . . . ."

"He's pretty good, huh?"

"Uh uh."

"He's very knowledgeable (about guns)?"

"I guess. I don't know that much about guns . . . he says he is."

"So you go to the range; what do you shoot with?"

"I'm shooting with my pistol and he's shooting with some kind of rifle."

"Have you seen that rifle before?"

"Uh uh . . . No. But he always has different guns . . . ."

"Keeps them in the apartment?"

"Sometimes. He buys them . . . trades them . . . ."

"Do they usually have scopes on them?"

"Most always . . . I don't like rifles."

"Are they lever-action? Do they have a bolt on the side?"

"He's had different kinds. Most have those bolts on the side."

"So why were you surprised that he had that rifle that night you were supposed to meet him?"

"It was . . . he didn't know I was coming . . . and it's who is there in his apartment . . . ."

"That surprised you."

"I didn't know that he knew them . . . but I guess that Jack . . . ."

"You can still see Roberto, can't you? You were really surprised that he was there?"

"Yes."

"Had you met him before that night?"

"Not before Saturday night."

"Had you seen him again after that Saturday night?"

"Yeah, he was in the club; in the club sitting at the bar."

"Did he ever talk to you? Did you talk to him?"

"No. Just that Saturday night at the party after hours."

"Who was he with?"

"Just five or six guys . . . five new guys."

"Were they with any of the girls?"

"Yeah. Lynn and Cathy are sitting at the table with two guys . . . but Roberto is sitting at the table with Jack and David (Ferrie) . . . he wants a Cuban Libra drink . . . so I go fix it and I set it down . . . and he's writing his name on a cocktail napkin."

"Can you see him writing it?"

"Yes."

"And what's his last name?"

"Guzman. And he writes it over and over and over . . . and (he writes) R.G., R.G., R.G., over and over . . . and then he starts to write on the tablecloth and Jack says, 'Don't write on the tablecloth you idiot!' "

"Take a deep breath. Just relax. (Sigh) Think of beautiful thoughts of peaceful feelings of people near and dear to you . . . times of very much joy and pleasure . . . peace of mind . . . that's it . . . nice . . . feels good . . . that's it . . . in a moment I'll count from one to three and when I say 'three' Beverly, you'll return to full consciousness feeling peaceful and calm as if a load has been taken off your mind and body. You will feel lighter . . . happier than you've felt in some time . . . realizing what a wonderful, wonderful day it is now, and how nice it is to be you.

"One, coming up slowly, easily gently.

"Two, returning to full awareness feeling perfect in every way–emotionally perfect, physically perfect, mentally calm.

"Now the next number; now, you will open your eyes take a nice easy breath and have a wonderful day.

"Number Three. Open your eyes."

(Sigh)

"You're getting better."

"How's that?"

"Oh, your responses are better."

"I feel weak. That is a strange feeling. It's the feeling you get after your leg or arm has been asleep and its returning to normal . . . a tingling sensation."

"Were you consciously aware of your responses?"

"I don't know. I would have to think about it."

"Any parts that you were surprised that came back to mind. If so, which were they?"

"Seeing Roberto in Larry's apartment; why he was there."

"The party was on Saturday night—that was very clear. Which must have been the 16th and that was Monday night because I used to bowl in a Monday Late Night League and that's why I wasn't going over there that night. But the other team didn't show up, so we just bowled our three games and we were through. They had to do a make-up. So I just drove over there; Larry wasn't expecting me. Seeing that rifle scared me."

Revisiting and experiencing her feelings that day in front of Larry's apartment, Beverly realized that episode was what caused her to break off relations with him, ultimately leading to the situation in the parking lot when he pulled a gun on her. Beverly then described the other man she saw with Larry and Roberto in more detail: he was dark-eyed, had dark complexion, and had a pencil-thin mustache and receding hairline. All of the men at the club that night had some kind of accent; but not necessarily the same nationality. Guzman sounded like a Cajun.

The sessions with Dr. Stower were successful. They provided a more detailed glimpse into those moments where Beverly's life crossed paths with history. But most importantly, Beverly doesn't have the recurring nightmares of that November in 1963. Now she can sleep through the night.

CHAPTER THIRTY-THREE

The Fake Ruby?

Larry Howard always approached new information on the J.F.K. case with caution. Taking the assassination public with the JFK Center was not easy and his visibility on countless JFK Specials led to death threats, critical information being delivered, and a sampling of strange fanatics. He learned not to form an opinion until he heard the entire story. Sometimes it required a personal meeting to verify information or just to read someone's eyes and body language to see if they are telling the truth. A wild-goose chase—an incredible find. Exposed film—a missing revolver.

When the call came from *Ms. Reynolds in Atlanta, asking for his help (on behalf of *Rachel and *Jake Glickman) to identify a man claiming to be Jack Ruby, Larry was excited at the possibilities; but cautious about proceeding. As the story of Thomas Kennedy unfolded, Larry had his reservations but was convinced that if it was a hoax, someone went to a lot of trouble. If it wasn't a hoax, then it would be the greatest scoop in the world. What if?

Beverly agreed to help Larry with the Thomas Kennedy case. It was the least she could do. Larry shared with Beverly all that he knew:

On September 8, 1980, Rachel Glickman received in the mail, a press-clipping with a typed note saying: *"Gene Dunbar" Jack Ruby, real name Jacob Rubenstein (signed with secret code).* There was no return address, but a Chicago, Illinois postmark. The press-clipping was an article about the JFK assassination by Mafia figure Johnny Roselli, and his subsequent murder.

Rachel recognized the name of Dunbar as someone she and her husband worked undercover with as information couriers for President Roosevelt. This was from March of 1933 to September 1945. She also knew that Gene Dunbar was the man she saw on television who shot Lee Harvey Oswald. The name Ruby was foreign to her. The secret code was right on target. Attempts to contact

Ruby while he was in jail had been futile. She remembered Dunbar to be an extroverted individual who enjoyed carrying lots of cash and dressing like he was important. He liked to go to the front of the line whenever he could and demanded special services wherever he went.

The Glickmans finally made contact with Kennedy through the Chicago want-ads and talked with him on several occasions. But they were confused by his answers. He couldn't remember the code but knew in great detail where they used to eat lunch and hang out. When asked the same question minutes later, he couldn't remember anything. After some time passed, Kennedy called the Glickmans. He remembered the code and asked that they fly to Chicago to meet him and to bring "the key." The Glickmans were astonished that he knew about the key. (Only Dunbar could have known about the key.)

Rachel eventually met with Dunbar and was quite taken back by his appearance. He told her he'd had extensive plastic surgery and was subjected to brainwashing; that's why he had a difficult time keeping things straight. Rachel asked Kennedy if she could comb his hair back the way she remembered him wearing it, thinking she would be able to see scars left from the surgery. She didn't see any scars, but she did see the small mole above his right temple, just like Gene Dunbar.

Rachel made another trip to meet Kennedy. This time she flew to Atlanta and took her husband. The Glickmans were waiting at the airport for Kennedy when Jake had to visit the men's room. While he was gone, Kennedy arrived and approached Rachel. He greeted her warmly as if he knew her and hadn't seen her in a long time. He was well-dressed and manicured, not like before, but looked completely different to Rachel. While they were talking, Jake walked up near where they were standing but stayed in the background to watch them without being seen. It didn't take long before Kennedy picked Jake out of the crowd and enthusiastically, walked over to greet him. The two men hadn't seen each other since 1945 but Kennedy had no problem recognizing Jake.

On the drive around Atlanta, Jake tried to fool Kennedy by making a series of wrong turns; but Kennedy knew exactly where he was. He even went so far as to point out where they used to buy hot dogs. He told them that he was now partial to cheeseburgers and strawberry milkshakes. He also had a sweet tooth for M&Ms. The Glickmans were impressed that Kennedy remembered minor details of their time in Atlanta and about the intelligence work they had done for President Roosevelt. Both Rachel and Jake were convinced that Kennedy was the man they knew as Dunbar.

When asked about the Ruby affair, Kennedy elaborated. He said there was a man in the hospital dying of cancer and that when he died, the media was informed that Jack Ruby had passed away. He, the real Ruby, was taken to the Dallas airport and flown to Mexico City by David Ferrie who had also flown him to Havana Cuba with Charles Flynn to meet with Trifficante. Six weeks later, Ferrie was found shot to death in his apartment.

While in a Mexican hospital, Kennedy said that they went to work changing his identity. Major plastic surgery and bone reconstruction were done. They even smashed his fingers to rid him of his fingerprints. Then the brainwashing began. Every day he was reminded that his new name was Thomas Kennedy. He was told that when he was well enough, he would be able to see his parents.

Kennedy didn't know why they chose to go to the extent they did to allow him to live when it was easier to dispose of him. He often broke down in tears when he talked about certain events. This was one of them. He was provided a fake Birth Certificate with the name Thomas Kennedy claiming it was just like the one he used for a black market baby he was trying to sell when working undercover.

Tired of playing Thomas Kennedy and wanting his real identity back, Dunbar asked Rachel to apply for his real Birth Certificate, in the name of Jacob Rubenstein, born April 16, 1912. Parents: Max Rubenstein and Rose Israel. He also told Rachel that he never told anyone his real birth date, so they kept getting it wrong in the papers. Instead of trying to get a Birth Certificate for Jacob Rubenstein, Rachel tried first to get one for Thomas Kennedy. There were no records on file for a Thomas Kennedy, she was informed by the Secretary of the State of Illinois.

One other thing that was mentioned by the Glickmans was Kennedy's addiction to cheeseburgers, shakes, and M&Ms.

Mrs. Reynolds told Larry that she thought she was on to something, because her office had been broken into and all her files pertaining to Rachel Glickman were taken, everything. That was followed up by a threatening phone call that she was not to handle any material provided by Mrs. Glickman.

Beverly was impressed with the story that Larry related. It was scary. Apart from the physical similarities, there weren't many people who knew how much

Ruby enjoyed eating shakes and burgers. Beverly said they often used to go to Keller's Drive-In on Northwest Highway, and occasionally to the Prince of Hamburgers on Lemmon Avenue. And the M&Ms—he always had a pocket-full of them.

However incredible the similarities were, there were two things that short-circuited a complete and total wonderment about Kennedy. First, there were too many credible witnesses to Jack Ruby in death, and secondly, Kennedy had blue eyes, Jack's were so dark brown they looked black. Larry could not find how that was possible without his wearing contact lenses—which he wasn't.

The list of questions Larry and Beverly had prepared for Thomas Kennedy were answered in full. The answers were interesting, but inconclusive. He remembered some obvious answers, but missed others. Some of his answers were a matter of interpretation. For instance, when asked who built the ramp (Jack Ruby called it a runway) in his club, he didn't answer that he and Wally Weston built it for Shari Angel. And when asked who he sent the money to from Western Union minutes before he shot Oswald, he couldn't remember.

One question that Kennedy did answer correctly came from Beverly. She asked him, "What was the only gift you ever gave me that you had gift-wrapped?"

Scrawled underneath the question, Kennedy had written—"a green and white polka-dot dress."

*Names changed for protection.

CHAPTER THIRTY-FOUR

The Never-Ending Story

The spectacle of Dealey Plaza is emblazoned in the minds of many people: those who were there; those who sat tight-fisted and teary-eyed while listening to the first news flashes; those who somberly watched Oliver Stone's movie, *JFK*; and even those too young to remember. What actually happened on November 22, 1963, is the single greatest mystery of our time. Was it one man with one gun and three bullets? Three teams of two men with three rifles and a handgun? An umbrella with a poisoned flachette? The CIA, the Mafia, the Cubans, the anti-Castro brigade? Who knows?

In the beginning, when investigators/researchers such as Jim Garrison, Mark Lane, Sylvia Meagher, and Harold Weisberg rolled over the corpse of the Warren Report—checked for fingerprints and verified records, they came to a simple conclusion: *The Report* was an impostor! It was not the actual *truth*. *The Report* was riddled with inconsistencies. Large gaping wounds and tangible evidence of tampering made it easy to see that it was not the whole body of truth; selective parts were missing. As *The Report* laid in state, the stench of foul play grew intolerable. The winds of justice tried to clear the air. Somewhere, somehow, someone was hiding the *real* truth.

The search for the real truth engaged and enraged researchers in a struggle from the beginning. Subject to slings of ridicule, stumped by codes of silence, stymied by inaccessible records, assassinologists waded through a political quagmire to find clues and try to come to an understanding of why, how, and who. Those clues that were found were placed on the table for others to contemplate: *On The Trail of the Assassins, Rush To Judgment, Accessories After The Fact,* and the *Whitewash* series. Ferreting through the facts, hearsay, evidence and the lack of it, interviewing those who were neglected, and re-interviewing others for accuracy, resulted in a picture that was not pretty.

Nothing was easy but speculation. As time went on and more information was uncovered, November 22 started to crystallize into an image that seemed concrete but was still interpretive–depending precisely on the angle from which the "facts" were viewed. As more years passed, for various reasons people started to talk and substantiate specific elements of the plot and its cover-up. Other books cut deeper into the "means and motive": *Cover-Up, High Treason, Reasonable Doubt, Best Evidence, Crossfire, The Ruby Cover-up, Mafia Kingfish, Contract on America, The Man Who Knew Too Much, Flashback,* etc. Medical evidence, physical evidence, missing evidence. Political suicide, *Coup d-ètat,* or random act of violence? An exciting game of theoretical and analytical Ping-Pong played by any and everyone with an opinion.

Hard work started to pay dividends. Misdirection and dead ends gave way to small discoveries in forgotten files and unsearched minds. Hope that the actual *truth* would be found started to become an issue with more and more people, and when Oliver Stone's movie surfaced, interest snowballed into an unstoppable worldwide event.

The single biggest "bobble" the Warren Commission made in trying to "pull the wool," was expecting that the public would believe the randomly-guided bullet fired from the sixth floor window, tabbed by unbelievers as "the magic bullet," could react the way it did and cause the damage credited to it. Having found only three bullet casings cast aside in the sniper's perch on the sixth floor of the School Book Depository, the Commission had a serious problem on their hands. There were too many wounds and too many stray bullet marks to reasonably account for only three projectiles. They knew that one bullet missed the mark and careened off the concrete on the south side of Elm street; one bullet struck the President in the head; therefore, the third bullet must have caused all the other damage: a hole in the President's back, a hole in his neck, and three wounds in Governor Connally–his back, his front and his wrist. As many researchers have said, without the magic bullet, the case for a single assassin falls apart.

But regardless of the angles, the number of bullet casings, computer-aided graphic analysis, a rusty gun and a bad scope, the simple fact of the matter is, too many flesh and blood people responded to gunfire coming from behind the fence to be ignored or discredited. They heard shots; they saw smoke; they smelled gunpowder. And a few saw the men. Two witnesses saw rifles. These weren't people who wanted or needed to create a controversy. They were simply responding to what was very real at the time it happened. The Commission chose not to include much of this information in their Report—and for good reason—they were directed not to. The investigation was at point "A" and point "B" was: Lee Harvey Oswald acting alone. While it's important to understand why the Commission was given point "B" and from whom the directive came, let's move on to the House Select Committee on Assassinations and the Dictabelt recording brought to everyone's attention by researcher Mary Ferrell. After conducting their audio analysis of the police-recorded tape of the gunfire, the Commission said that there was evidence that gunfire emanated from behind the fence; therefore—there was a conspiracy. They also threw in that there was probable cause that the Mafia was involved as well. End of the seven-million dollar Committee.

The Dictabelt issue was later brought to issue by another group of interested parties. To the human ear, it is nearly impossible to hear any gunfire at all, let alone distinguish four shots instead of three, therefore they must not be real.

To further discredit the one-gunman theory is the gory motion-picture taken by Abraham Zapruder, bought by Life, sequestered by the government, and made public, thanks to researcher Robert Groden, and Geraldo Rivera and his staff. Anyone who isn't sure that Kennedy's head snapped back because of a speeding bullet fired from the front is looking at it with his or her eyes closed. The explanations provided by some diehards that the backward movement was the result of a "jet effect" propulsion of the head cavity releasing pressure, or that the President's back brace prohibited his head from moving forward defies science and common sense.

Setting the Zapruder film aside for a moment, what about Beverly's film? She knows she loaded the camera with film. She knows that she pressed the record button. She knows she started filming when the limousine made the turn onto Elm Street and continued filming until it sped away with a dying President. She knows that Regis Kennedy with the FBI took it. Why didn't he (they) give it back?

On behalf of Beverly, Gary Shaw made several inquiries concerning Beverly's film when the House Select Committee was meeting. Regis Kennedy, the FBI Agent Beverly identified as having taken it is now deceased. Surprisingly at first, the news seemed encouraging. In February of 1979, FBI Special Agent James Hosty told Ron Libert, a researcher in Florida, that the Committee had the Babushka film for some time and that he knew for a fact that they have viewed it. In a phone conversation on March 13, 1979, Gary spoke with Dallas researcher Gary Mack who quoted Robert Groden, a photographic consultant to the committee, that he was "almost certain" that the committee had the Babushka film. Then, on April 10, Shaw spoke with Dallas Times Herald reporter Earl Golz who told him that Robert Blakey was in Dallas as an advisor for the Texas School Book Depository, and that they had spoken. When Golz asked Blakey if he knew about the Babushka film Blakey was vague. When Golz described the film, Blakey said, "Oh yeah, I'm pretty certain that they have it but it doesn't show much."

Ten days later, Shaw followed up by calling Blakey at Cornell University and asked if he had the film or if it had even been found. Blakey said that it positively had not been found. When Shaw quoted the Times Herald that a "high official of the Committee said it had been found" Blakey replied that there was no higher official on the staff than he and that he knew nothing about it. He went on to say that the news media was a big source of misinformation.

On August 26, 1993, author John Newman (*JFK and Vietnam*) made a phone call to Washington, D.C. to the Federal Bureau of Investigations National Headquarters and inquired about getting Beverly's film back. They were told that their request had to go through channels and formal requests. As of this writing, a formal motion is being prepared requesting delivery of the film back to its rightful owner.

The tug of war between conspiracy theorists and the Warren "Reporters" has reached new heights and new lows. In print, on the radio, and on television, the public is being bombarded by more information than it probably wants to deal with, some believable—some not. And like a political campaign bout, the inevitable has happened. Researchers are fighting among themselves, and accusations of unsubstantiated claims and unqualified analysis has clogged the wheels of progress. While some researchers are diligently sharing information with one another, others are safeguarding theirs with the attitude of a miser. It seems that some researchers are turning the focus of their investigation from actively pursuing the assassins to critically analyzing to death every element of the assassination story expounded upon by other researchers. Many veteran television newspersons are playing by their own rules, or that dictated by management, and guilty of not advancing their understanding of the case and prejudicing their interviews with well-planned questions guaranteed to result in supporting their biased view—usually in favor of what they believed and reported thirty years ago. This is not what this case needs. While disagreement is inevitable and critique is in order, slander and railroading can only serve to discredit everyone and sidetrack the real issues with petty complaints. This case needs to be brought before the public in a legal forum that is fair to all sides, weighs all the facts, and places judgment in the hands of a well-informed public. While there have been several worthwhile symposiums and mock trials, it is time to get more serious.

Maybe Oswald was the shooter behind the window, maybe he was not; that's not the debate here. What about the assassin behind the fence? Are we just going to forget about him? The majority of the House Select Committee members believed that there was a shooter back there and their report substantiated it. There are forty-three earwitness accounts who believe that shots came from the fence, and at least three eyewitness who saw suspicious activity behind the fence; one claims to have seen men with rifles. How can we as citizens disregard the importance of this information or accept the fact that we have a murderer who has gotten away scot-free? Is he still walking among us? And more importantly—who gave the orders and why aren't we as a nation of justice concerned and actively pursuing the biggest unsolved murder case of the century? Why? Don't Presidents count?

Some citizens would prefer that the entire Kennedy issue be forgotten; that too much has been made of something that happened long ago; that our government is too sacred and honorable to be involved in such an insane scheme. Some people agree that Kennedy was assassinated by rogue elements of the government operating with the underworld, but feel that in the interest of National Security, the public should not be told the entire truth.

Should the case be reopened regardless of who is still alive to account for the crime? Is there anything to be gained? If it happened once, could it happen again? If you don't know the answer to these questions, ask yourself, "If my father, or brother, or husband, was murdered; and I knew that the person or persons who issued the orders and pulled the trigger had not been brought to justice, would I sit still and let bygones be bygones?"

President Kennedy and his brother were not perfect people; nor were they perfect politicians. However, they were elected to public office to serve our country, and they deserve justice. Both men were visionaries at a time when America needed them. They were entrenched in fighting for the same liberties our forefathers fought for, but faced with far greater and more complex problems; and, had far more powerful adversaries. Our democratic society is founded on very altruistic values which necessitate that its people rely on virtue as its guiding force. Without applying ethical standards at every level in our government and our daily lives, our republic is vulnerable to dissent and misdirection from uncontrollable forces. Life, liberty and the pursuit of happiness might seem antiquated to some people. However, in all its simplicity, it is what America is all about. We cannot take for granted what our soldiers have fought and died for, and are currently fighting for. As cumbersome and complicated as life seems as we approach the twenty-first century, we cannot ignore our obligations to future generations or the responsibility of learning from our mistakes. We cannot allow the government to become stagnant and bureaucratically unresponsive to the majority of its citizens. Our constitution lays the framework for the people of the country to make the laws and to vote its leaders in and out of office. There can be no room for the extreme of a coup d'état. Our government cannot make strategic alliances with an underworld it is trying to fight. As citizens of the United States, it should be our rightful obligation to insure that this process is safeguarded. It is important that history be corrected. November 22, 1963, should not be a gray area for our children's children's children. We need to know. If we understand the forces behind President Kennedy's assassination and the attempt on Governor Connally's life, the more mature we can act today as a nation dedicated to the pursuit of civil liberties. Let us not allow the judge in this case to be this book or any others like it. The Warren Commission, for whatever reason, didn't finish the job (the House Select Committee on Assassinations even said so); and, neither did the House Select Committee finish the job it was commissioned to do.

The serious fact is, that the murder of President John Fitzgerald Kennedy has not been solved. It is time for America to wake up and demand justice for a President who loved his country; to insist that the case be reopened; every file be made available; and every avenue of investigation pursued. America must stand accountable for her past in order to move forward as one nation under God, indivisible, with liberty and justice for all. For this to happen—*the truth must prevail!*

Beverly Oliver (the Babushka Lady) travels across the nation speaking to audiences about her life story. She has been seen on Geraldo, 48 Hours, Larry King and in Nigel Turner's documentary, *The Men Who Killed Kennedy.* Beverly also served as a consultant in the making of Oliver Stone's *JFK.*

Coke Buchanan is a graduate of the University of North Texas and is the Editor of *Dateline: Dallas,* a quarterly publication of the JFK Resource Group.

Nightmare In Dallas is the hard-hitting account of the "Babushka Lady," who at the age of seventeen was an eyewitness to the assassination of President John F. Kennedy. Beverly had been coined "the Babushka Lady," due to the inability of anyone being able to identify her and the scarf she wore around her head at the assassination. It is a story that, for years, many people wanted to hear in its entirety. Beverly stood across the street from Abraham Zapruder and, like him, filmed the assassination. The following Monday Beverly's film was confiscated by the FBI.

Beverly was a personal friend of Jack Ruby, married to the Mafia, and the featured singer at the Colony Club, located next door to Jack Ruby's Carousel Club. She witnessed many of the strange comings and goings of people linked to the conspiracy to kill our president. Ruby introduced Beverly to his "friend from the CIA" Lee Oswald. Beverly also met and conversed with David Ferrie, who many believe to be one of the masterminds in planning the "crossfire" in Dealey Plaza.

Nightmare In Dallas is more than a book recounting Beverly's experience on that fateful day in Dallas and how she has been terrorized by what she knows. It's a book about the salvation, protection and deliverance of her Lord and Savior, Jesus Christ, her marriage to an evangelist, and how she continues to cope with the criticism of some who don't understand, and others who are still trying to cover it all up.

Nightmare In Dallas is a solemn reminder that President Kennedy had an altruistic vision for America that transcended politics and racial boundaries. It is a tribute to his legacy, dream for global peace, and belief that America owes its allegiance first and foremost to God.

If you would like to order an autographed copy of this book with a personal comment, please give us the name and comment you want to appear in the book by going to the CONTACT US page on our web site: *www.theholybearstore.com*.
Photo contribution by Robert Groden, Coke Buchanan and Beverly Oliver Massegee.